MYSTERIOUS
CAMBRIDGESHIRE

MYSTERIOUS
CAMBRIDGESHIRE

Daniel Codd

PUBLISHING

DEDICATION

For Josie, Tom and Charlie, and all the family.

First published in Great Britain in 2010 by
The Derby Books Publishing Company Limited
3 The Parker Centre,
Derby, DE21 4SZ.

ISBN 978-1-85983-808-2

Printed and bound by Cromwell Press Group, Trowbridge, Wiltshire.

CONTENTS

ACKNOWLEDGEMENTS

My thanks to the staff at Peterborough Museum; the staff at Fitzwilliam Museum (Cambridge); staff at Cambridge County & Folk Museum; staff at King's College (Cambridge), Queen's College (Cambridge); N. Codd and J. Codd for their helpful suggestions for photographs; Josie Mae Skinner for her assistance in Cambridge! Ely Ghost Walk, Peterborough Ghost Walk; C.M. Tilbury (and www.burwell.co.uk); the staff at the Norris Museum, St Ives; Ely Tourist Information Centre; Cambridgeshire Libraries and Information Service; L.C. for her information regarding the aerial haunting at St Ives; Peterborough Tourist Information Centre; wardens of St Mary Magdalene's Church, Warboys; staff at Elton Hall; staff at the Golden Lion, St Ives; the Lion Hotel at Buckden; wardens of Buckden Towers; staff at Ely Cathedral; warden of St Paul's Church, Gorefield; owners of Hannath Hall (for their fine plum cherries!); K. Lawrence; Cambridge Ghost Walk; staff at Trinity College, Cambridge; staff at Queen's College, Cambridge; J. Beatty and the staff at Flag Fen; Elizabeth Stratton and Peter Newstrubb at Clare College; Sarah Key at the Haunted Bookshop; staff at Old Ferry Boat Inn, Holywell and the many people who have brought particular stories to my attention whom did not wish to be included by name, or whose name I shamefully neglected to record. All photographs are copyright D. Codd.

FOREWORD

It is impossible to describe the many faces of Cambridgeshire in so short an introduction as this. When condensed, a picture is painted of a region frequently touched by revolt, rebellion, conflict and drama throughout history. The county has seen revolts against the Roman forces and resistance to the Danish and Norman invaders; bloodbath clashes between 'town' and 'gown' in Cambridge; the carnage of the Peasant's Revolt in 1381; an agrarian uprising in 1549; Civil War skirmishes and violent rebellion against the drainage of the Fenland; corn riots during the reign of King George II; and fierce clashes in Littleport and Ely following the Napoleonic Wars. In the 1940s the flat landscape of parts of Cambridgeshire proved perfect places from which to fight the German bombers, and the runways of many RAF bases quickly began to appear across the county. Many historic sites, from the ancient Stonea Camp, where Roman legionaries suppressed a tribal uprising among the Iceni, to the grassy mound of Burwell Castle (where the rebel and bandit Geoffrey de Mandeville was assassinated), can be sought out nowadays. They stand as plaintive and often lonely testament to the monumental events that have occurred in Cambridgeshire throughout history.

But in prestigious Cambridge itself it is different: this bustling city has become famous for the University of Cambridge, one of the most renowned seats of learning in the world. Its 31 Colleges (of which Peterhouse is the oldest, being founded in 1284) have spawned an almost mind-boggling list of British luminaries that almost reads like a 'who's who' of success in every field from science and politics, to literature and music.

As I have said, it is impossible to reduce Cambridgeshire to a soundbite; hopefully the rest of this book will help provide a clearer picture of the many secrets, treasures, triumphs and enigmas the county holds.

In referring to 'this county', I have chosen to include all parts of what has (since 1972) been classed as the county of Cambridgeshire, following a seemingly endless series of boundary changes throughout the centuries: therefore, included within are the districts of East and South Cambridgeshire (including Cambridge), the formerly independent counties of the Isle of Ely (Fenland) and Huntingdonshire, and the Soke of Peterborough – which for ceremonial purposes is (presently) part of Cambridgeshire. I have also chosen to include in very small part some stories of Stamford, Lincolnshire, given its strategic importance and proximity to the Soke of Peterborough, as well as occasionally some information regarding other places on the periphery of Cambridgeshire. This last mostly concerns the region where the county boundary of the South Holland region of Lincolnshire and northern Peterborough/Fenland join, known as the Bedford Level, or the North Level.

A word also needs to be said about the geography of parts of Cambridgeshire. It is important to remember that in some places, notably the Isle of Ely, the area thereabouts was once a vast, stinking, waterlogged morass of swampland where conditions were inhospitable and unhealthy. The hardy folk there earned names like 'Slodgers' and 'Fen Tigers', and they travelled by flat-bottomed boats and stilts. These peoples eked out a living in wattle huts beside the mosquito-infested waterside, passing the day by snaring, fishing and cutting reeds. A gazetteer of Cambridgeshire describes the Isle of Ely in these times as: '…an inland island, surrounded on every side by lakes, shallow meres and broad rivers which became broader still in the season of rain, there being few artificial embankments to confine them…when the autumnal or the spring rains swelled the meres and streams, and covered the flats, they formed so many detached islets. Though surrounded and isolated they were never *covered* with water, therefore it was upon these heights and knolls that men in all times built their towns and churches.' Although the waters did subside (and in those months it was possible to farm livestock and grow crops in places) for the most part it was a very hazardous existence and a strange way of life. In the Norris Museum in St Ives can be found an atmospheric reproduction of a charcoal etching depicting those times: a solitary Fenman sits in his coffin-shaped flat boat, sailing gloomily past a spit of land. In the fog beyond, the waterlogged landscape is so vast that it almost mirrors the sea. I only bring this to the reader's attention since this was the Fenland landscape until Dutch engineers were imported to undertake a breathtaking drainage project that changed this landscape forever in the 17th century. Therefore, readers should bear this in mind given the frequent references to 'waterlogged landscapes' within this book.

This is clearly a far cry from the lives of those who resided in Cambridge itself, and compare the Fenman of times past with the joyful punters that can now be seen every day on the River Cam in Cambridge. It is a case of 'so near yet so far', and it is difficult to imagine that in the past (and perhaps even today) these different parts of Cambridgeshire ever really felt any affiliation with each other. But perhaps it is this diversity which has ensured that Cambridgeshire remains one of the most fascinating and legend-ridden parts of the whole of the United Kingdom: a land of myths, mysteries, folklore and ghosts.

Many years ago I was lucky enough to obtain a copy of Enid Porter's now difficult-to-locate *Cambridgeshire Customs & Folklore; With Fenland Material Provided by W.H. Barrett* (1969). This book astounded me, with its mix of history, mystery, folklore and superstition, and is one of those books (much like Ethel Rudkin's *Lincolnshire Folklore*) which is sadly long out of print despite its being such a definitive and locally important work. Ms Porter served as curator of the Cambridge and County Folk Museum on Castle Street between 1948 and 1976 and has her position in Cambridge history secured as the region's leading authority on all manner of customs, dialect, place names, local history, stories and beliefs. *Mysterious Cambridgeshire* is of a somewhat different calibre, however, for there was much outside of witchcraft, legend and ghosts that did not warrant Ms Porter's attention and which I have decided to largely concentrate on. Cambridgeshire is rich in folklore, yes, but it is also rich in many other types of strange stories: curious weather phenomena, rains of fish, 'living' fossils, UFOs, bizarre crimes and disappearances, out-of-place animals, phenomenal human ability, general curiosities and an abundance of more recently reported ghostly anecdotes and urban legends. Where archive sources have been drawn upon I have tried to remain faithful to the text of the original source, so as not to generate falsities. Except in the cases of first-hand accounts, the many and varied sources drawn upon are included within the text, and hopefully, between that and this book itself, this will give other researchers a good starting point if they wish to delve further (although please remember that many of the sites featured herein are private property, such as Hannath Hall, the old rectory at Barnack and Woodcroft Castle, so please be careful).

Come, then, and take a trip round mysterious Cambridgeshire: from the haunted and gloomy Fens and the Lincolnshire borders to the urban heartland of the historic Soke of Peterborough; and from the beautiful waters of old Huntingdonshire to the venerable city of Cambridge itself. But most of all enjoy a journey into this part of Great Britain's hidden corners: its folklore, supernatural heritage, legends, curiosities, mysterious animals and weird phenomena of every shape and form.

CHAPTER I

ENIGMATIC EVENTS FROM COUNTY HISTORY

INTRODUCTION

Often it is the very landscape of Cambridgeshire itself that has provided the basis for some of the county's best-known legends and mysteries. For instance, there is a long-standing belief that Cambridge, like Rome, was founded strategically on seven hills. For my part, however, perhaps the most intriguing historical riddle is the suggestion that the semi-mythical Trojan Wars of pre-history were actually fought in Britain and not in the Turkish Dardanelles, as has long been suggested. The events – among the most important in Greek mythology – were drawn upon in Homer's epic poems *Iliad* and *Odyssey* and supposed by Greek scholars to have occurred in the Mediterranean between 1194-1184 BC. A Belgian named Theophile Cailleux, who in 1879 questioned assumptions made about Homer's ancient narrative and inconsistencies regarding topographical and geographical detail, proposed the unusual stance that events in fact occurred along the chilly shores of Britain. He proposed the idea that 'Troy' was situated in East Anglia – on the range of low chalk hills south-east of Cambridge now known to us as the Gog Magog Hills. He went to great lengths to explain that rivers cited by Homer – Scamander and Simoeis, for example – were in fact the rivers Cam and Great Ouse in Cambridgeshire, and that other locations in the saga were in fact in Spain and not Greece, as popularly assumed. This idea has been drawn upon by others, not least by writer Iman Wilkens, whose *Where Troy Once Stood* (1991) offers the most comprehensive analysis of the argument yet provided. In it, he argues that the Trojan Wars were a prolonged conflict among Celts over access to British tin mining areas, and that Homer's poems were repetitions of an oral tradition circulating in north-west Europe. The huge and ancient Fleam Dyke and Devil's Ditch, whose actual purpose has been the subject of much argument by scholars (and of which we shall learn more of later on), are argued to have been war dykes intended to defend 'Troy' from a seaborne assault via the great bay of the Wash. Wilkens suggests the famed Isleham Hoard is evidence left over from this conflict: the hoard is the largest ever deposit of Bronze Age relics to be found in Britain and consists of thousands of pieces of weapons and armour (even ceremonial equipment for horses) found in 1959 at Isleham, east of Soham.

These arguments are controversial. But it is nonetheless interesting to speculate that such household names as Helen of Troy, Paris and Achilles, etc, and incidents such as the 10-year siege of Troy, finally being ended by the Trojan Horse ruse, may actually have been inspired by events that took place millennia ago in Cambridgeshire.

Maybe the region even has its own Atlantis as well. *A History Of The Fens Of South Lincolnshire* (1897) appears to be the first publication to record the almost forgotten legend of Dalproon, a town that had stood somewhere in the vicinity of the South Holland Sluice. Apparently it was completely obliterated in November 1236 when 'the sea broke in and made great havoc.' The event spawned a local rhyme:

When Dalproon stood,
Long Sutton was a wood:
When Dalproon was washed down,
Long Sutton became a town.

Just like Atlantis itself, the story appears to be a legend built on shaky foundations – for there is no contemporary evidence that 'Dalproon' ever existed. There does, however, appear to be better evidence for another obliterated town at the county's other extremity on the Essex border, the fate of which is still shrouded in mystery.

Chrishall is actually in Essex and just shy of Cambridgeshire's border, but deposits of brickwork and tiling were occasionally unearthed just to the north, in Cambridgeshire itself – indicating that 'Old' Chrishall at one time stood on a different location near to Chrishall Grange. Enid Porter's influential *Cambridgeshire Customs And Folklore* (1969) put to paper a story about this discrepancy that had been collected by the Women's Institute some 15 years prior. Locally, they said, Old Chrishall had been annihilated by a devastating blaze some five centuries previously. This fire was suspected of being a deliberate act aimed at ridding the village of the plague. It was said that the plague victims were afterwards tossed into a huge pit, and that if they were ever unearthed – even today – the deadly disease would once again sweep the region, causing catastrophic fatalities.

Equally fascinating are the occasional unearthing of mass graves, suggesting some forgotten calamity from prehistory, the circumstances of which we can now only guess at. During excavations at the Iron Age hill fort known as the War Ditches, at Cherry Hinton, a suburban area east of Cambridge, a number of skeletons were uncovered. Analysed by anthropologists in 1904, the remains were found to be of young and old, and both sexes. They displayed evidence of having been decapitated, or otherwise violently wounded, and had been thrown into a fosse where they were discovered with pottery and the remains of domestic animals. They were tentatively dated to the Romano-British era, but of course we will now never know what political, religious or tribal motives brought about such a massacre.

Also curious are later stories of odd, out-of-place human remains in Cambridgeshire. It is recorded that in 1756 some workmen employed in refitting a seat within All Saints' Church, Landbeach, made a remarkable discovery within a pillar next to the chancel on the north side. Four feet above the flagstones, the workmen were forced by circumstance to remove a decorative stone rose, and behind it they found a small alcove. Within this were two wooden dishes bound together with linen, and upon this strange container being prised open it was found to contain 'the muscular part of a human heart' that had evidently been mummified by embalmers and wrapped in linen. Quite whom this heart belonged to is unknown, as is its whereabouts – it was apparently presented to the British Museum but at some point became lost. Similarly, in St Andrew's Church, Soham, a parishioner was buried in a standing position, according to a will of 1607. A skeleton was also discovered buried as though standing beneath the earth in the vicinity of St Mary's Church, St Neots, around 1853. There is even a suggestion in Marr's *Handbook To The Natural History Of Cambridgeshire* (1904) that the border with Norfolk may have been home to a pre-historic tribe of 'almost pygmy proportions', following specimens that were found near Brandon.

In times of conflict there have always been rumours of conspiracy: on 1 April 1941 an air-raid shelter marshal named Alice Stutley was led by a small boy to the corpse of a man slumped in a shelter on Christ's

Pieces, Cambridge. The man had shot himself through the head and proved to be a bogus scientist allegedly from Holland who was staying in Cambridge while he worked on fossils. His name was Dr Jan Willem Ter Braak, but this proved to be an alias. His frequent visits to Whitehall, London, had attracted the attention of MI5 who had searched his rooms while he was away and found a transmitter, another pistol and a file on PM Winston Churchill's movements. They were waiting for Ter Braak to return to his rooms when they learned the scientist had been found dead elsewhere in Cambridge. There was a strong suspicion that 'Ter Braak' had been planning to shoot Churchill dead on behalf of the Nazi regime, although his true plan and motives remain shrouded in wartime secrecy. Others said he had in actual fact been a Soviet spy posing as a refugee from the Nazi-controlled Netherlands.

Cambridgeshire has, of course, seen much conflict over the centuries. But in quieter times stories of enigmatic characters, unsolved or bizarre crimes and legends with possibly the barest basis in fact have surfaced to perplex us.

MYTHICAL ORIGINS OF CAMBRIDGE

Although utterly impossible to prove, and in all probability complete myth, there are several stories detailing how Cambridge came to exist.

In *c*.1136 the Welsh churchman and renowned scholar Geoffrey of Monmouth produced his expansive *History of the Kings of Britain*, drawing on as much local lore as actual fact. It covered a time period that began centuries before Christ up until the year AD 800 and told the story of how refugees from Troy, under Brutus the Trojan, fled to the island of Albion, guided by the goddess Diana. This island was Britain, and the Trojans defeated a race of giants that inhabited the place before setting up a capital called New Troy (modern-day London). This, Geoffrey tells us, was around 1070 BC.

Born of this line of Trojan leaders was one Gurguntius, who ruled England sometime around 375 BC. According to Geoffrey, Gurguntius' rule was a mostly peaceful one (except for a war with Denmark) during which he allegedly directed a huge number of exiles from Spain to settle on the uninhabited island of Ireland. One of these exiles, named Cantaber, was a prince and he was given the hand of King Gurguntius' daughter Guenolena. This royal couple ruled eastern Britain, and on the River *Cante* built a large city with temples housing astrologers and learned philosophers brought over from Athens, the city where the exiled Spanish prince had himself been educated.

It was here at this so-called 'City of Scholars' that the learned Athenians Anaximander and Anaxagoras are supposed to have taught (although the dates do not really match). Later, the British chieftain Cassivellaunus is supposed to have granted privileges to the scholars at this university (by now in existence for some four centuries) until the Roman invasion, when Julius Caesar removed some of the scholars to Rome. The death-knell for the university, however, occurred in AD 303 when an army of pagan British marauders raided the town and massacred the Christian students.

There has been evidence of a 3,500-year-old settlement in Cambridge unearthed, at the site where Fitzwilliam College stands today. But the 'truth' of Cambridge's mythical origins is highly questionable. Geoffrey of Monmouth's 12th century *History* is the earliest record of much of Britain's mythological heritage, and this was allegedly based on earlier Anglo-Saxon works, folklore and a lost source of Breton legends Geoffrey had apparently translated. Historically, it is almost unimaginable that tribal Britain of 2,000 years ago had such a long-established seat of learning, with scholars of such renown that the sophisticated Romans would feel the need to steal them; although it is possible that the Romans took 'wise men' and Druids back to Rome as curiosities. The whole story reads as though it is an attempt to unnecessarily provide Cambridge with an antiquity befitting of such an important town, and there is a similar legend of the 'World's First University' being at Stamford in Lincolnshire in the ninth century BC. But despite the feeble evidence for Cambridge's origins, the story is an intriguing one nonetheless, especially if one can stretch their imagination to the extreme possibility that those mythical characters had just the tiniest basis in fact.

THE DANES

In AD 870 there supposedly occurred the 'Massacre of Peterborough'. The monastery of Medeshamstede (modern-day Peterborough) was at the time a wonder of the era, its library unrivalled, until a marauding party of Danish invaders under the warlords Hinguar and Hulba sought it out and began to lay siege to it. It is said that many people, fearing the Danish advance through the Fens, had congregated at Medeshamstede, and during the confrontation Hulba's brother died when a rock catapulted from the monastery tower struck his head. Enraged, Hulba himself executed all the friars, including the ancient and worldly Abbot Hedda and scores of his monks. Folklore has it that the abbot was one of the most learned men of the period whose journals, charters and many other writings were destroyed when the monastery was put to the torch. The blaze is said to have raged for 15 days. After the massacre, dozens of monks lay dead, together with an unknown number of townsfolk. Writing in 1866, a church historian noted that 'in the cathedral of Peterborough is shown a monument called Monk's-Stone, on which are the effigies of an abbot and several monks. It stood over the pit in which fourscore monks of this house were interred.' Nowadays this unique piece of Saxon stonemasonry is known as the Hedda Stone and resides within Peterborough Cathedral. Archaeologists have disputed whether this 'memorial of the Danish massacre in 870' is actually what tradition says it is, but it does indicate that even in Victorian times the violence of the Danish era was stamped into the land; indeed, the Danes had for centuries been despised as a collective 'bogeyman figure'.

There are some noteworthy legends pertaining to this. AD 870 is also supposed to have been the year that an Anglo-Saxon named Wilburtus was murdered by the Danes south-west of Ely, a circumstance that led to the settlement where he was martyred becoming (what is now) Wilburton. The curious composition of the soil in parts hereabouts – red and sand-like – no doubt prompted stories that its discolouration was due to the blood that the earth soaked up during the era. The year following Wilburtus' murder Cambridge itself was burnt to the ground by the hordes of Danish invaders.

It was for a long time said that a heroic member of the Longueville line had been slain fighting the Danes near Overton (Orton) Longueville on what is now the southern fringes of Peterborough. Lord Longueville had managed to kill the Danish king; and this was in spite of receiving a wound so severe that his guts had spilled from his belly. It was said locally that he had wrapped his entrails around his left arm and continued to wield his sword with his right before falling on the battlefield.

Perhaps the most familiar story concerns the Brave Man of Balsham, originally recorded (albeit briefly) by Henry of Huntingdon in *Historia Anglorum* and which drew upon an event rumoured to have taken place when the forces of Thorkell 'the Tall' occupied East Anglia for three months in the year 1010. A number of regional towns were razed to the ground, including Cambridge, and Thorkell's army made their way

Holy Trinity Church at Balsham. Did a single villager defend the church against the Danes?

across the Gog Magog Hills to a 'very pleasant country near Balsham.' Here, the inhabitants were butchered, the children being tossed into the air to be impaled on the points of the Danish invaders' spears. However, at Holy Trinity Church, one lone villager, 'whose name ought to have been recorded', made his way up the steps of the tower and thus fortified by his position and his own courage managed to successfully defend himself single-handed against the pillagers.

Although enlarged in the 13th and 14th centuries, Holy Trinity did by all accounts exist in the Anglo-Saxon era in a more primitive form. Standing in the church grounds in the bright sunlight of May 2009 it is somehow difficult to evoke the carnage that must have occurred here 1,000 years ago. The lack of other corroborative evidence indicates that perhaps this legend was based on an ancient folk memory of events already over 100 years distant even by the time Henry of Huntingdon wrote of them. Most historians agree, though, that it is likely to be based on a factual event.

It is interesting to note that at Castor, according to the 18th-century antiquarian Revd William Stukeley, the monastery there was also destroyed by the 'barbarous Danes' around AD 1016. Here, 'much Daneweed still grows upon the Roman road in Castor fields.' Dane-weed, or Danewort, is actually the European Dwarf Elder plant. As at Borough Hill, Northamptonshire, there was a general belief that when cut, the Dane-weed thereabouts secreted human blood – for the ground itself had been soaked in the blood of the slain at Castor, and from the saturated earth the Dane-weed sprouted...

LAWLESSNESS IN LITTLEPORT

One of Cambridgeshire's most famous stories concerns the days when the area now known as the South Level was a vast, gloomy expanse of swampland, sparsely inhabited by pockets of higher-lying hills referred to as 'islands'. During the reign of King Cnut (AD 1016–35) the monarch himself spent time at Ely, so the story goes, after the clergy there had asked him to advise on flood defence. While there the king obtained for himself a punt and, using a pole, sailed out on his own into the inhospitable insect-infested morass of decaying plant vegetation that formed much of the inland shallows of the Fens. The king was hoping to catch for himself some eels, but before long appalling weather conditions forced him to beach his punt at the low hill of a stretch of land arising from the murk. Finding a rough shack, the king knocked on the door and was greeted by a man named Legres, who invited him in and fed him with stewed eels and homemade beer. Thanking his saviour, the grateful king announced that the spot where his punt had beached would be known as Punt Hill and that the parcel of land would be known as 'Littleport', as this land had been a 'little port' to him during a storm.

As they talked by the fireside, it transpired that Legres was employed by the monks of Ely to make beer for them at a monastery farm nearby called the Grange. Some of the monks were presently there, the king learned, feasting and making merry, and Legres suggested that the king should ask them for accommodation at the Grange, which would be more suitable than his own meagre quarters.

However, the monks drunkenly told the king and Legres to clear off, and seeing that the king was furious Legres took the opportunity to confide that he hated the monks: 18 years prior they had abducted his wife and thrashed Legres himself almost to death with whips. In attempting to rescue her, the monks had unleashed their dogs on the couple and Legres' wife had been mauled to death. Legres and his wife had had a son, and on the boy's birthday every year Legres had, in revenge, quietly abducted one of the monks off into the swampy darkness of the Fens and slit his throat.

An alternative to this is that Legres cut a notch in his staff for every monk that drowned in the Fens, but either way King Cnut was forced to stay the night in Legres' humble abode that evening – an experience he found so dismal that he chose to sleep in his punt, the little vessel tied to a stake so it would not drift off in the night. The following morning Cnut awoke to the bizarre sight of a teenage girl plastering herself with mud on the banks of one of the river tributaries: it gradually dawned on him that another of Legres' 'sons' was in fact a daughter obliged to obscure her beauty with muck and filth so as to pass herself off as a 'son' and thus avoid the attentions of the monks. Cnut was appalled that so beautiful a young woman should have to undergo such an indignity, and after breakfast he rode up to the Grange intending to use his royal authority to arrest the monks. Unfortunately, the attempt failed and a bloody and chaotic fight ensued in which the king and Legres killed a number of the monks before the king's soldiers arrived and ended the monks' rebellion. Following this battle the king officially named the land Littleport and made Legres its royal brewer and mayor, giving him overlordship of the monks – whose duty it became to work in the brewery. The nuns were ordered to spend the rest of their lives making shirts for the kingdom.

Legres' daughter is subsequently supposed to have married a relative of Cnut's, while Legres himself remarried and named an infant son *Canute* after the monarch. In fact, every first-born son was named Canute until one year the tradition died out following the death by drowning of the heir to this family tradition. The surname Legres, however, persisted, and this was the legend passed to Walter Henry Barrett in the early 1900s by an old Fenman named Chafer Legge to account for his curious surname and the origin of Littleport. It seems quite amazing that such a piece of family lore could have passed through generation after generation for almost 1,000 years without being recorded elsewhere, and it is likely that the old tale of how Littleport began developed gradually as an explanation for certain street names and other places in the locality, a circumstance that Barrett suggested in *Tales From The Fens* (1963). These included Crown Lane – supposedly the spot where King Cnut raised his crown and it caught the sun, the flashing signalling his whereabouts to his soldiers.

Barrett wrote, 'At a ripe old age Chafer died in his sleep, the last of the real old Fen tigers…'

Whatever the truth of such tales, the true horrors that occurred in this era indicate that such a story was at least plausible. For example, in early 1036 the scheming Aelfgifu, Cnut's concubine, connived with Earl Godwine of Wessex to have Aelfred the Aetheling, the most immediate threat to her own son Harald's position as future king, captured when he returned to England upon the king's death. Aelfred and his retinue were ambushed west of Guildford, and the event turned into a massacre of horrifying proportions: hundreds of Aelfred's supporters were beheaded and disembowelled, and the young prince himself was grabbed and brutally blinded as he boarded a ship. He was then dragged naked behind a horse to the monastery at Ely where he died on 5 February, the weapon used to gouge out his eyes having cut into his brain. It was a time of utter barbarity on a scale that can scarcely be imagined these days.

IN SEARCH OF HEREWARD THE SAXON

Scraps of ancient evidence that throw light upon semi-mythical figures, such as King Arthur or Robin Hood, are always fascinating. In fact, the site of the Battle of Camlann is said by some to have occurred along the banks of the River Cam. This was the decisive clash that took place around AD 537 (according to the ancient *Annales Cambriae*) in which the legendary King Arthur was finally slain by his enemy and relative Mordred. In the Fens, however, no other character has provided a longer-enduring legend on so little historical evidence as Hereward the Wake.

Although undoubtedly a real person, the very life and times of Hereward are shrouded in uncertainty. Romance has painted him as a brave freedom fighter, but he was no Robin Hood. At times he was a cunning, brutally ruthless barbarian credited with taking part in the violent raid on Peterborough Abbey on 2 June 1070. This assault was carried out by the forces of King Svein Estridsson, who had mustered his Danish fleet in the Humber and then sailed south intent on plundering a nation in utter turmoil. His forces set up a base in the Isle of Ely, where English rebels resisting the Norman invasion of 1066 subsequently joined them. William the Conqueror had just appointed a Frenchman named Turold to the abbey at Peterborough and provided scores of soldiers to protect him – but the English got there first and, emboldened by their allegiance with the Danish, entirely plundered the abbey. A rare near-contemporary reference to the incident in the *Anglo-Saxon Chronicle* notes that 'Hereward and his gang' took part, indicating he was at the time already notorious. For Hereward, a *thegn* from south Lincolnshire, the attack was a direct challenge to the authority of England's new rulers, the Normans.

Hereward's story is the stuff of legend. His cause drew many influential supporters, including Morcar, a Northumbrian earl and veteran of the anti-Norman cause. King William managed to secure a truce with the Danes and get them to leave England, but his inability to secure the Isle of Ely merely enhanced the rebels' standing; the Isle, surrounded as it was by a barely navigable wilderness of swampy marshland, became a tiny pocket of free England after the rest of the kingdom had submitted to the Normans. The rebels withstood repeated land and sea attacks, and the king was forced to begin building a two-mile-long causeway of stones, earth and wood across the treacherous marshland from Aldreth to get to the island. The beginning of the end came when William seized all the lands of the monks of Ely Abbey, drawing them out of the marshes and bribing them to reveal a safe passage through the swamps. On 27 October 1071 the king's forces finally breached the impenetrable stronghold in the Isle of Ely and took it by storm. Earl Morcar was arrested and the rebellion was crushed.

There is another near-contemporary reference to Hereward in the *Anglo-Saxon Chronicle* that briefly explains how he managed to escape the storming of the island, bravely leading a band of followers to safety. There are further shaky indicators as to the background of the man himself in the *Domesday Book*. But beyond this there are few clues. The 12th-century *Gesta Herewardi* was comprised largely of oral anecdotes about the man that were chronicled at various periods in the century after the siege of Ely. Although much of it allegedly drew upon first-hand accounts, it is clear that there was an almost mythical dimension in the common mind regarding Hereward, and this hero-worship had begun almost immediately after the rebellion was over. Tales of his noble birth, his personal reasons for joining the rebellion and how he would use disguises to sneak into King William's camp to steal attack plans were the very stuff that romance was made of. Much of the *Gesta* was based on rapidly disintegrating papers allegedly scribed by one of Hereward's chaplains, Leofric, which dealt with the fabulous and the fantastic as much as the truth. The anonymous compiler of the original *Gesta* found himself the first to experience the frustratingly difficult task of separating man from myth, even a mere 50 years after the event.

Hereward was, then, certainly long dead by the time *Gesta* was compiled; although his demise as recorded once again speaks to rumour. He apparently made peace with the king and was rewarded by having his Lincolnshire lands in Bourne returned. But, despite this, *Gesta* notes he is supposed to have been murdered by his son-in-law during a violent quarrel. Geoffrey Gaimar's later *L'Estoire Des Engles* (*c*.1140) elaborates: it recounts how Hereward died violently battling a band of vengeful Normans who invaded his home. He managed to kill 15 before being stabbed in the back, and there is the inescapable feeling that by this point researchers were being told by the peasantry a version of how they believed their hero *should* have died.

Gesta also noted numerous supernatural feats popularly ascribed to Hereward and his men. It is the first to hint at the legend that, following the assault on Peterborough Abbey in 1070, during which the abbey's fabulous treasure and relics were looted, Hereward was visited in his sleep by a vision of Saint Peter. It was midnight and Saint Peter in his fury brandished an enormous key. The holy man then ordered the rebel warrior to restore the treasures (and a kidnapped abbot) to the abbey. This vision terrified Hereward and he did as he was bid.

Following the storming of the Isle of Ely in 1071, Hereward and his men took to living the life of an outlaw band. They escaped the Fens and made the thick woodland of the *Bruneswald* their home, from where they engaged in skirmishes and carried out guerrilla attacks on royal targets. Following an attack on Stamford, Hereward and his men became hopelessly lost in the impenetrable forest of the *Bruneswald*. Saint Peter saw them and took mercy, and in thanks for Hereward's piety in returning the treasure to Peterborough Abbey he sent a gigantic white hound, which led the warriors through the dense woodland of the midnight forest. Furthermore, Will-o'-the-Wisps lit the tips of their spears to illuminate their passage. As dawn broke, Hereward and his men recognised the path that they had been led to and at this noticed that the white hound was in fact a spectral white wolf, sent by Saint Peter; the animal promptly disappeared into the forest.

The *Bruneswald* forest is nowadays vastly reduced, its name remembered in the village of Newton Bromswold, Northamptonshire, just shy of the Bedfordshire border. Although highly romanticized, Charles Kingsley's *Hereward The Last Of The English* (1866) essentially drew on and elaborated the original *Gesta*. He describes the white wolf thus: 'A huge wolf met them, wagging his tail like a tame dog, and went before them on a path.' Hereward and his men took the animal for a dog, and felt compelled to follow it, only realising at daybreak that it had in fact been a *wolf* that had saved them: 'And as they questioned amongst themselves what had happened, the wolf and the candles disappeared, and they came whither [realised] they had been minded, beyond Stamford town, thanking God, and wondering what had happened.'

The stories of Hereward's exploits have been the stuff of popular culture for almost 1,000 years now. In 1926 Fenland folklorist Christopher Marlowe wrote of him as being born '...of Earl Leofric and his gentle wife Lady Godiva...a son, whose flashing blue eyes and long flaxen curls earned him the nickname "fair".' However, most of what has been written – from *L'Estoire Des Engles* to Kingsley's *Hereward The Wake* – draws upon the original *Gesta* to one degree or another. And it is this that is fascinating. *Gesta* is the nearest thing to an *actual* account of Hereward's life, and while it is clear that much of it is drawn from the popular imagination, there is also much of it that reads as though it is a narrative with a historical basis. Hereward is not a typical hero; he is portrayed as cunning, brutal and occasionally barbaric. The author himself notes how, in compiling *Gesta* 50 years after the events at Ely and Peterborough, he saw for himself skeletons in Norman armour being dredged out of the swamp at Aldreth – which he supposed were casualties of a disastrous attempt by soldiers to storm Ely via the hand-built causeway. *Gesta* moves from fanciful storytelling and near-fabrication to folklore, historical narrative and alleged first-hand accounts to tell the tale of Hereward: so much is unknown, but folklore often has a *basis* in reality. The story of the vision of Saint Peter and the white wolf may have been an attempt by a contributor to *Gesta* to 'legitimise' the often-brutal hero, but the story of Hereward's 'miracle' was nonetheless apparently common currency by the time *Gesta* was put together.

One assumes the same contradiction of the man himself. A picture is painted of a man prepared to wreak the utmost carnage on the invading Norman army – his ruthlessness, through two successive generations, very quickly earning him the reputation of a heroic 'freedom fighter'.

LEGENDS OF BURIED TREASURE

There are numerous fantastical legends of buried treasure in the region. According to a local legend, King John's treasure – a fabulous hoard supposedly lost in the Wash in 1216 – was actually stolen by his servant and a girl who had shared the king's bed during a stopover at Wisbech Castle. The hoard ended up being buried beneath a ramshackle hideaway at Gold Hill for centuries, although by the time Fenland folklorist W.H. Barrett was told of this by his great-uncle the treasure was lost once more. Apparently it was revealed by drainage in the 1640s and almost instantly spirited off as word of the discovery reached the ears of the so-called Fen Tigers – the hardy, primitive and murderously cunning folk who peopled the Fens. Gold Hill is a small mound at the suspension bridge over the Hundred Foot Washes north-east of Littleport. Alternatively, in 1858 a contributor to *Notes And Queries* wrote that on the southern side of the Long Sutton to King's Lynn road, now the A17, he had as a boy had a spot pointed out to him as 'King John's Hole', a dark stagnant pool of water: '…it was said that some of the treasure had been dug up while draining the land on the banks of this pool.' This location *might* have been somewhere between Sutton Bridge and Walpole Marsh.

Enid Porter noted in 1969 that in Horseheath, between Linton and Haverhill, there was a road locally known as Money Lane, haunted by the ghost of a miser who had secreted his hoard hereabouts. On the night of the full moon it was whispered that people would be startled by an ethereal voice commanding, 'Pick up your spade and follow me!'

Near Cambridgeshire's border with Essex can be found the Bartlow Hills, an ancient group of four almighty burial mounds, or tumuli. According to an 1819 history of Essex, these mounds were raised over the bodies of slain Danish warriors following a bloody clash between the forces of King Cnut and Edmund Ironside, the Saxon king, in 1016: 'Near Hadstock it is said to have raged with the greatest fury, to have been declining at Bartlow, and to have ceased entirely at Ashdon.' Excavations since 1835 have revealed the Bartlow Hills to be considerably older, however, and many Romano-British artefacts have been turned up: but no sign of the treasure chest that for over 150 years local legend has said Oliver Cromwell hid here during the Civil War.

Perhaps the most fabulous treasure of all was nearly found in the 1800s. For generations it was said that a golden coach lay buried within the ancient tumulus known as Mutlow Hill, south-east of Cambridge at Great Wilbraham. During excavations at the Bronze Age earthworks in 1852, the archaeologist R.C. Neville, Lord Braybrooke, turned up only evidence of Roman pottery – and sadly no evidence of the fabled golden coach. Who knows, maybe it is still buried thereabouts!

LEGENDARY CRIMES

In 1088 Cambridge and the surrounding county were virtually destroyed by 'fire and sword' when the Earl of Shrewsbury, Roger de Montgomery, rebelled against the king in support of Robert, Duke of Normandy. His marauding army must have claimed many lives, but there are no *details* in spite of the scale of the devastation. This reinforces the fact that sometimes there are crimes where the evidence is so scant we can

in his fatal coat, with the disease quickly spreading and sweeping through Ramsey with terrifyingly deadly consequences.

Throughout Cambridgeshire history there are many instances where a single death has become the focus of speculation. For instance, in the north-east corner of St Michael's churchyard, Stamford, lies the remains of Cassandra King who was executed in the town in 1704 for a burglary at Wothorpe. The merciless treatment meted out to her for such a minor crime has become the basis for a tradition that, according to George Burton's *Chronology Of Stamford* (1846), 'after her execution, proof of her innocence was discovered, and this is the alleged reason for discontinuing capital punishments here.' In fact, no execution was ever carried out in Stamford again, but the story of Cassandra's 'innocence' appears to be folklore rather than fact.

Still, sometimes it is the details of a demise itself that are remarkable, rather than the aftermath. In Cambridge, Dr John Peachell, Master of Magdalene College, having been rebuked by Archbishop Sancroft of Canterbury for drunkenness and setting a generally poor example to the University, proceeded to literally starve himself to death in penance in 1690. And some deaths are simply grimly comedic. In December 1728 a bell ringer named Henry West at King's College met an unusual death when he was crushed by one of the five great bells falling on him during an exhaustive ringing session. On 8 September 1741 a windmill in the parish of Bourn was buffeted by such violent gusts that it collapsed, killing a man and a boy.

A wife's dedication to her husband's love of beer led to a curious discovery in May 1762. An inhabitant of Whittlesey had passed away, and as he was being buried his friends found the coffin underside to be unaccountably soaked. Cautiously they prized open the coffin lid and found two gallons of strong beer sloshing around the corpse inside. The widow explained that her husband '...loved ale, and she was willing that he should not want it [i.e. be without] when he was dead.' Surely this was a wife that some men might be proud of!

More sinister are the whispers of dark and brutal deeds. When the body of PC Thomas S. Lamb was fished out of the River Ouse in February 1842 there were rumours of foul play. The young constable had vanished just before Christmas the previous year, and among his colleagues there was a strong suspicion that he had been assaulted and tipped over a bridge in Huntingdon into the freezing water during some violent fracas with a gang of ne'er-do-wells. But some suspected crimes were simply strange in their details.

On 16 March 1901 the *Cambridge Daily News* reported the bizarre circumstances surrounding the death of 72-year-old Lavinia Farrar, a blind woman of 'independent means' found badly beaten on her kitchen floor in Cambridge. Her face was bruised and her nose broken, but she had actually died from a stab wound to the heart. However, the fatal wound was not discovered until the victim was undressed for post-mortem examination. Somehow, it appeared the victim had been stabbed while undressed, and had then been dressed up after the fact in the four layers of clothes she was found dead in; although she could not have performed this feat herself as death from the knife wound had been instantaneous. It was also established she could not have stabbed herself through the openings in her garments, as they were too far apart from the injury. A knife was found on the kitchen floor, which was spattered with blood, but this only compounded the mystery. It was established that Ms Farrar's wound had bled very little with only tiny specks dotting the innermost of her garments, so it appeared that the blood on the knife and the kitchen floor might have come from somewhere else. Nothing had been stolen from the property and an open verdict was returned.

CHAPTER 2

SIGNS AND WONDERS

INTRODUCTION

In Peterborough towers the jewel of the River Nene – Peterborough Cathedral, or more properly the Cathedral Church of St Peter, St Paul and St Andrew. As befits such an imposing, Gothic landmark, with its awe-inspiring triple-arched West Front, the history and antiquity of this place is truly remarkable. The Saxon foundations of what would become Peterborough Cathedral allegedly stood on an even earlier monastic settlement called Medeshamstede, founded by Seaxwulf, who became the first abbot, in *c.*AD 655. The mediaeval *Peterborough Chronicle Of Hugh Candidus* tells us that the stone used for this monastery was procured from Barnack and 'so large were the blocks, that eight yoke of oxen could scarcely draw one of them.' He also wrote that the scale of Medeshamstede was such that, 'the daughter of Rome might through him [i.e. the cathedral] have liberty and sovereignty in England.'

As we have seen, Medeshamstede is traditionally supposed to have been razed by the Danes in AD 870, but it is suggested that divine retribution was wreaked on the perpetrators of the so-called 'Massacre of Peterborough'. The Danish Earl Hulba, who led the sacrilegious rampage, lost most of the booty plundered from Medeshamstede to the treacherous Fenland marshes and rivers as his bandit army retreated. Nonetheless, the remnants of the building rose once more in the form of a Benedictine Abbey in the mid-10th century, being dedicated to Saint Peter and with the surrounding town earning the name Peter-*burgh*.

Peterborough Cathedral.

The re-foundation of an abbey at this site is itself supposed to have been due to a miracle: Aethelwold, Bishop of Winchester, is said to have been 'warned of God in the night' that he should repair the monastery at Medeshamstede. Accordingly he travelled to Oundle, Northamptonshire, which he mistook for the correct place until a second dream ordered him to follow the course of the River Nene to reach his true destination. Upon visiting the completed abbey, Edgar, king of England at the time, is said to have wept upon his realisation that his kingdom now housed a 'second Rome.'

Thomas Craddock's *Peterborough Cathedral* (1864) tells us that during the tenure of Abbot Elsinus in the early 11th century the abbey became famous for its collection of alleged saintly relics. So industrious was Elsinus that pilgrims flocked from miles around to view, among other relics at Peterborough: a piece of the holy manger, the garments of the virgin, a sliver of the cross and the relics of Saint John the Baptist, Saint Paul and, of course, Saint Peter himself. However, it was during this period (incidentally a time when the Danes were once again ravaging the region and imposing heavy taxation upon the abbey) that Peterborough acquired its most famous saintly relic: the preserved arm of Saint Oswald.

Oswald was a Saxon king of Northumbria, an exceptionally pious Christian ruler whose fortunes changed when he was killed in battle by his rival King Penda of Mercia in the Welsh Marches in AD 642. Oswald was beheaded and his arms chopped off as the spoils of war, and the rest of his corpse was buried on the battlefield. In *c*.675 the slain king's remains were unearthed by his niece, Queen Osthryth. In the century that followed, miraculous cures were reported in both humans and animals at the site of his slaying and a huge hole was dug there by peasants who believed the earth possessed miraculous healing qualities. Oswald's relics – his arms, torso and head – were highly prized and ended up in such diverse places as Lindisfarne, Gloucester and Bardney in Lincolnshire. Of these, his arms were the most highly revered: there was a story that, when alive, Bishop Aiden of Lindisfarne had taken hold of Oswald's hand and said 'May this hand never perish' after being moved by the king's generosity to the poor. When he had died in battle, Oswald's arm and hand had been severed from his torso and yet had remained intact and miraculously incorrupt. There is a persistent accusation that the mummified arm was stolen to order, but either way this was the relic that Abbot Elsinus managed to procure for Peterborough before his death in 1055.

Naturally, the preserved arm of Saint Oswald drew thousands who had heard of the miraculous cures occasioned by the relic. The ailing and the sick came from all parts of the country, and the monks themselves are supposed to have used its marvellous properties. Whenever the arm was washed, the water so used was bottled and carried to the farthest reaches of the land – where if drunk, it effected the same miraculous cures in the ill and desperate. The arm in its silver case is even supposed to have been among the treasures plundered from the abbey in 1070 by the Fenland rebel Hereward before a vision of Saint Peter made him return it. (Of this incident Craddock reserved doubts, and considered that if Hereward did steal the relic then it was 'recovered either by treaty or cunning.')

King Stephen of England (1096–1154) came to see the arm for himself, and by this time the abbey had grown greatly in stature. Following a disastrous fire at the abbey in August 1116, in which most of the building was destroyed with the exception of the chapter house and the dormitory, work on the cathedral was begun again two years later. The Norman-style design was reflected in the architecture, and the cathedral as we know it today, including its unique decorated wooden ceiling within the nave, grew with every block of Barnack limestone hauled to the site until the job was completed.

In 1177 an attempt by the deposed Abbot William de Waterville to steal Saint Oswald's arm ended in carnage. He had stormed into the cathedral backed up by a band of soldiers, but the monks managed to defend the shrine housing their collection of relics, although several were killed in the pitched battle. Even by this time the arm is still supposed to have remained incorrupt: a lifeless limb of withering flesh and mouldering bone, complete with sinews and nails.

As indicated by this outbreak of furious violence, it is interesting to note that the monks at Peterborough Cathedral could be less than spiritual. During the tenure of Robert Kirton, who became abbot in 1496, it is even recorded that a shameless monk stole jewellery from the shrine of Saint Oswald in 1510 to pay a prostitute in the town of Peterborough; other monks could be found drunk and brawling with locals in a nearby tavern, the situation on occasion approaching a near-riot.

These days Peterborough Cathedral is history before one's eyes. There is a suggestion, probably false, that a 16th-century sexton named Robert Scarlett was the inspiration for the gravediggers in Shakespeare's *Hamlet*. 'Old Scarlett' was a well-known figure in Tudor Peterborough; he died on 2 July 1591 aged 98, and he had the distinction of interring two queens in Peterborough Cathedral following their deaths. The first was Catherine, the divorced wife of King Henry VIII, who died at Kimbolton Castle in 1536, and over 50 years later Old Scarlett was also responsible for interring the body of Mary, Queen of Scots, following her execution at Fotheringhay, Northamptonshire, although her body was subsequently removed to Westminster Abbey. Apart from these, Old Scarlett had buried two generations' worth of his fellow townsfolk, and his portrait in all its Tudor splendour hangs high up in the west transept. Chambers' *Book Of Days* (1832) observes: 'And what a lively effigy – short, stout, hardy and self-complacent, perfectly satisfied, and perhaps even proud of his profession...'

But the real curiosity here was the ancient mummified arm that once graced the great interior of this extraordinary, noble building. In St Oswald's Chapel in the south transept there can be observed a curious watchtower with internal stairs once used by the monks to guard Oswald's arm, the design of this tower being such that it would not allow the monk on guard duty to lie down and potentially nod off. But today the arm is lost, and quite what became of this priceless relic is unclear; it apparently vanished or was destroyed some time during the Reformation – a period in history roughly gauged as being the early-to-mid 1500s. Perhaps 'Old Scarlett', then, knew what became of Oswald's arm or saw who came to take it away. There were even some that doubted whether the arm had actually ever arrived at Peterborough Cathedral in the first place – William of Malmesbury, the respected 12th-century historian, was unwilling to take at face value the claims that the sacred arm was actually within the shrine supposed to contain it. However, later that same century the venerable Bishop of Lincoln, Hugh of Avalon, believed the sainted relic was genuine enough to cut a sinew from it to add to his own collection of relics at Lincoln Cathedral.

The whole story is an intriguing enigma, shrouded in folklore, faith and probably even some truth, and it is just one of many such tales from Cambridgeshire. Ramsey Abbey and Ely Cathedral also stand out as shining examples of religious devotion, as we shall see. In fact, the Fenland of the region has been colourfully described by folklorist Christopher Marlowe as being the place where '...came all the great teachers and preachers of history – John the Baptist, Buddha, Mohammed, the Hebrew Patriarchs and Prophets, the Saints and the monks of later years. Here they founded monasteries and dwelt in isolated cells for the purpose of closer communion with the spirit world.'

The 19th-century historian W. H. Bernard Saunders noted that there could be found a curious epitaph on a tombstone in the grounds of All Saints' Church, St Ives: *A crumb of Jacob's Dust lies here below; Richer than all the mines in Mexico*. Jacob, of course, was a Biblical patriarch who according to the *Book Of Genesis* was accorded the rare honour of experiencing the vision of a ladder to heaven, complete with angels ascending and descending, during his flight to the Biblical city of Haran (in modern-day Turkey). What the cryptic inscription at St Ives means can only be guessed at; but clearly it is good to know that faith in Cambridgeshire has, from whatever quarter, apparently never dimmed, and this chapter is designed to illustrate the miraculous, the mysterious and the marvellous attached to such faith. Cambridgeshire, it seems, is a land of miracles.

THE STORY OF SAINT ETHELDREDA

The story of Saint Etheldreda is possibly the best-known legend concerning religious phenomena in Cambridgeshire. Etheldreda (or Athelthryth, or more informally Audrey) was born *c.*AD 636, one of four daughters of King Anna of East Anglia. Around 652 at the age of 16 she was forced into a marriage with a princeling of the southern *Gyrvii* (i.e. the Fens) named Tonbert. During the three-year marriage Etheldreda kept her virginity and for the most part confined herself to the Isle of Ely, at the lonely site of a primitive, ruined church; which upon Tonbert's death in 655 came fully into her possession since

he had given it to her in dower prior to his death. However, a few years later she was again manoeuvred by her parents into a political marriage with Egfrith, the 15-year-old son of King Oswy of Northumbria, and forced to leave the solitude of her beloved Ely.

After 12 years of marriage, during which she denied Egfrith any kind of physical contact, she took herself to a monastery in Scotland. Finally, word was brought to her that the enraged and humiliated Egfrith intended to come and take her by force, at which point she took the decision to flee to the relative safety of Ely. Her long, harsh and dangerous trek southwards to Cambridgeshire, accompanied by her two handmaidens Selbenna and Selvera, and a priest named Huna, is the stuff of legend. Along the route (according to the 12th-century retelling of the story by Thomas of Ely) there were numerous instances of divine intervention that saved her life: for instance, when she was suffering from fatigue at Stow

Ely Cathedral.

in Lincolnshire she stuck her staff into the ground and then fell asleep. When she awoke the staff had put forth leaves and branches that shielded the holy woman from the sun's rays. It afterwards grew into an immense ash tree that towered above all the others for miles around. It was the largest ash tree in Lindsey, a gift from heaven to protect Etheldreda from the heat of the sun.

Upon her return to Ely, Etheldreda was warmly received and her first task was to oversee the building of a double monastery for monks and nuns near the site of the older, ruined church near the River Great Ouse – this is reliably supposed to be on the site where now stands Ely Cathedral itself. Etheldreda gave over the whole island to her monastery and petitioned Pope Benedict; from him she received great immunities and privileges. With the founding of the monastery in AD 673 Etheldreda was made abbess until her death on 9 July 679.

While it is true that Etheldreda died from a tumour under her jaw, it is often said that she considered the disfigurement divine retribution for her vanity in youth when she wore jewellery about her neck. However, it would appear more likely that the tumour was caused by an outbreak of plague, or some other fatal malaise, that also killed others at the monastery. In 695, the then abbess, Etheldreda's own sister Seaxburgh, ordained that her saintly predecessor's remains be unearthed from its grave and brought within the church at Ely. All were astonished to observe that despite the passing of some 16 years, Etheldreda's body remained miraculously intact and showed no sign of decay: nor did the shroud that she had been buried in, and furthermore the tumour on her jaw which had brought about her death had somehow healed

itself and was now no longer visible. The monks of Ely, desiring a suitable sepulchre for their long-dead founder, set sail by water through the gloomy marshlands of the Fens until they reached land and subsequently found 'a desolate city called Grantaceastir [Grantchester], near the walls of which place they discovered a tomb of white marble, of elegant workmanship, with which they returned to their monastery.' It is said that the marble sarcophagus fitted her perfectly, as though it had been made to order. Over the years, and throughout the centuries, the sick, dumb, lame and blind made the hazardous pilgrimage to Ely, with many miraculous cures written of there.

Ely supposedly met the same fate as Crowland, Peterborough and other places in Cambridgeshire in the year AD 870, when the Danish marauders forced the nuns out and the restored church was burnt to the ground. It would seem, though, that Etheldreda's saintly remains were somehow

Tapestry depicting Saint Etheldreda in Ely Cathedral. In 2008 I learned that during a famine she saw to it that the inhabitants of Ely were sustained by the milk from two female deer.

spared the atrocity for they continued to reside at Ely. Ely Cathedral (the Cathedral Church of the Holy and Undivided Trinity of Ely) subsequently grew on the site of the monastery when refoundation began under Abbott Simeon of Ely (1082–94), with the cathedral being dedicated to Etheldreda. Writing in the 12th century, Henry of Huntingdon noted that Ely Cathedral now had a remarkable new relic linked to Etheldreda. By the altar hung a pair of iron shackles which in *c.*1115 a prisoner named Bricstan claimed had spontaneously broken when the ghostly vision of Saint Etheldreda had appeared before him in a dazzling ethereal light and touched them.

Bricstan, 'a very pious man' who came from Chatteris, had fallen afoul of the Bishop of Ely and the Abbots of Ramsey and Thorney, and thence had been carted off to a London dungeon where he was locked away. As he wasted away in his filthy cell, he did not cease to pray to Saint Etheldreda until on one occasion the gloom of his confines was brilliantly lit by the spectral appearance of Saint Etheldreda the Virgin, who was accompanied by Saint Benedict and Etheldreda's sister Seaxburgh. Queen Matilda is said to have sent an envoy named Ralph Basset to investigate the strange events, and this man, upon pushing open the cell door and seeing the shattered irons before him, burst into tears of raptuous joy and hugged the prisoner as though he were his own brother. The queen desired these shackles for her own curiosity but Bricstan denied her them – under any other circumstances a rebuff that would have resulted in severe punishment. But he had argued that the relics belonged to Ely and the queen accepted this, allowing him to travel unmolested with them to the cathedral. While there, people are said to have rubbed injuries and wounds against the iron and recovered their health. As a postscript to this curious tale, we are told that Bricstan retired to Ely and donned the habit of a monk. A local trouble-causer named Robert Malart, who had initially caused Bricstan to be arrested after accusing him of hoarding unearthed treasure, was himself subsequently arrested and condemned to death. Bricstan, according to Fenland folklorist Christopher Marlowe, 'did [not] cease, throughout his long life as a monk at Ely, from rendering thanks to the saints for his remarkable preservation.'

Many churches across England are dedicated to Etheldreda, and within Ely Cathedral itself can be found both a slate marking the former site of her shrine and also the 100-year-old Etheldreda Banner, which is usually used during processions at the cathedral and upon her two feast days: 23 June and 17 October (this second date being the date her remains were moved from their common wooden coffin to the mable sarcophagus). As at Peterborough, the relics of Saint Etheldreda are now lost to history: they disappeared in 1541 along with the saintly remains of her sister Seaxburgh, and also those of her nieces Ermenilda and Werburg. Saint Etheldreda's shrine was destroyed at the time, as were so many historic treasures, and these days the actual location of her remains is unfortunately unclear; however, a piece of Saint Etheldreda's hand *does* survive and is kept in a bejewelled casket in St Etheldreda's Church in Holborn, London. The loss of such relics has generated entirely predictable rumours that a ghostly discoloured, perishing hand – Etheldreda's own – slowly creeps about certain sites in Ely in an attempt to find its way back to the cathedral.

LADY CONYBURROW'S WAY

A Victorian gazetteer describes an ancient trackway to the south-west of Castor thus: '...the way, called by the inhabitants the Lady Conyburrow's Way, which, from all conjectures appears to be nothing but a paved Roman way, leading from a fortress on the other side of the River Nyne to the castle or principal fort on the other side upon the hill, where now the church stands, which was the residence then of the Roman governor, or chief commander. The city was destroyed by the Danes.'

The Roman settlement referred to as being situated south of the River Nene was that known as *Durobrivae*, and Lady Conyburrow's Way was apparently a thin pathway meandering northwards to Castor that had at one time been paved but now presented itself as a barren track through 'Castor-field.' As to how it had obtained its name, there was an odd story. The person that the Victorians referred to as 'Lady Conyburrow' is supposed to have, in life, been Kyneburgha – another Anglo-Saxon saint who was a contemporary of the aforementioned Etheldreda and whom Castor's huge, prominent church is dedicated to.

Kyneburgha is thought to have been a daughter of Penda, the King of Mercia, and later the wife of Alhfrith of Deira – a son of the rival royal house of Northumbria. Penda died during a bitter battle along the banks of an unknown river called *Winwaed* (near Leeds) in AD 655, and Alhfrith disappeared from history after apparently clashing with his own father at Whitby in AD 664. However, it would seem that long before these events Kyneburgha had already chosen the life of a Benedictine nun, founding an abbey for both monks and nuns at Castor (known at this time as *Dormundescastre*) around the year 650. She was later joined there by her kinswomen Kyneswitha and Tibba, both of whom succeeded Kyneburgha as abbess at Castor upon her death *c*.680. All three women were buried here at Castor, but in the early 11th century her bones were carried to Peterborough – an act which enhanced the standing of her cult among the peasantry of the region. One of her bones even made it as far as Canterbury, where it was kept until the Reformation. Her feast day is 6 March.

For centuries the old Roman trackway was used as a route to Castor and it may have been an offshoot of Ermine Street (the route of which can still be observed). Until around the turn of the 20th century this track was called 'the Lady Conyburrow's Way' on account of the popular belief that during her time at Castor the holy lady had found it necessary to navigate Castor-field by moonlight and a barren pathway had miraculously presented itself through the rough, overgrown land north of the bank of the Nene so as to lead her back to the abbey. Other versions of the same story were told as well – the most common being that at one time she was forced to run through the fields to escape the attention of a would-be attacker, and ever after the route of her flight was marked upon the ground as evidence that she had made her escape and kept her purity. Some even said that during the pursuit thick bushes spontaneously grew from the ground and entangled the attacker, allowing Kyneburgha to make her escape.

Ermine Street stretches in a north-westerly direction from the old Roman settlement of *Durobrivae*, and there are a number of old pathways between Castor and the Nene, although it is unclear nowadays which one is Lady Conyburrow's Way. It may be the one that follows Splash Dyke. But the legend that the track was named in veneration of Kyneburgha keeping her virginity is a curious one: she may, in fact, have been the mother of King Osric of Northumbria who ruled till his death in AD 729.

The Family Memoirs Of The Rev. William Stukely note how in September 1737 the antiquarian visited Castor on a fact-finding expedition. Here, he noted among other things that the superstitious held that 'Lady Ketilborough' was said to haunt the old Roman road: a few nights before Michaelmas the ghostly apparition of the holy lady could be seen in a phantom coach pulled by six spectral horses. Nonetheless, the parish church of Castor now (allegedly) finds itself unique in Great Britain, being the only church to be dedicated to Kyneburgha.

ST WENDREDA OF MARCH

The noble and Gothic church that stands on Church Street, off the B1101, on the southern outskirts of March, is dated to 1343 and dedicated to Saint Wendreda – another seventh-century Anglo-Saxon saint who was a sister of the venerated abbesses of Ely, Etheldreda and Seaxburgh.

Very little is known about Wendreda, although she is supposed to have settled in March at a time when it was an island, and (like her sister Etheldreda) opted for the life of an anchoress. She is said to have been baptized as an infant in a spring of pure water at Exning, Suffolk, that subsequently earned the name St Wendreda's Well, and to have (in later life) developed a great skill in healing both humans and animals using herbal remedies that she took with her when she settled in March. Folklore has it that royalty and peasants sought her out for her curative powers. A nunnery was supposedly built at March (on the site where now stands the church) dedicated to healing. Her death date is unclear, and in fact so little is known of her that Murray's *Handbook For Essex, Suffolk, Norfolk And Cambridgeshire* (1875) questioned whether she ever actually existed; although tradition stated that when she died she had been given a lavish funeral at March, being interred in a bejewelled coffin. However, around AD 1030 what were said to be her relics were taken from March to Ely under the instructions of Abbot Aelfsi, where they were richly enshrined in gold. Upon the building of the church in March, these relics are supposed to have been returned by the then Abbot of Ely, where they suffered a fate that is all too commonly repeated throughout this chapter: they disappeared during the Reformation. One is left with the feeling that somewhere there must be a deposit – of utterly incalculable value – of bone fragments, shrines and other relics belonging to Cambridgeshire's saints.

PEGA'S-KIRK

Alongside Etheldreda ranks a woman named Pega as one of the county's most important saints. In the early eighth century, *The History Of Wisbech And The Fens* (1849) reminds us that, 'a few miles from Crowland, a pious woman, named Pega, had so invested the place of her residence with sanctity, by a life of devotion, that a hermitage and church were built there by the flourishing monks of Crowland, and the place [was] called Pega's-kirk or church and [is] now known as Peakirk.'

Pega (or Pege) was born around AD 673, of the royal line of Mercia, although little is known of her life. She was the sister of the famous Crowland hermit and saint Guthlac, and like her brother chose to live an existence of Christian solitude in a part of the country which at the time was widely viewed as inhospitable marshland, populated only by lawless, primitive tribespeople and haunted by unearthly demons.

Guthlac lived the life of a hermit in the remote borderland between Lincolnshire and Cambridgeshire that we now call the Bedford Level; shortly before his death on 11 April 714, Guthlac bade that Pega come to him in Crowland to help take care of the funeral. She came to oversee the burial accompanied by Guthlac's disciples Bettelin, Egbert, Tatwin and Cissa, and the group are reputed to have made their lonely pilgrimage by boat, navigating their way eastwards along the mist-enshrouded River Welland. During this journey Pega is said to have encountered a blind man from Wisbech, who recovered his sight after being blessed by her.

Following Guthlac's burial Pega is supposed to have inherited his book of psalms and the scourge with which his devotees believed he had battled demonic forces of supernatural evil during his residency at Crowland. For the record, the type of nightmarish creatures that haunted this region and which menaced

Guthlac, and probably Pega as well, are described by folklorist Christopher Marlowe as being: 'horrible shapes with great heads, fiery mouths, scaly bodies, pointed chins, crooked legs and unwinking eyes as big as saucers…' There is a legend that at one time the Devil came to Guthlac in Pega's likeness and tried to get him to break a holy vow never to eat before sunset. Pega, upon learning of this, is supposed to have taken herself off and not returned to the area till summoned by her dying brother in AD 714. At any rate, these relics Pega later presented to Abbot Kenulph at Crowland Abbey.

Pega is also believed to have been responsible for exhuming her brother's body 12 months after his death in order to have it moved to another tomb. When the leaden coffin was opened, all those present were astounded to see that Guthlac's body lay therein totally uncorrupted by decay; it looked as though he were merely sleeping. Marlowe writes that as the assembled throng stood in silent amazement Pega 'was filled with joy and gave thanks to God for so miraculous a preservation.'

This contradicts Ingulph's *Chronicle Of Crowland Abbey*, however, which says that Pega returned by boat to Peakirk, where she settled in a cell and lived in a state of 'tearful lamentations' for another two years and three months. Pega subsequently took herself on a pilgrimage to Rome, where she died *c.*AD 719. It is written that when she arrived in Rome, weak with cold and hunger, all the bells of the great city spontaneously chimed and rang for a period of one hour. Ordericus Vitalis, a mediaeval English chronicler who died around 1142, wrote that in his time Pega's relics were housed in an unnamed church in Rome where miracles were alleged to have occurred, but this is – sadly – the last that we hear of Pega's earthly remains.

Her legacy in Peakirk, however, has never really faded from public consciousness, perhaps due in part to the rarity of women anchorites. A monastery is believed to have been erected at the site of her cell, only (like so many others here) to have been attacked and destroyed by the Danes in AD 870 and again in 1013. St Pega's Church is now supposed to stand on this site. And in the surrounding countryside, an 1827 survey of Wisbech noted that a certain part of the turnpike road 'between Wisbech Saint Mary's and the adjoining town of Thorney beyond Guyhirn is called Peakirk drove' on account of the saint. This was presumably somewhere along what is now the A47. An ancient cross also once stood in the vicinty of Guyhirn as further veneration. In Victorian times it was noted that the village at the site of Pega's cell had become known as Peagkirk, or Pequirk. In Northamptonshire she was known as Saint Pee, in southern Lincolnshire as Saint Pege. Today, the village sign bears a depiction of the saint, proudly ensuring that the legend of this remarkable Anglo-Saxon lady of whom we know so little is not forgotten.

THE EELS OF ELY

The famous Northumbrian monk, historian and scholar the Venerable Bede grew up in the years following the death of Etheldreda. Albeit a long way from Ely, Bede noted that the area had been coined *Elge* since the island where the monastery stood was surrounded by water and marshes that were teeming with eels. Some 600 families inhabited the district of the 'East Angles' and lived off this plentiful food source.

This was in the early eighth century, so the following legend can be more or less discounted historically, as well as because of its sheer unlikeliness; nonetheless, it is one of Cambridgeshire's best known stories. It is simply said that in the 10th-century Archbishop Dunstan of Canterbury (d.AD 988) visited Ely on a mission to rid the church of fornication. With the consent of King Edgar, he 'pressed the married clergy to put away their wives' and those that refused were defrocked and monks moved into their quarters. These

This mural can be found at the site of an ancient priory in St Neots today. During the reign of King Edgar, in AD 974, the priory was either presented with (or stole) the miracle-working bones of Saint Neot, a Cornish saint allegedly only 15 inches in stature.

monks, it would seem, put the story about that all those who had disobeyed Dunstan's orders at Ely had been supernaturally transformed, along with their wives and children, into a huge mass of eels, that had surged and slithered their way into the waters of the surrounding marshes.

This, so the story went, was why the isle had gained its name of Ely. This is a very well-known myth, but various antiquarian sources describe it as a Catholic legend extolling the virtues of celibacy and warning against sin, and there is an indication the legend may have begun with a Dr Prideaux in the later 1700s.

THE FOUNDING OF RAMSEY ABBEY

W.H. Bernard Saunders' *Legends And Traditions Of Huntingdonshire* (1888) tells us that Ramsey Abbey was supposedly founded following a sequence of miraculous 'signs' that a humble fisherman had been told would evidence that the Almighty wished for an abbey to stand at that exact site.

Events are said to have occurred in the late 10th century, when the fisherman was plying his trade in 'Ramsey-Mere' but having no luck whatsoever: the nets remained empty, and, finally, after hours of unrewarding attempts, he fell into an exhausted sleep on the floor of his primitive boat. As he slumbered the fisherman dreamt that he was visited by a vision of Saint Benedict, who told him to try again at daybreak – when he would find that his nets would be full of fish. The largest of these, the fisherman would present to his master, a man of wealth and resource called Ailwin. Ailwin was to take the gift, and (the fisherman was instructed to tell his master) thence build a religious house, the exact site of which would be indicated by the behaviour of a bull. The bull would be seen to tear up the ground with its hoof and this was to be the site of the altar of the church. If Ailwin was not convinced by the fisherman's story and wanted further signs that this was a divine instruction, then he would find that his gout (which had ailed him for many a year) would vanish if he complied with Saint Benedict's instructions. As a further sign, the fisherman would find one of his fingers bent and crooked – and that his master Ailwin would straighten it without difficulty.

Armed with this information, the fisherman awoke at daybreak and with several companions he proceeded as instructed in his vision. He fished and the nets were full; the largest fish he presented to Ailwin, telling him that Saint Benedict had asked of them to build a church, the site of which would be marked by the behaviour of the bull. The fisherman's finger had been bent crooked during his expedition, and Ailwin found that he could twist the man's finger back into place with no effort or pain on behalf of the afflicted man. Thus convinced by the fisherman's tale, Ailwin ordered a horse and then rode out to the water's edge. Here he then took a boat to the large marshland island where his cattle resided, and found that all the animals had lain down and formed the shape of a cross. All, that is, except for a bull in the centre that was snorting and thumping its hoof three times into the ground. As he stood there in amazement, Ailwin felt his gout-ridden feet, that had afflicted him for years, slowly begin to feel better until the pain had subsided altogether.

This, so the story goes, is how Ramsey Abbey was founded; such was the fame of the event that it had been built in less than five years and Dunstan, the Archbishop of Canterbury, and Oswald, the Archbishop of York, consecrated it on 8 November 974. It was dedicated to the Mother of God and St Benedict himself, and W.H. Bernard Saunders also tells us that the first abbess, Elfled, herself performed a miracle within the grounds of the foundling abbey. She was reading the lesson in choir one day when the lighted candle flickered out. At this, her finger ends lit up so brightly that the entire church was filled with radiant, divine light. He adds, 'She died in the year 992 and was buried in the Lady Church at Ramsey with great veneration.'

Ramsey, we are told, remained a site of learning and piety until it was 'scattered and destroyed by those who called themselves Reformers in the 16th century.'

FROM SLEPE TO ST IVES

In Saxon times the historic Huntingdonshire market town of St Ives was called *Slepe* until about the year AD 1001.

The story is that in the year *c.*600 a Persian archbishop called Ivo travelled across Europe to England to preach the Gospel and died at the primitive Anglo-Saxon settlement of Slepe. He is said to have spurned a life of priviledge in his homeland, and eventually (with three followers) chosen the life of a hermit among the wilds of the Fens, as would a number of future anchorites. He died there around AD 660.

The common version of the story is that on 24 April 1001 a ploughman discovered the stone coffin and corpse of a man 'in pontifical habit and *entire*' as if he had just been buried (according to Huntingdonshire folklorist W. H. Bernard Saunders in 1888). The skeletons of his three fellow anchorites are also supposed to have been unearthed at the same time, and subsequently a local villager employed as a smith experienced a sequence of visions in which he learned from a man clad in bishop's robes that the remains were, in fact, those of the legendary Christian missionary Ivo and his followers. As the fame of the event spread throughout the county the stone sarcophagus became a focus of pilgrimage where miracles are alleged to have been wrought. A Benedictine priory was erected at the site by Ednoth, Abbot of Ramsey, though after a while the relics of all four of those so discovered were transpoted to the (at the time) 50-year-old Ramsey Abbey, under whose influence Slepe fell.

Around AD 1095 a Canterbury monk named Goscelin wrote his *Vita*, dedicated to Ivo, which drew upon the earlier writings of the third abbot of Ramsey and *his* allegations of further miracles at the site where the sarcophagus was transported. According to legend, a healing spring is supposed to have spontaneously gushed forth there, which further drew many pilgrims to the relics to experience their health-giving properties. Ultimately, however, the monks of Ramsey are believed to have taken the saintly remains back to Slepe — there is a suggestion in *Vita* that many of them were opposed to Ivo's cult — which over the years earned the name St Ives in recognition of the events that occurred here. There is a further suggestion that the stone sarcophagus thought to contain Ivo was actually of Roman origin and that its origin as ascribed to Ivo was in fact a misremembering of Celtic, not Persian, missionaries preaching here centuries earlier. However, by the year 1110 the then Abbot of Ramsey procured a grant for a fair, and thus, as observed by one Victorian commentator, St Ives owed 'its fair and its name to a miracle.'

INGULPH OF CROYLAND AND THE BAILIFF

In the year 1076, as the region was recovering from the rebellion of Hereward the Wake, an acrimonious dispute arose between Ingulph, the Benedictine abbot of Croyland (Crowland) Abbey and the abbey's bailiff, a man called Ashford.

Ingulph had complained that Ashford was trying to extort from him a meadow which belonged to the abbey, and so both parties were ordered to appear before the king's justiciars in Stamford. Somewhere between Helpston and Stamford (probably along what is now the B1443) Ashford's horse unaccounatbly threw him to the ground, where the land-grabbing bailiff died.

Ashford's body was recovered by his relatives and placed on a wooden bier. As the grim procession made its way back in the direction of Helpston, a huge thundercloud darkened the entire sky and rain fell heavily; in the confusion the bier broke and the corpse of Ashford the bailiff tumbled limply into a muddy field — the very meadow he had been trying to extort from Croyland Abbey.

At this point, the relations are supposed to have seen Ingulph himself, standing in the lane amid the downpour, and observed that the whole sequence of events indicated divine judgement in favour of Ingulph and the abbey.

Ingulph died on 16 November 1109 and the story turned up in the *Croyland Chronicle*. It was originally supposed to have been a contemporary account of the incident by Ingulph's own hand. However, it has since been found to be mediaeval fable-spinning; although the anonymous author may have been drawing upon a long-standing Croyland legend.

A PRAYER TO SAINT GILES

In around 1092, a woman called Hugoline became dangerously ill in Cambridge. Since she was the wife of Picot, the county sheriff and baron of Bourne, no expense was spared in attending her: the king's physician and other eminent doctors of the era were brought in but none could do anything for Hugoline. On her deathbed, she vowed that if she might recover then she would build a church and dedicate it to God and Saint Giles, to whom she made her desperate prayer and whom she looked upon as her patron. Her husband consented to this wish.

Within three days, Hugoline had completely and miraculously recovered. Together with her husband she consulted both Anselm, the Archbishop of Canterbury, and Remigius, the Bishop of Lincoln. Both agreed to the construction of a church dedicated to Saint Giles, near the castle at Cambridge, which fell under the supervision of the canon of Huntingdon, and the patronage of the sheriff Picot.

This was according to one Alfred of Beverley, writing in the 12th century. These days all that remains of the castle is the motte, known as Castle Mound, on the eastern side of Castle Street. The site where the original St Giles Church was built is at the bottom of Castle Hill near the Magdalene Street crossroads. The church was almost entirely rebuilt in 1875, although the process was essentially begun the previous century when the semicircular arch seperating the nave and the chancel was 'beautifyed' in 1713; however, its interior has retained some of the original Norman architecture.

HERBERT OF HUNTINGDON

A curious and sad story briefly alluded to in the mediaeval *Chronicle Of Melrose* illustrates the way religion has been twisted in the past and actually used as a justification for persecution. The era saw numerous instances of alleged 'ritual murders', and brutal killings linked to the Jewish population were rumoured to have been carried out at such places as Lincoln, Northampton, Norwich and Bury St Edmunds.

These accusations fuelled an ugly period of anti-semitism in England. For 150 years England's wealthy Jewish community had been expanding and yet was frequently subject to attacks, a circumstance that prompted them to be among the first to build stone houses. Among the charges of atrocities made against the Jews, the *Chronicle Of Melrose* noted the instance of a boy called Herbert of Huntingdon who was tied to a stake and whipped by his Jewish father before being drowned *c.*1180. It is supposed that the boy Herbert wished to convert and so was martyred, but the story appears to be rumour-mongering – there may not even have been a Jewish community in Huntingdon in the 12th century. Nonetheless, we know from other instances (such as the story of 'little saint' Hugh of Lincoln, or that of John of Stamford in Northampton) that the discovery of such crimes was often attended by multiple instances of miraculous relgious phenomena, and it is likely that if this enigmatic story has *any* basis in fact then rumours of such would have swept Huntingdon accordingly.

In *c.*1272 there was a mysterious crime in 'Melbourn Field' when a wealthy Jew named Saul was found slain in the dirt along with two Christians, Peter de Logges and Henry de Logges; who killed them all is unknown, although the deaths may have resulted from a violent fracas over money. In many ways, this was a sign of the times. After a century and a half of accusations and occasional outbreaks of violent rioting and massacres, things finally came to a head in 1290 when a royal edict expelled the Jews from England. The 'official' reasons were the laws of England that now enforced loans from them, burdened them with taxation and confiscated their property to such an extent that, with the coffers of England bulging, the once-royally favoured Jews had nothing more to give the state. The 3,000 strong Jewish community had also failed to comply with a 1275 statute that forbade them from pursuing their tradional occupation as money lenders. The third reason, as the tale of Herbert of Huntingdon illustrates, was sadly prejudicial superstition and the desire to promote negative propoganda: the chronicler at the time did not even think it necessary to *say* the boy's murderous father was Jewish – it was deemed self-evident.

BISHOP HUGH OF LINCOLN

Of exceptionally worthy memory was Bishop Hugh d'Avalon of Lincoln, formerly Prior of Witham, Somerset, and a learned man who earned the respect of the clergy, royalty, three popes and all the common people for his generosity, sense of justice and his spreading of the faith in the 12th century.

By all accounts Bishop Hugh was an extremely attractive and witty man, whose personality embraced all. Men, women and children all warmed to his human charm. Chroniclers recorded anecdotes about him playing with babies, where the infants would gurgle happily, much to the evident joy of the bishop. He was thoroughly chaste and took his vows of celibacy extremely seriously, but unlike some of the clergy he entertained widows and mothers at his table, blessing them and listening to their fears and problems. His charm even extended to members of the animal kingdom, notably his famous swan, whose behaviour wildlife experts still have some trouble in explaining. Such stories of an entirely human bishop no doubt fuelled the fondness that almost all felt for Hugh, who had come to England of noble Burgundian stock and ultimately went on to champion a diocese for 14 years that at that time extended from the Humber to the Thames.

Bishop Hugh of Lincoln statue in Buckden Towers.

Bishop Hugh died on 16 November 1200 at a house owned by the bishops of Lincoln, during a visit to London. There were numerous miracles that were purported to have occurred in Bishop Hugh's lifetime (and beyond) which are described fully in Father Herbert Thurston's *The Life Of Saint Hugh Of Lincoln* (1898). Among these was a remarkable incident that occurred at Alconbury when Hugh was introduced to a one-year-old boy who had swallowed an elegantly fashioned but very sharp piece of steel. The baby's father believed that his son could not be saved and would shortly die, but Hugh stood over the infant and pressed the boy's throat and gave him his blessing. On the following Sunday the boy vomited the iron out of his system, and afterwards recovered; this incident was confirmed as fact by the Abbot of Sawtry and the Prior of Huntingdon.

A CAMBRIDGESHIRE MARTYDOM

John Foxe's *Book Of Martyrs* recorded the grim and bizarre details of the execution of Revd John Hullier in 1557. He died for 'opposing the superstition of the papists' during the reign of the Catholic Queen Mary – 'Bloody Mary' – and his death is an extreme example of the faith that some can display when faced with the inevitable prospect of a violent, unjust death.

Hullier was brought up at Eton College, Berkshire, and in due course became rector of *Babram* (Babraham), south-east of Cambridge, before transferring thence to Kings Lynn, Norfolk, where his religious rhetoric caught the attention of Mary's Catholic spies. He was brought before the Bishop of Ely, Dr Thirlby, and then thrown into gaol at Cambridge Castle. After a while he was removed to the 'Tolbooth prison' and three months later moved once again to St Mary's Church, Cambridge, where he was sentenced to death by Dr Fuller for heresy in promoting the cause of Protestantism.

On Maunday Thursday, Hullier was dragged to the stake to be burnt on Jesus Green, before Jesus College. He was undressed and placed in a pitch barrel atop a pile of reeds and wood, chains binding him to the stake. As this was done, Hullier cried out that his death was in a just cause, and as a priest named Boyes pressed the Mayor of Cambridge to silence him, the wood blocks were set alight.

The manner of Hullier's death is very curious to the modern reader. Having said his piece, Hullier began to pray quietly. The direction of the wind fanned the flames against his back, at which he began to pray more fervently. His friends directed the executioner to fire the pile 'to windward of his face', which was immediately done. Books were thrown onto the pile to feed the flames, one of which Hullier caught. It was the *Communion Service*, which he began to read aloud in much joyful rapture. In his death agony, he continued to read without screaming or apparent distress, until the billowing smoke blinded him. At this point he pressed the book to his breast and thanked God for what he saw as a 'sign' from heaven in his moment of suffering. The day was hot, and the fire raged furiously until the Revd Hullier appeared to have succumbed. However, as the executioner and others moved to put out the flames, the supposedly-dead man suddenly exclaimed, 'Lord Jesus, receive my spirit!' In panic, gunpowder was thrown onto the pile, but it was clear that Hullier was at last dead. Even so, the fire continued to rage until all the crowd were afforded the 'singular spectacle' of Hullier's bones – still chained erect against the stake – presenting the image of it having been a skeleton that had been so treated.

It was noted that after this grim spectacle the crowd descended on the pile to touch the remains and grab relics of what they saw as divine intercedence during a 'martyrdom'.

The history of religion in Cambridgeshire is full of such remarkable characters, and a different kind of 'martyrdom' is recorded as having taken place the following century. It concerned a Yorkshire local, James Naylor, of Ardesley, who experienced a sign while ploughing a field in 1651. He was aged about 35, and Naylor had 'heard a voice bidding him to go forth from his father's house, and had a promise given with it that the Lord would be with him.' Believing that he had heard the voice of God, he was converted to Quakerism in Wakefield by George Fox and endeavoured to spread the word; he embarked upon a remarkbale four-year 'crusade' to preach conversion, where in London the brilliance of his speeches was marked by the wonder that God had provided sustinence for him as he travelled (he had been exceptionally nervous about leaving his home parish). Naylor seems to have been very charismatic and he developed an adoring female following who referred to him as 'The Everlasting Son of Righteousness', an appellation that subsequently began to threaten his reputation. Although he acknowleged such titles, he said that they referred to Christ within him, and not he himself. The authorities, however, saw it differently, and after a bizarre visit to Bristol (in which a shaven-headed acolyte and devout female followers spread scarfs and handkerchiefs under his feet) the convoy was arrested.

Naylor was accused of blasphemy, although in reality he seems to have been exceptionally devout and very humble. The court failed utterly to prove he had ever spoken a blasphemous word in his life, and he vocally denied that he believed himself to be Christ personified; merely that, spiritually, Christ was in him. It seems

HOLY WELLS AND SPRINGS

Much like the afore-mentioned 'healing well' at Exning, Suffolk, Cambridgeshire has its own holy wells and springs. The folklorist Thomas Sternberg observed in 1851 that there was the celebrated 'holy spring' of Saint Lawrence, Peterborough, that was attributed with miraculous healing qualities. The fact that it was popularly ascribed to the saint apparently angered the Bishop of Lincoln, Hugh d'Avalon, in the late 1100s, who believed such associations were a superstitious embarrasment. By 1851 the spring was speculated to have been entirely lost, although local historians thought the chapel of St Lawrence, 'the chancel of which is yet standing', was probably built over such a well 'supposed to be possessed of supernatural virtues.'

Evidence of some healing springs can still be sought out, such as the stonework of the well between St John the Baptist Church, Holywell, and the River Great Ouse. The historian W.H. Bernard Saunders wrote of this spot that a natural spring that fed the well produced 'very soft water' that 'was reputed to possess healing qualities, which caused it to be visited by large numbers. Some witers have urged that in pre-Reformation times its healing qualities were ascribed to a "miraculous agency", but there is no evidence of this.' Another spring can be found between the Longthorpe Housing Estate, Peterborough, and the A1179. This one was supposedly dedicated to Saint Cloud, an ancient hermit who lived by the well but of whom virtually nothing is known; in all likelihood it dates to the mid-1600s.

As in neighbouring Northamptonshire, belief that such wells possessed miraculous properties was very common, and W.H. Bernard Saunders noted others in the region. A mineral spring had once existed at Somersham, but by the time of writing in 1888 this had become entirely neglected. The Somersham Spring had been discovered by a Dr Layard in 1759, and the learned doctor wrote a discourse on its remarkable healing qualities; however, it survived not 65 years before falling into neglect. North-west of St Neots, by the River Kym, two mineral springs were discovered at Hail Weston around 1597, 'the water being looked upon as a certain cure for scrofula, eruptions, dimness of sight etc.' The water from one was described in Tudor times as 'verrie sweet and fresh', from the other 'brackish and salt.' By 1770 they were still being sought out for their remarkable curative powers; but as in the rest of the region, the fad for 'healing wells' itself dried up and the Hail Weston wells fell into disrepair. The *History, Gazetteer And Directory Of Cambridgeshire* (1851) notes that a mineral spring of 'much repute' near Bourn called Jacob's Well had also recently

The holy well in the grounds of Holywell's church.

Here at Eltisley, so legend says, lies buried Saint Pandonia, the daughter of a Scottish king who fled to a nunnery hereabouts in order to keep her chastity. She died c.AD 904 at the nunnery, which fell into disrepair some 1,000 years ago. She was buried near a pure spring (now lost) called St Pandonia's Well, before she was unearthed and transported into the village church in 1344.

closed up, whereas another spring – possessing remarkable healing qualities – had been discovered in 1845 within 100 yards of the old one.

Around this time it was observed that the water in Croxton Park, Croxton, was of such an extraordinarily excellent quality that a well was dug to the remarkable depth of 303ft to tap it. Another, called Gorman's Pond at Godmanchester, was alleged locally to cure leprosy. In the north-west of the county, Gutch and Peacock's *County Folklore Vol. 5* (1908) notes that a religious house 'inhabited by pious women' near Stamford once had a healing well within its grounds that supposedly cured blindness.

There were curious echoes of this theme in March 2008 when local and national media picked up on a story from Trinity Church in the village of March, where every day the cellar was observed to be mysteriously flooded with some 200 gallons of water. It was a constant job to pump the water out, but the church steward at Trinity commented at the time that maybe it could be bottled and marketed as 'holy water', although quite where it was coming from was not clear. Anglian Water took samples of the water, however, and declared it unfit for human consumption as it had become 'environmentally contaminated.' They decided it was likely to have come from an old drain near Trinity Church, but admitted that it was not mains water or sewage and that it was just as likely that it came from a natural spring or an old well that had been disturbed in a recent eathquake that had centred on neighbouring Lincolnshire. Wherever it had come from, however, the church steward had himself partaken of the water when it began rising in the cellar – and had not suffered any ill effects.

CHAPTER 3

SUPERNATURAL EVIL

INTRODUCTION

In 1127 King Henry I of England gave the abbacy of Peterborough to an abbot called Henry of Poitou. The 12th-century Peterborough chronicler Hugh Candidus recorded how there was much protest, as the abbot's acquisition of Peterborough Abbey was a strategic move aimed at reaping profits; thus, 'miserably was the abbacy given between Christmas and Candlemas at London.'

As soon as the abbot arrived 'on the Sunday which one sings "*Exurge, quare obdormis, Domine?*"', a Hellish spectacle was visited upon the area which was chronicled as fact and talked about across England. In the deer park in the town of Peterborough, and in all the woodland between Peterborough and Stamford, a ghastly, demonic hunt was seen crashing through the trees, through Lent and up until Easter.

Many reliable witnesses saw these huntsmen, and the monks heard the winding of the horns at night from deep inside the forest. It was reckoned that there were some 30 demonic huntsmen in all: 'These huntsmen were big, black and ugly, and all their dogs were black and ugly with wide eyes, and they rode on black horses and black goats.'

The entire story is clearly a criticism on the excesses of the abbot, but it is possible the huntsmen were real: many people of 'unquestioned veracity' saw and heard them, and Hugh Candidus certainly believed the rumours: 'This was on his [Abbot Henry's] arrival. Of his departure we cannot yet speak. May God provide!'

This incident is still alleged to be one of the most reliable instances of some form of supernaturally evil visitation appearing in the region, although it is not the oldest. For generations, the folk of Peterborough grew up with the story of Werbode and his diabolical end. Werbode was a pagan knight and steward at King Wulfhere of Mercia's court in the seventh century, and the king's two sons – Wulfade and Rufine – forbade that Werbode marry their sister Werburgh since she was raised a Christian. Werbode's solution was to assassinate the two princes as they prayed; however, he instantly repented and took himself before Bishop Chad to confirm himself converted to Christianity. Because of this, a short time later Werbode was openly strangled before the king's palace in Medeshamstede (Peterborough) by the Devil himself – who took his soul off to Hell. Another account states that he became as though *possessed* by the Devil, and tore the flesh from his arms with his own teeth – a prolonged period of self-inflicted violence that brought about his death shortly thereafter. For centuries stories such as this must have terrified generations who grew up in this part of Peterborough. One Walter of Whittlesea tells us that this event was the reason for re-founding the early monastic building here *c.*655 at the site of what would become Peterborough Cathedral. The sequence of events is said to have so terrified the Mercian king Wulfhere that he went to Bishop Chad and promised to undergo whatever penance the holy man saw fit to rid his kingdom of the evil malaise that pervaded it. The bishop told him that this could only be achieved by undertaking to 'restore the Christian religion and the ruinated temples thereof, and likewise build new ones.' Wulfhere is supposed, at the time, to have drifted from the Christian faith, hence his inner torment. His faith was restored anew, however, when he saw Bishop Chad take off his vestment following prayers in the oratory and hang it on a *sunbeam* as though it were a coat hook.

Belief in the Devil manifested itself in many curious forms throughout the centuries. In the Fenland areas, following drainage, it was common for fossilised molluscs to be turned over, and these curved valves – Gryphaea – were superstitiously referred to as 'Devil's Toenails'. In Cambridgeshire, it was observed in 1834 that there was a peculiar ritual which was performed upon the discovery of such a fossil. Young men would spit into them and then lob them over their shoulder without looking to see what had become of them. Thus, the Gryphaea became a 'Lucky Stone'; unless, presumably, it hit someone behind the thrower. It is highly likely that certain bizarre natural phenomena were also laid at Satan's door: between the river Cam and Newmarket Road in Cambridge (at what was then called *Barnewell*), the Bishop of Ely was giving orders at St Giles Priory when a sudden 'tempeste of raine and thunder' shook the building to its very foundations. Flashes of lightning entered the priory, giving it the appearance of having been set afire. A 'filthie stench' then caused many of those within to fall so ill that it was feared they might die. This was in 1223, and it is likely that the 'filthie stench' was viewed as the sulphurous smell of the Devil himself.

The region itself was also the setting for one of the earliest recorded incidences of witchcraft. An anonymous Anglo-Saxon charter dated 1044 notes that around a century earlier one Wulstan Uccea was a *thegn* in the East Midlands who held estates at Kettering and Ailsworth. This latter had come into his possession because a neighbouring widow had had a grudge against his father, Alfsige. When the widow's house was searched an effigy was found of Alfsige, with an iron pin stabbed into its heart, and following her conviction on a charge of witchcraft the widow was carted off to London Bridge where she was drowned in the Thames. Her Ailsworth estate thus passed to her victim's family, with King Edgar's blessing, while her own son was forced to flee after being branded an outlaw. And so this chapter is largely concerned with not only the sites where they say the Devil lurks, but also the legacy of witchcraft in Cambridgeshire: a county where unbelievable accusations of demonically supernatural incidents at Warboys were written as fact, and a land where the 'Witchfinder General' Matthew Hopkins (a man undoubtedly more evil than those he sought out) presided over tyrannical trials and barbaric executions. And a county where the lingering, rural belief in witchcraft survived until much nearer our own time than you might think…

WHEN THE DEVIL VISITED CAMBRIDGESHIRE

It is well known that, in the past, the Fens was a demon-haunted landscape. The Anglo-Saxon hermit Guthlac, we are told, suffered the nightmarish visitations of demons described as 'many horrible shapes with great heads, fiery mouths, scaly bodies, pointed chins, crooked legs and unwinking eyes as big as saucers.' By the 13th century, civilisation had touched the Fens and some of the landscape had been given over to meadows and arable farmland. Nonetheless, it must have seemed like the Devil had possessed two visiting canons of the Priory of the Holy Trinity, London, who came to such high words over where the boundaries of Ramsey and Ely were drawn that one brutally murdered the other on St Peter's Day 1256. Around this same time, Wright's *Memorials of Cambridge* (1845) observed that, 'the ancient encampment of *Vandlebury*, on the summit of the Gog Magog Hills, was believed to be haunted by unearthly beings', which may be a reference to demons.

The philosopher Henry More (d.1687) recorded that a coven of witches were reckoned to gather at the house of one Mother Lendall of notorious reputation in Cambridge. The table would be well stocked with guests and meat during these meetings, but at the head of the table 'there sat one in black' who clearly commanded the proceedings. The leaders of the party would talk in a strange tongue that could not be understood by most, and it is clear that More was implying these parties were hosted by the Devil himself. All things told, Satan seems to have taken a frighteningly frequent interest in our county.

One of the most famous antiquarian landmarks in Cambridgeshire is the Devil's Dyke, or the Devil's Ditch, an immense earthwork consisting of a bank and a ditch that stretches nearly eight miles in a north-west direction from (approximately) Woodditton. The massive embankment then follows a line parallel with the July Course at Newmarket Racecourse to the village of Reach. The structure is truly impressive to behold, although its origins are unclear. It is generally thought of as Anglo-Saxon, although some thought it had earlier origins. At some point labourers digging through the ditch on Newmarket Heath, near Exning, unearthed artefacts bearing Roman inscription, leading to speculation that it had been manufactured in that era to defend against an unknown enemy threat from either the south or south-west. This was assumed by the fact that the ditch was on the 'southern/western' part of the structure. Today's archaeologists are of the opinion that the Devil's Dyke was not a single structure, but more likely an earthwork that was refortified by different peoples in different eras over a period of centuries. Whatever its true age and purpose, a contributor to *Notes And Queries* remarked in 1845 that the Devil's Ditch would always 'retain the mysterious appellation conferred on it by popular superstition.'

The dyke's satanic name, however, appears to be relatively modern: prior to the mediaeval era, the earthwork was apparently called St Edmund's Dyke, but it may have then earned the name *D'Aviler's Ditch* on account of a rebel baron called D'Aviler who laid waste to Cambridgeshire in 1266 during the reign of Henry III. But to the peasantry of the region, this mysterious landmark must have seemed to have been made by the Devil himself, and 'D'Aviler' perhaps over time became substituted by 'Devil.' The Tudor traveller William Camden noted that the structure had 'the common people wondering greatly at, as a

The Devil's Dyke at Swaffham Prior.

worke made by devils and not by men.' Some said that other huge earthworks at Thetford, Norfolk, were made by the Devil scraping his shoes after he had dug the ditch at Newmarket Heath. Others said that the dyke was created by the Devil's fiery tail as angry residents chased him from the parish.

Worryingly, there are many places in Cambridgeshire with similar associations to the Devil. As we have already seen, a 1647 disappearance at St John's College, Cambridge, was blamed on the Devil. And at Ely, when Doctor John Frankland died in 1730 the people of the Fens sung a peculiar rhyme. Franklin was a Fellow and Master of Sidney Sussex College, Cambridge – 'a very fat and rosy-complexioned man', who died soon after becoming Dean of Ely. He was succeeded as dean by Dr Peter Allix, described as 'a meagre, weasel-faced, sworthy man.' It seems neither were particularly popular: for the rhyme explained that:

> *The Devil took our Dean,*
> *And picked his bones clean.*
> *Then clapt him on a board*
> *And sent him back [to us] again.*

Some clearly even considered the great Oliver Cromwell to be the Devil incarnate, and it is a remarkable truism that he has split opinion (to this very day) ever since the 1640s. We have already seen that some thought his victories and escapes from death were evidence of divinity. On the flip side of the coin, in the early 1700s the then owner of Cromwell House, Huntingdon, Edward Audley, would take care to point

Remains of the stone cross at March.

out to visitors to Oliver's bedroom that in 1599 the future Lord Protector had been born within sight of the Devil, who had hidden behind the bedroom door. He was referring to an old tapestry that had hung there at the time of the Cromwell family's residence, but the allegory is clear.

Enid Porter explained in *Cambridgeshire Customs And Folklore* (1969) that many years ago there was an attempt to build a church near the Market Place in March. This was thwarted by nightly appearances of Satan, who would invade the town and tear down the walls of the fledgling church: the Fens, of course, was a demon-haunted land in days gone past, and 'the Devil hated to see any house of God being built' there. The townsfolk thus erected a great stone crucifix – much to the dismay of the Devil, who fled March and retreated back into the gloom of the Fens. Ms Porter noted that this legend was still common currency

Ruins of the chapel at Reach, where Satan was said to appear.

well into the 20th century. The church in question is supposed to have been the 14th-century St Wendreda's on Church Street, at the B1101-Job's Lane junction; the remains of the stone cross can be found to the north on the western side of the B1101 along the stretch known as The Causeway.

Near the Norfolk border at Leverington, in late Victorian times, they still baked a delicacy known as Whirlwind Cakes on the Sunday in mid-Lent – known here as 'Whirling Sunday', according to the Revd Frederick Carlyon of that village, in a contribution to *Fenland Notes And Queries* in 1891. Some said that this day, which had once observed a kind of bank holiday in the village, had earned its strange name (and its cake!) because of a strange incident long ago. A woman had been making cakes for some visitors on a Feast Sunday when the Devil appeared in a whirlwind and swept her up out of her kitchen, over the steeple of St Leonard's Church and away forever.

There is also an ancient superstition that if one were to run seven times round St Etheldreda's Church in Reach then his Satanic majesty would appear in all his glory at the ruinous remains of the old chapel archway behind the church. But should anyone harbour a desire to actually meet the Devil that badly, then maybe this old ritual will work. Throughout the Fen country there was a tradition of 'gathering the Devil's harvest'. At midnight on St Mark's Eve the aspirant had to go to a bracken fern and hold beneath it three pewter plates that all rested upon one another. Christopher Marlowe wrote in 1926 that the seeds of the bracken were supposed to fall *only* at this time of year. While they were so small that they could hardly be seen, they nonetheless fell with great violence, smashing the first two plates but being caught by the third. Immediately upon the advent of this, the Devil rode up on a black hog, willing to grant all requests – provided that the one who had performed this peculiar ritual was willing to sign their soul away first.

In 1895 the British occultist and magician Aleister Crowley attended Trinity College in Cambridge. Crowley is often described as the 'Wickedest man in the world', and according to folklore he spent his time at Trinity in the study of poetry and the occult. Thanks to his orgiastic depredations in later life, he is often popularly depicted as Satan incarnate. However, these days Satan himself seems to have taken his attention elsewhere. But, before you breath a sigh of relief, it might be worth bearing in mind the words of C. L'Estrange Ewan, the demonology expert. In 1936 he noted, 'A band of Satanists have their rendezvous not far from the city of Cambridge…'

THE WITCHES OF WARBOYS

In 1585, some eight years before the famous 'Witches of Warboys' drama, there had been a less well-known incident of witchcraft in Cambridge. Henry More, a Fellow of Christ's College, obtained from an eyewitness a strange, true story. A mother and daughter were on the point of being hanged for witchcraft, and the pair were urged to forsake the Devil. The woman stoutly refused, and so hanged unrepentant. But this seemed to affect the daughter, who began to pray loudly in sincere penitence. The Devil's anger was immediately displayed: it was a calm day, but a furious wind whipped up out of nowhere, and threw the executed mother's body against the ladder violently and shook the gallows platform so tremendously that spectators were forced to grab the posts to stop the whole contraption collapsing. What became of the daughter is not said, but the event proved a strange forerunner to the Warboys saga some years later.

In 1593 a pamphlet was published part-entitled *The Most Strange And Admirable Discoverie Of The Three Witches Of Warboys*. It evidenced a bizarre sequence of events that had begun four years earlier in this village south of Ramsey – a story that in many ways conforms to the archetypal Stuart-era idea of witchcraft accusation, and an example of the frightening way in which events could spiral out of control.

In November 1589 Jane Throckmorton, the 10-year-old daughter of a well-to-do squire living in Warboys called Robert Throckmorton, began suffering from a series of seizures. During one of these fits, Alice Samuel, a neighbour, came to the Throckmorton household to see how the child was doing. During the visit, the afflicted little girl pointed at the old woman in the corner of the room and said, 'Look where the old witch sitteth…did you ever see one more like a witch than she is?' Alice Samuel was at the time sat by the chimney with the youngest Throckmorton baby in her lap when Jane made her accusation before proceeding to go into a fit, writhing, convulsing and shrieking terribly. She then appeared to go into a trance, and when she recovered she glared at Alice Samuel and cried, 'Take her away, I cannot abide her – she is a witch!'

At this point the child's mother and grandmother excused the child's behaviour and sent her to bed; however, her fits did not cease and returned with an increasing frequency. It was at this point that events began to slide out of control and into the realm of the surreal. Within the space of a month, it was not just Jane who was having fits. Two other daughters of Robert Throckmorton – including the eldest, 15-year-old Joan – had begun to display similar symptoms. Joan suffered a fit apparently worse than any that had gone before, during which she sneezed, shrieked and groaned, and suffered convulsions so violent that she had to be forcibly held down on the bed to prevent her from injuring herself. All three children blamed old Alice Samuel for their torment, and Joan was now beginning to make prophecies: 12 within the household would be possessed, she shrieked. By the end of January 1590 five of the Throckmoton girls (aged between nine and 15) and seven of the family's female servants were suffering fits and making the same claims to bewitchment. Doctors were brought in, but none could explain what was going on: and so the family physician, Dr Barrow of Cambridge, put forward the sinister suggestion to Mr Throckmorton that, '…some kind of sorcerie and witchcraft [was] wrought towards his child.'

where the Devil suckled, but in actuality likely to have been a mere wart) from her mother's body, it did no good. A steady trail of people queued to give information to the Justice of the Peace in order to condemn Ann Symes.

In both instances it is unclear what fate befell the accused women. However, their cases served as forerunners to the nightmare of Puritan tyranny that was to be visited upon East Anglia later that century.

'THE WITCHFINDER GENERALL'

In the 1640s, chaos reigned in England. The nation had been reduced to anarchy in the face of civil war, and many villages found themselves lacking protection from taxation, outbreaks of sickness, hunger and the abuses of the undisciplined armies that marched through the parish. Many saw the hardship their communities suffered as symptomatic of a larger war than that between Royalty and Parliament; it was the very struggle between good and evil itself. Into this mix was thrown Matthew Hopkins, the 'Witchfinder Generall', a figure demonised for over three-and-a-half centuries now…a man who rode from remote parish to isolated village, accompanied by a male assistant and a female searcher. Hopkins boasted he could alleviate the villagers' sufferings by identifying the evil that plagued them: witchcraft, and those practising it.

Many such places had lost most of their male population, who had gone to fight in the war. By the time the long-haired, bearded Hopkins, in his familiar cloak and black steeple hat, rode into Huntingdonshire with his assistants in 1646, he had been travelling East Anglia and the English Midlands 'curing' the curse of witchcraft for two years. There was never a shortage of those who wished to have their neighbours prosecuted for harming livestock or relatives. Although the true number of luckless 'witches' identified by this time is unclear, hundreds had been accused and Hopkins had presided over scores of executions – all the while dubiously claiming to have been given the task by Parliament and charging fees wherever he uncovered a suspect. The Edwardian-era writer Wallace Notestein studied the panic in his *History Of Witchcraft In England From 1558-1718* (1911) and wrote of Hopkins' appearance in the county as supposedly having been foreseen by the 'detested creatures', meaning the witches. Hopkins' brutal reputation had gone ahead of him, at any rate.

Following a visit into Northamptonshire, Hopkins' course led him into Huntingdonshire around March 1646, where the usual pattern of events played out. Frightened, ignorant and malevolent parishioners turned upon each other as the justices of the peace began to gather evidence prior to Hopkins' arrival. One Elizabeth Chandler of Keyston had dispatched an imp called Beelzebub to harm a neighbour who had not invited her to a party. The subsequent gathering was ruined when the frumenty (broth) boiled over and all but flooded the house. The fact that this 'imp' bore a striking resemblance to a wooden log seems not to have mattered; Ms Chandler also employed another imp called Trullibib that looked suspiciously like a stick. But these were supernatural creatures, after all, and Elizabeth Chandler apparently confessed to employing them to hound the family of William Darnell, a blacksmith. His daughter Elizabeth, aged nine, had at some point been hit round the head by Ms Chandler, and three weeks later the child had died screaming that, 'Goodwife Chandler did come to her and would kill her.' The necessity for two inanimate objects to be classed as 'imps', or familiars, is perhaps the most curious detail in the narrative. Even by the standards of the time, this is strange: far more typical, for instance, were the demons that were supposed to have visited a suspected witch called Margaret Flower on 30 January 1618 in Lincoln

Castle's gaol. Around midnight, '…one stood at her bed's feet, with a black head like an ape and spake unto her, but what, she cannot well remember, at which she was very angry because he would speak no plainer.'

One so accused was dragged before the inquisition and attempted to cast the blame on others. He recalled a conversation with 'Clarke's sonne of *Keiston* [Keyston]' in which the latter had declared, 'I do not believe you will die a witch, for I never saw you at our meetings.' John Gaule, the incumbent clergyman at Great Staughton, was so outraged at the terror that was being fostered among his parishioners that he bravely began to preach against Hopkins. In a letter to one parishioner in the village, Hopkins stated, coldly and matter-of-factly, 'I intend to give your towne a visite suddenly…I intend to come (God willing) the sooner to heare His singular judgement on the behalfe of such parties.' The vicar of Great Staughton was not intimidated, however, and shortly hereafter produced a work rubbishing Hopkins' crusade – cleverly dedicating it to Colonel Walton in the House of Commons to ensure that it appeared he had political support. Walton was a townsman, and a brother-in-law of Oliver Cromwell. Nonetheless, although Great Staughton appears to have been spared, the rest of Huntingdonshire suffered in March and April.

The accusations voiced at the inquisitions were surreal, bizarre and outrageous. In Great Catworth, Elizabeth Weed confessed that 21 years prior she had been granted three spirits: a young man, whose duty was to 'lie with her carnally, and he did so often', and two small dogs. A white one, Lilly, whose job was to kill her enemies, and a black one, Priscill, whose job it was to kill livestock, were employed by Ms Weed. In nearby Molesworth, Ellen Shepherd confessed to being tempted by a demon that took the form of something like a speaking rat: '…but smaller, of an iron-grey colour, which said, "You must go with me".' On 6 April Jane (or Joan) Wallis, also of Molesworth, confessed that six weeks earlier she had been making the bed and had been shocked by the sudden appearance of a shape in black clothes that resembled a man. Contemporary notes of the events suggest that beneath the black garb, this 'man' had cloven hooves, or 'ugly feet uncovered.' The strange guest told her his name was Blackman and he promised her two familiars, Grissell and Greedigut, to do her bidding. Before he vanished, she noticed his 'ugly feet' and how his stature appeared to grow and shrink as he stood before her. Three days later the two familiars arrived, and bore the form of talking dogs that had thick, bristly hog-like hair upon their backs. Although the strange and sinister Blackman 'had use of her body' she chose not to employ the demonic Grissell and Greedigut, so they played their own tricks. On one occasion they pulled a man from his horse and robbed him, bringing mistress Wallis the money.

All this was established in some instances even before Hopkins and his retinue turned up. Some 20 were accused in Huntingdonshire, and several (the exact number is not known) were executed. The terrifying fragility with which the suspects' lives hung in the balance is evidenced by the surprise acquittal of one woman who was twice searched unsuccessfully and who once suffered the 'swimming' ordeal, somehow managing to survive it.

In 1648, Hopkins' assistant John Stearne published an account of his and Hopkins' conduct entitled *A Confirmation & Discovery Of Witchcraft* in which he absolved himself of any wrongdoing. He also commented that Hopkins had died peacefully after a long consumptive illness the previous year. His writing also makes reference to what would seem to have been a purge in the area of the Isle of Ely in 1647, speaking of 'those executed at *Elie*, a little before Michaelmas last…also one at *Chatterish* (Chatteris) there, one at March there, and another at Wimblington there, now lately found, still to be tried.'

Again, some of the accusations – and accompanying confessions – are truly weird. In Stretham, south of Ely, Dorothy Ellis stood before Justice Thomas Castell Esq on 30 May 1647 and admitted that *c.*1617 she had been approached by the Devil, who appeared in the likeness of a great cat and demanded that he suck her blood. This perverse act enabled Ms Ellis to bewitch her neighbours and their livestock – including making one villager lame, an intriguingly named fellow called John Gotobed. A suspicious neighbour accused Ellis of bewitching to death her granddaughter, Mary Salter, who had died in bizarre convulsions aged just a year-and-a-quarter. One Alice Wade accused Ellis of touching her child's cheek, whereupon the child's face swelled on that side and one of its eyes fell out. It is likely Ms Ellis was executed, but the outcome is unclear. A Robert Ellis (presumably a relative, perhaps her husband) certainly suffered in Stretham though: he would not confess to witchcraft and so was pulled apart after his limbs were tied to wild horses. At Sutton, a woman named Moore was hanged after apparently confessing to sending an imp to bewitch a vendor who subsequently died. At the same time here a couple named Bonham were accused; both had previously been suspected of murdering their son, although the case had collapsed. It seems the hysteria of the moment had presented the villagers with another opportunity to vent their spleen on the couple; John Bonham is subsequently supposed to have confessed to keeping a 'familiar' – a mole-like creature – which he fed with blood pricked from his finger and which he would send to attack livestock. In Haddenham another woman was similarly accused of making a covenant with the Devil and sending an imp to bewitch a child and ruin crops; the accused allowed herself to be 'scratched' by the child, which Stearne thought an attempt to rid herself of the plague afflicting her; in all likelihood she saw this performance as her only means of appearing repentant before the justices. It is likely that she was executed nonetheless.

It is difficult to say what the most unnerving dimension of these outbreaks of hysteria is. But as author Wallace Notestein commented on this case in *History Of English Witchcraft* (1911), perhaps we just cannot understand the era: 'It is quite impossible to grasp the social conditions, it is impossible to understand the opinions, fears and hopes of the men and women who lived in Elizabethan and Stuart England, without some knowledge of the part played in that age by witchcraft.'

SHAPE-SHIFTING

One of the phenomenal abilities laid at the door of suspected witches (due to their pacts with the Devil) was the ability to shape-shift, usually into the form of an animal. The theologian Dr Henry More, in a submission to Glanvill's *Saduscismus Triumphatus* (a 1681 book on the 'reality' of witchcraft), wrote of a strange incident in Cambridgeshire in the mid-1600s, although he did not specify exactly where it had taken place.

He noted a 'credible report' of an old witch who was reckoned to have roamed the villages and countryside in the form of a great cat, until an old man apparently grabbed the animal after finding it before his hearth and broke its spine with a fire-fork. The suspected witch was, that very same night, found dead in her own bed, her back broken in a like manner. A similar incident was written of as occurring during the witch-hunting hysteria of the 1640s, but for once (amazingly) sanity appears to have taken hold.

A Cambridge man was sure that a certain widow had bewitched him, and one evening as he lay in bed he struck out at a black cat that had invaded the room and hit it on its back. The animal disappeared, and the following day the man made enquiries about his antagonist and found that she had a sore back: an injury she must have incurred while in the form of the cat. A surgeon, Mr Day, was brought to the widow where he brought an abrupt end to the 'bewitched' man's triumph by exclaiming that the widow had a huge boil on her back, and had not been dealt any injury. Possibly the two stories noted here are a misremembering of the same event; nonetheless, E. Lynn Linton's *Witch Stories* (1861) cites this as an example of 'a marvellous allowance of common sense, remembering the times.'

Nonetheless, this belief that witches were able to 'shape-shift' persisted. A man in Thorney told folklorist Enid Porter in 1956 that his grandmother (who had died in 1897) would never eat jugged hare. The reason behind this was a genuine suspicion that she 'might be eating a witch.' There was also a general belief in Cambridgeshire, recorded by Ms Porter in 1934, that 'a hen crowing like a cock' was a witch in disguise.

PURGING CAMBRIDGESHIRE OF WITCHCRAFT

During these times it was not just village eccentrics or troublesome neighbours who were targeted. The 17th century also saw the growth of dissenting religious houses, such as the Religious Society of Friends – the Quakers – whose new way of thinking quite often led to superstitious finger-pointing and violent assaults. In 1659 a pamphlet entitled *Strange And Terrible Newes From Cambridge* told its readership of the bewitchment of one Mary Philips by Quakers, who turned her into a 'bay mare' while she slept peaceably in bed beside her husband. While thus trapped in the form of a horse, the Quakers rode the woman from 'Dinton [Buckinghamshire] to the University', until at length she found herself in a town near Cambridge among a Quakers' gathering. Here the 'snaffle coming out of her mouth' (i.e. her distress at being trapped in horse form) led the Quakers to release the spell. Mary's sides were subsequently found to display vicious cuts and injuries as though she had been 'spurred', and she pointed the justices squarely in the direction of the group of Quakers. Two were dragged before Cambridge Assizes to answer the allegations. Despite the physical evidence – Mary Philips' hands and feet were also bruised and blackened, and her smock bloodied – it seems the allegation was *too* outlandish this time. The two Quakers from the group, Robert Dickson and Jane Cranaway, were acquitted, and one can only guess at the circumstances that prompted Mary Philips' bizarre accusation. She had, it seems, been drawn into this circle of Quakers, but after a few weeks she returned to the Church of England. Maybe her minister encouraged her somewhat in her subsequent allegations.

Such persecution continued throughout the 17th century. Francis Hutchinson's *An Historical Essay Concerning Witchcraft* (1718) notes that a witch was convicted around 1679 at Ely but reprieved from the gallows. Others were not so fortunate: numerous witches were tried by swimming in 1692 in Northamptonshire and the surrounding counties: 'Some drownd in the tryal.' This was the year of the famous witch trials in Salem, Massachusetts – clearly back home the scourge of witchcraft was still being taken just as seriously.

If we are to believe the contents of a 1716 pamphlet, such events continued into the 18th century. A Huntingdon man named Hicks was said to have taken his nine-year-old daughter Elizabeth to Ipswich, Suffolk, where she spotted a vessel out at sea and told her father she could play a trick. She took a basin of water and stirred the contents about, and the father was aghast to see that simultaneously a storm whipped up out at sea that threw the ship about – and would likely have sunk it had he not made his daughter stop. (However, in *Witchcraft And Demonianism* (1933) folklorist C. L'Estrange Ewen interpreted the site of this incident thus: 'By ship is no doubt meant some small craft suitable for the Ouse.') Their

THE INFIDEL'S BIBLE

C.F. Tebbutt's *Huntingdonshire Folklore* (1952) records how the author learned the strange story of the *Infidel's Bible*. On the eastern outskirts of Great Gransden, east of Mandean Bridge at the Mill Road and Primrose Hill junction, can be found the antiquity known as Great Gransden Mill.

In the 1850s the windmill was worked by Thomas Webb, and Tebbutt was told a family tradition relating to the Webb family's time here. The sails on the windmill one day simply ceased to work, and for some three years the Webb family abandoned the mill, unable to get it working. Some time later, the grandson of the family learned from his grandmother of a mysterious family heirloom called the *Infidel's Bible* – an ancient book of sorcery, black magic and necromancy that had long been lost. Tebbutt wrote, 'In the course of his exploration of the mill he [the grandson] chanced to find the book and bore it in triumph to the house.' The book was ceremonially destroyed – and immediately after the mill began working once more.

Tebbutt wrote that he had observed a newspaper cutting, dating to about 1920, in which one of the family, Richard Webb, had told of this strange family legend. Tebbutt noted that the last miller of Great Gransden was one William Webb, who died around 1890, and whose ne'er-do-well brother-in-law (who died at the mill house) was suspected of hiding the cursed book within the mill.

The Infidel's Bible was allegedly hidden here, at the mill.

NECROMANCERS, WISE MEN AND TOAD-MEN

In 1441, received in Cambridge were part of the remains of Sir Roger Bolingbroke, a priest and astrologer who had been executed at Tyburn on 11 November that year for 'practising necromantic rites in order to procure the death' of King Henry VI. Other body parts were sent to other parts of the kingdom as a warning against mixing sorcery and treason. In 1466 there was further excitement in Babraham when a certain Robert Barker of that village was hauled before the Bishop of Ely, William Grey, who heard his confession to necromancy. Barker recounted how he had obtained a number of magical artefacts from one John Hope: 'A great book, and a roll of black art containing characters, circles, exorcisms and conjurations; a hexagonal sheet with strange figures; six metal plates with diverse characters engraved; a chart with hexagonal and pentagonal characters and figures, and a gilded wand.' With these implements, Barker intended to raise ghosts who would direct him to hidden hordes of gold and silver. The bishop had him punished and his magical tools ceremonially burned by the hangman in Cambridge's Market Place.

It is remarkable to note that the dubious practices of such necromancers, 'cunning folk' and wise men were still being employed in the later Victorian era. A contributor to *Notes And Queries* narrated that during a recent visit to Barnack his hosts had talked of 'the Wise Man' – a 'sort of witch' who lived at Stamford and who was believed to have the power to foretell the future and inflict evil spells upon people in the region. In one instance, it was said, a servant girl had robbed a fellow-employee of some money, so the latter travelled nearly 20 miles to see the Wise Man for justice. Not long afterwards the thief was afflicted with a painful wasting disease that was blamed on the Wise Man issuing a curse on behalf of his client. Such supernatural powers were often laid at the door of a pact with the Devil.

A modern incarnation of these 'Cunning Folk' could be found in eastern England between the two world wars. Their abilities bridged the gap between witchcraft and the so-called 'wise-men', and modern-day psychics. They were referred to as 'Toad-men', and to become a Toad-man one had to carry out a peculiar ritual, of which there were regional variations but which broadly followed these lines. The would-be Toad-man took a toad and buried it in an ant's nest. When the toad's body had been picked clean the man could recover the bones and toss them into a running stream at midnight, on the advent of a full moon. All the bones were swept away downstream – except one, which was key shaped and could easily be recovered from the water. A certain ritual – of which the details are unspecified – was then performed and the leftover bone empowered the Toad-man with the ability to psychically control animals, particularly horses. To tire out the horse, all the Toad-man had to do was touch its shoulder; to get it moving again, all he had to do was touch its rump. It was also rumoured that those possessed of this gift were able to exert their influence over unwary women. Enid Porter wrote in 1969 of numerous instances where those who possessed these dubious powers were reckoned to be involved with Satan himself.

Ms Porter learned of the Toad-man ritual that sometimes the bones were supposed to scream as they were thrown into the water. Some believed that the ritual actually prompted the Devil to appear, and Ms Porter was given enough examples of this to at least indicate a sincere *belief* that Toad-men's powers were given to them by the Devil. In 1949 she was told by a retired horse-keeper at March that one aspiring Toad-man had carried the bone (recovered from the stream) to some stables on three consecutive nights at midnight. On the third night the Devil appeared before the fellow and engaged him in a fight, during which Satan drew his blood and thus fully initiated him into the mystic fellowship of the Toad-man. As late as 1950 a woman at Comberton related that her grandfather had imparted some details of the initiation ritual to her, and actually claimed that Satan had manifested before him in the moonlight when he had gone to retrieve the toad's bone from the brook. In 1936, one E.G. Bales had recorded an anecdote told to him by a Wisbech resident, who some 60 years before had worked for a Wisbech farmer – whom everyone at the time had reckoned was a fully-initiated Toad-man capable of somehow controlling his own, and his neighbour's, horses. At one time this farmer, upon arriving home drunk, had let slip to his housekeeper that he was on friendly terms with the Devil, and that he could see him stood there. He would even say to her 'Can't yew see him Mary? I can!'

Ms Porter noted 'In 1956 the question of Toad-men was discussed at an adult evening class. The members agreed that Toad-men were known to exist in Cambridgeshire between 1918 and 1938; whether their influence over horses was obtained by the use of drugs or herbs or by some supernatural means could not be decided.' Her *Folklore Of East Anglia* (1974) explained how in Willingham one Jabez Few was believed by many to be a wizard: 'He kept some white rats, which the villagers called his imps; he delighted in playing all kinds of practical jokes with them.' Jabez Few died as recently as 1920, and the family plot can be found in St Mary and All Saints' Church. I suspect that there are many people alive in the county today who recall hearing similar tales to this, and maybe even some that can actually recall the resident village Toad-man. Maybe there are even those who recall the ritual, which superstition has it was still conjuring up the Devil in Cambridgeshire well into the 20th century...

This plaque mark's Judy's Hole in North Street, Burwell. A mysterious woman named Judy – who some believe was Burwell's last witch – is said to have died here.

CHAPTER 4

PORTENTS, CURSES AND SUPERSTITIOUS BELIEF

INTRODUCTION

*T*he *History, Gazetteer And Directory Of Cambridgeshire* (1851) poses an almost unanswerable question of the Fenland topography in the days before drainage: 'How, or by what revulsion of nature, has this extraordinary phenomena occurred, by which this great tract of land, which was once a forest, then a morass, and is now by the industry of man converted into rich pastures and fertile corn fields – how had it become so deluged as to resemble a large lake studded with small islands, isolated from the neighbouring counties and extending nearly 100 miles from east to west, and nearly 40 miles in breadth?'

Christopher Marlowe's *Legends Of The Fenland People* (1926) answers this conundrum with the myth 'How the great level became a Fen' – a story of a disastrous event of almost Biblical proportions in Cambridgeshire's past that was blamed on a curse. Events are said to have taken place during the reign of Emperor Valerian (*c.*AD 200–260) when England was subject to the rule of Rome. According to the legend, the British tribesmen of the Iceni were subject to harsh repression and casual tortures by their Roman masters. Upon the abduction of a girl named Rowena, the daughter of an Iceni priest named Mandru, rebellion began to ferment. The mutiny was cut short when Roman soldiers invaded a gathering of British plotters and hacked them to pieces, and although Mandru was captured he managed to escape from the Roman town of Isinnis.

Many months later a stranger arrived at the gates of Isinnis, clad in rough-hewn garments and sporting a long, white beard. He had the venerable bearing of a holy man, which is why whenever he approached a British slave and told them, 'Friend, arise this night and be gone. Destruction comes fast upon this city', they took him at his word, gathering their families and leaving town. Very soon, a kind of mass migration was taking place; families of Britons were leaving the towns and heading for the thickly-forested land that at that time covered this part of East Anglia. All told the same story, of the bearded stranger with his portentous message; and before long he appeared among them, revealing himself to be the long-missing Mandru and saying, 'The Gods are angry with Rome and purpose to destroy every Roman city. It has been revealed to me where I shall lead you.' Thus, Mandru led the swelling hordes of thousands of Britons to 'a group of hills fast by the father of rivers', which is possibly meant to mean the Gog Magog Hills.

This dire prediction, within a few nights, came true. By now the Roman town governors had realised that something was amiss and were raising a huge army to hunt down the Britons. An enormous tempest resembling a hurricane had, however, gradually materialised off the east coast and was making its way inland, and the storms it brought with it prevented the Romans from leaving the towns in pursuit. Word began to spread that a column of solid water had been observed to raise itself some 300ft high far out in the sea, and after a while many Roman families themselves began to pack up their belongings and leave the settlements. Soon, the gigantic tidal wave roared over the land, obliterating many settlements and killing thousands: a curse reigned down upon the Romans for their mistreatment of the Britons and supposedly the origin of the unique landscape of the Fens. As Marlowe wrote: 'Attempts were made to undo the work of the sea-God, banks were constructed and roads made through the district, but the Fen country remained for centuries as it was after the deluge – the haunt of birds and fish and of a peculiar people who walked on stilts, amid the quagmires and boggy islands of the neighbourhood.'

Although some of the ingredients of the story are factual, the story itself must be a myth. The Roman historian Tacitus mentions that in AD 47 (some 200 years before Valerian's reign) a violent, bloody confrontation occurred between the Iceni and Roman auxiliaries at a small natural island in the flooded landscape of the Fens following an attempt to disarm the tribesmen. This is thought to have been at Stonea Camp, the Iron Age hill fort south-east of March, so it is clear that any flooding as late as c.AD 260 cannot have been responsible for the topography of the Fens. Evidence of sacrifices at Flag Fen, a Bronze-Age religious site comprising a small artificial island (where corpses, daggers, swords and jewellery were ceremonially tossed into the marshland) also tells us that the Fens were 'historically' waterlogged well before the Romans came and were largely so until drainage began in earnest in the 1600s.

Although this story does imply in many ways that dire predictions and portentous events were synonymous with divine retribution, at the other end of the scale superstitious rituals to procure good fortune or avoid misfortune were much more universal, diverse and day-to-day in Cambridgeshire, as this chapter illustrates. For example, it was noted in the later Victorian era how – even among the educated – there was a belief in the Fenland of Cambridgeshire that should 13 people sit down together at a dinner table, one of those so present would be dead before the year was out. We may scoff at these types of portentous superstitions, but maybe – just maybe – the future can be read by the behaviour of animals, the weather and all manner of day-to-day occurrences. More worryingly, is the proof of forthcoming disaster all around us, only we have forgotten how to see it?

Even the royal family were not immune from such superstition. In 1603 England and Scotland were united when Mary's son, King James VI of Scotland, was also crowned King of England. In 1612 he ordered that his mother Mary's body be exhumed from Peterborough Cathedral and reburied in Westminster Abbey. Turner's *History Of Remarkable Providences* (1677) recalled that there was a long-held belief here that to exhume a corpse in this manner '…bodes death or some terrible calamity to the surviving members of the deceased's family.' Apparently King James chose to ignore this warning, given to him by a Kentish man named Thomas Fludd, despite being told that it always 'bodes ill to the family when bodies are removed from their graves. For some of the family will die shortly after, as did Prince Henry, and, I think, Queen Anne.' Of course, the king's son Charles would be executed in 1649. Following a similar theme, it was also commonly believed in Cambridgeshire that the failure of a crop of ash keys (the seed vessels of the ash trees) portended the death of a member of the royal family.

Many events believed to foretell bad luck were considered supernatural. Other portentous oaths came in the form of a curse: the father of Fenland storyteller W.H. Barrett (1891–1974) was told that neither he nor his offspring would die in bed: a circumstance later proved correct, according to the folk tale *The Gipsy's Curse*, a piece of family lore that Barrett swore were true and which was retold in Briggs' *Folktales Of England* (1965). And so this chapter is concerned with miscellaneous portents of death and disaster, curses laid against enemies, superstitious rituals of luck and love and evidences of the general belief that folk in Cambridgeshire could shape their environment – and even predict the future…

WARNINGS ABOUT THE WEATHER

In 1236, on the day after the feast of St Martin, the Fens suffered a flood of catastrophic proportions during a storm that had raged for several days. The chronicler Holinshed wrote of events, 'The marsh counties near to the sea were drowned and overflown, beside great herds and flocks of the cattle that perished.' The sea rose for two days and nights without ebbing, mighty winds creating surging tidal waves, and Wisbech and the surrounding villages were virtually destroyed. The human toll is not accurately recorded, but Holinshed provided a glimpse of the scale of the disaster: 'In one village there were buried 100 corpses in one day.' It would seem that there was a portent of these events, for it was rumoured the disaster was preceded by 'strange meteors and wonderful appearances in the Heavens.'

The weather itself played an important part in the lives of county folk in more than one sense. It was often regarded as an omen of misfortune – if not the very word of the Lord himself. William Perkins (d.1602), the clergyman and Cambridge theologian, noted that it was common for the peasantry to cross themselves upon hearing thunder, or seeing lightning flash; he himself would often recount the cautionary tale of a county man who had mocked thunder as being merely the work of a cooper thumping a barrel – only to be instantly hit by a flash of lightning and killed on the spot.

Marlowe's *Legends Of The Fenland People* (1926) relates the legend of another disastrous tempest similar in many ways to the one mentioned earlier. The story goes that in Wansford, a recluse and suspected wizard named Doctor Stefan, of Nercots Grange, had been arrested on suspicion of being a witch. He had been witnessed pacing up and down in his dwelling, with a great book under his arm and his other hand making strange signs and passes in the air. Many gathered at the market cross to see the reputed wizard being thrown into a tiny barn that functioned as a cell, but that night, when the hubbub had died down, an old shepherd named Barnaby snuck past the drunken parish constable and liberated the imprisoned doctor. Barnaby did this deed since he was grateful to Doctor Stefan, who had cured some of his sheep of ague. In return for his freedom, the doctor uttered a terrifying prophecy: in 13 days time, disaster would be wrought on the region, 'when ye see the heavens black and a ring like silver around the moon.' The Doctor, after providing this dire warning, then vanished, and the following day the alarm was raised and a posse of locals began to scour the countryside for him – fruitlessly, as it turned out.

The shepherd, Barnaby, on the other hand, spent his time watching the skies for the portent he was warned of, and on the 13th night he did indeed see the curious aerial phenomenon he feared. At this, he selected a number of his fattest and purest livestock and drove them into the church (presumably St Mary's Church) and thence into the tower. Barnaby's curious behaviour quickly excited the local population, and a crowd swelled in the churchyard. Here, the local publican began to suspect that Barnaby's strange antics indicated that he had been forewarned about some event – presumably by the missing wizard. As their curiosity turned to anger, Barnaby the shepherd slammed the church door in their faces, barricaded it and drove the sheep further up the steps of the church tower to the highest vantage point. From up here, Barnaby gazed across the wide expanse of the Fenland in the direction of the sea – where, to his horror, an immense wall of water was steadily advancing across the marshes.

Barnaby and his livestock survived the catastrophic tidal surge that devastated the eastern coast of England, but his frantic exertions in ringing the church bells to warn the villagers had little impact – there was no time. For two days, from the church tower, Barnaby surveyed a flooded landscape: 'Out over the marshes stretched an endless sea, its course broken here and there by islands of marooned houses, tall oaks and ruined barns...'

Ramsey Abbey gatehouse.

And at Ramsey, they sang in similar belief:

> *Should a hare in hasty flight*
> *Scamper through Ramsey Whyte*
> *Be sure before three days are gone*
> *A fire will blaze in Ramsey town.*

The thoroughfare 'Ramsey Whyte' is supposedly named after the chalky-coloured façade of Ramsey Abbey's gatehouse, but quite how such a random belief arose is not clear. Something must have happened in the dim and distant past to bring this superstition about, and it was also thought of as a truism as far away as Wellingborough, Northamptonshire.

In 1878 it was observed of Huntingdonshire folk that they believed if a cat leapt over a corpse then it portended bad luck. The folklorist C.F. Tebbutt also recorded in 1952 that the howling of a dog at night was a sure omen of doom. And as with all this the question arises as to what combination of events brought about such beliefs so thoroughly that they were considered a truism?

DEATH FORSEEN

Around 1770 John Cowper, brother of the poet William Cowper (d. 25 April 1800), saw to his horror an elderly, stooped and haggard woman on the walks behind St John's College garden in Cambridge.

The reason for his dawning terror was very real. Cowper had often reflected to his fellow collegians on a disturbing incident that had occurred in his childhood, before ever he saw Cambridge. Cowper would enthral his friends with the story of how he had come into contact with an old woman, a fortune-teller, who had outlined for the young boy many details of his own and family history. Pointing a bony finger at the young lad, she had then warned him that the next time he set eyes on her he would die shortly thereafter. Where this unnerving encounter occurred was not remembered, although it may have been near his father's house in Hertfordshire.

Years later, when Cowper glimpsed the old woman near St John's, then she had either sought him out or else it was a ghost that he was seeing. Maybe he was mistaken, and it was not her at all. But either way, white, trembling and clearly disturbed, he told his friends that the old fortune-teller had come for him and he was doomed. Soon afterwards, he fell ill and died.

A friend of Cowper's, who had heard the tale first hand, submitted it to *Notes And Queries* in 1801, commenting, 'Such is this plain unvarnished tale, left to yourself and readers as of undoubted authenticity.'

GHOSTS AS OMENS OF DEATH

The Huntingdonshire folklorist C.F. Tebbutt explained that in 1757 the ghost of Thomas Hussey was glimpsed in his eldest daughter Mary Anne's bedroom by both Mary herself and her maid at Upwood Manor House. The women took the apparition to be a real person, despite being somewhat confused since Hussey was at that time thought to be in the capital. Hussey had, in fact, just died during his visit to London, although neither of the women knew this at the time. This spectre had apparently appeared on the point of death to his beloved daughter. In this instance the spiritual appearance was benevolent, perhaps a dying old man's desire to see his daughter one last time before he deserted this earthly plain, but sometimes it was the witness themselves who were in danger if they saw a ghost.

Sightings and manifestations of ghosts were often regarded as omens of impending death, and the connection between the witness, the ghost and an immediate death is a wide-ranging one. In some instances it was the mere glimpse of a supernatural entity from afar that was fatal; however, spiritualist John Ingram recorded an extremely intimate example of this phenomenon in *Haunted Homes And Family Traditions Of Great Britain* (1888). On the night of 28 July 1706, between 11pm and 12pm, the rector of Souldern in Oxfordshire (a former scholar of St John's College called Shaw), was visited by his former friend, a man named Naylor. Shaw and Naylor had been close friends in Cambridge, only Naylor had died some five years previously…and yet now stood before Shaw 'garbed apparently in exactly the same clothes, and in exactly the same manner' as when the rector had known him at St John's. Shaw spoke with this phantasm for upwards of an hour and a half, without fear, during which the spirit told him that several of their old collegians from St John's were about to die, including a famous Fellow named Arthur Orchard, and – distressingly – Shaw himself. Naylor vanished at the end of the grim conversation, and the next day Shaw made a will.

Shortly after, a severely shaken Mr Shaw was paid a visit by another fellow collegian of St John's; although this time it was a real, living friend called Mr Grove, who was travelling westwards and had stopped by. Shaw told Mr Grove the story of his recent ghostly visit, and also of his fear that he would soon be dead. Not long after, Shaw suffered a fit of apoplexy, slumping from the pulpit while delivering a church service and later dying.

Mr Grove, already shaken by the death of his friend, was further shaken to learn while passing through Clopton that the aforementioned Arthur Orchard had also died on 6 August.

Perhaps the most intriguing element of the ghostly conversation was the response to Shaw's question, 'Mr Naylor, how is it with you in the other world?' To which the spirit had replied simply, 'Very well.'

Naylor's ghost had also elaborated that he had 'but three days allowed to him' to impart his grim information.

Sometimes it was possible to make sure you saw ghosts. In common with many other parts of Britain it was often said that if you hid in a church porch on St Mark's Eve (24 April) you would be able to see a spectral procession of those doomed to die the following year making their way through the sturdy church door. At St Mary and St Andrew's Church, Whittlesford, they used to believe that at midnight on this date the ghosts of those who were to die in the parish in the next 12 months could be observed drifting into the church grounds. There, they would lie down in a vacant plot of land where the earth would submerge them. At Helpston (in the mid-1800s when *Helpstone* was part of Northamptonshire) a village eccentric named Ben Barr would hide by St Botolph's Church and wait until midnight to see this procession of the damned. Thus, he claimed to know the fate of everyone in the village. Around the county at large, there was great fear of something called the 'death-coach', which doomed all who saw it. By the mid-19th century, although it was no longer seen, it '...is still *heard* rumbling along the old lanes.'

A number of Victorian spiritualists recounted the bizarre tale of Captain G. Wheatcroft of the 6th Dragoon Guards. The captain was, at the time, away fighting in India when on the night of 14 November 1857 his wife awoke in bed at their Cambridge house to see her husband stood at the bedside. Curiously, Mrs Wheatcroft had been dreaming of her husband at that precise moment, and upon waking she now found herself *actually* looking at him. The captain stood there, in full uniform, but his pale face bore an agitated expression and his hair appeared dishevelled. He clutched his hands to his breast, and he appeared to be trying to say something; however, no sound came from his lips and then he bent forward as though in pain and slowly faded from view. In all, he had been visible to his wife for about a minute.

The following morning Mrs Wheatcroft related this to her mother, convinced by now that her husband had been either killed or seriously injured. In due course a telegram arrived at her home bearing the grim news that her husband had died in combat at Lucknow on 15 November 1857.

Even more remarkably, the captain's ghost appeared at *exactly* the same time before a medium called 'Mrs N.' in London, only in this instance he spoke, stating that he had died that day and at the time of his appearance. His body was not yet buried: 'The thing that I wore...is not buried yet.' Both women were put in contact by an astounded mutual acquaintance called Wilkinson, although no one could quite understand why the ghost insisted that it had died on the 14th, while the telegram stated that it had been the 15th when Captain Wheatcroft had fallen. This discrepancy was cleared up when a fellow officer who had survived the assault on Lucknow confirmed in a letter that the captain had in fact died on the 14th – the ghost had, after all, been correct.

SUPERSTITIONS

It is clear that superstition played a major part in the lives of county folk in days gone by. All manner of rituals and beliefs, affecting all walks of everyday life, were practised without any sensation that it was a ridiculous fancy, and it is my own personal belief that some of the rituals must have 'worked' to one degree or another to have persisted for so long. Somehow the belief in a 'bigger picture' affecting the lives of villagers and townsfolk appears a strange loss in these more cynical times.

In 1878 it was observed that should a child in Cambridgeshire speak of itself in the third person, or give itself a soubriquet (an assumed nickname) it was a forewarning of an early death for that child.

Ms Porter's *Cambridgeshire Customs And Folklore* (1969) cites many such examples of what were thought to be portents of doom, and indicates just how thoroughly anything out of the ordinary – or even the ordinary itself – was viewed with the fear of impending disaster. A retired district nurse in Histon explained in 1965 that should rigor mortis be slow to set in following a death then there would be another death in the same family within a year, and that one fatal collision on a road was in all likelihood expected to be followed by two more within a week. In Wilbraham Ms Porter learned that soot hanging or falling from old-fashioned grate bars had to be swept away upon sight if it was long and oval, as this represented a coffin. However, in Coton, Ms Porter was told that this meant something else – that a stranger would come to the house. A sudden spark jumping to the back of the fire, and then extinguishing itself, meant in Cambridge itself that a close friend, relative or neighbour would soon die. Wearing green was also thought to be unlucky, and many elderly women still looked for 'coffin marks or coffin folds' in freshly laundered linen. In 1965, a Cambridge woman explained that to leave a room and close the door, without extinguishing the light, meant that there would soon be news of a death. And in Thorney, a man explained in 1957 that should there be a thunderstorm on the day that a coffin was laid out in a house then there would be another death in that same household within 12 months.

Omens must literally have been spotted everywhere. Ms Porter wrote, 'The howling of dogs, the hooting of owls, the flying of a robin into a house, the bringing of certain plants and flowers indoors, the refusal of cats to stay in a sick person's home – all these were though to be omens of death in a family. The sudden stopping of a clock or watch in a house where one member of the household is seriously ill still means, to some Cambridgeshire people, that the patient will surely die.'

I myself was brought up in the 1970s with the notion ingrained in me that it was extremely unlucky to put brand new shoes on a table or other surface until after they had been worn. Presumably in many cases such beliefs are symbolic (i.e. if the shoes do not touch the ground first, then by association the wearer is likely to be not walking in them, possibly even laid out in a coffin on a raised surface).

CURSED PLACES

In the summer of 1924, during excavations at a Romano-British cemetery at Guilden Morden, the archaeologist and psychic researcher T.C. Lethbridge was part of the team. He observed a number of strange phenomena, including the mysterious failures and accidents that bedevilled the cars transporting the skeletal remains to Cambridge. These included unexplained brake failures and on one unnerving occasion the sudden disappearance of the near side front wheel while driving between Royston and Melbourn. This near-accident occurred near a woman pushing a baby in a pram, while travelling at about 30 miles an hour. Although the car was brought to an uneventful halt Lethbridge and his passenger were forced to take the box of skulls they were transporting the rest of the way by bus. Worse still, when Lethbridge later showed his host – Mrs R, the canon's wife – a skeletal finger, still with an ancient ring attached, she exclaimed in horror, 'How very unlucky!' The very next day this lady suffered an apoplectic fit and died as doctors tried to resuscitate her. When Lethbridge wrote of this strange episode 37 years later in *Ghost And Ghoul* he wondered what part these 'boxes of grinning skeletons' played in the sequence of events.

Folklorist Edwin Radford noted another 'cursed' site in Cambridgeshire in 1949. Apparently there was a piece of land in Wisbech that must forever 'remain sacred' on account of it being a Quaker burial plot. This piece of land was at 'the corner of Quaker Lane and Silk Lane', and as of 1946 was being rented by one Charles Beakley. Quakers were buried there, deeds prevented the ground from being 'dug, delved or ploughed' and the ground must at all costs remain undisturbed. It is unclear, however, where 'Silk Lane' is, although it is possible that Stow Lane was meant.

During the course of researching this book I was told that the level crossing on Conington Fen, east of the village of Conington, was supposedly cursed. This belief appears to be based on two disastrous accidents that occurred within eight months of each other at the crossing, formally designated Occupation Crossing No. 85. On 1 March 1948, very early in the morning and during thick fog, a lorry belonging to the Huntingdon War Agricultural Company was struck by a train at this spot, killing three outright and fatally injuring another three. All six victims were German prisoners-of-war. Then, on 16 October, Colonel A.H. Mellows died when a train ploughed into his motor car as he returned from a shooting trip. The *Railway Gazette International Vol. 90* observed that conditions at the crossing were highly unsatisfactory, especially after dark, with a high volume of traffic even by 1948. On 5 March 1967 there was further carnage when an express train derailed near Conington and killed five passengers. An investigation into this tragedy concluded that the signalman at the Conington South signal box purposely altered the points just as the express passed over them, flipping the sixth coach. The signalman was charged with manslaughter; he was eventually jailed for two years, there being an almighty question mark in the mind of Ministry of Transport investigator K.A. McNaughton as to whether these actions had been accidental, panicked or deliberately malicious.

There is a strong belief locally that not only is the crossing 'cursed' but that it is also haunted as well because of these accidents.

ECHOES OF THE PAST AT 'CURSED' NORMAN CROSS

Perhaps unsurprisingly, it is the site of the former barracks for French prisoners-of-war at Norman Cross, south of Peterborough, that is nowadays reckoned to be cursed. Work began on the barracks in 1790 and when finished it occupied 40 acres of land and was capable of interring 6,000 French soldiers taken during the Napoleonic Wars. By July 1804, it held 1,600 prisoners that Bonaparte boasted were his 'army of England', and the site was the focus of frequent spirited escape attempts and uprisings: one in October 1804 led to the infantry corps being called in from Peterborough to maintain order. Following the insurrection it was revealed it had been designed to misdirect the soldiers from the fact that a 34ft-long tunnel had been dug towards the Great North Road, through which a number of inmates had escaped. Some were never caught and presumably made it back home to France.

The casualty list was horrendous. Between 1796 and 1814 some 1,800 people are reckoned to have died at the barracks from neglect, suicide, battle injuries that went untreated, accidents, illness and violence. In January 1812, for example, a French prisoner threw a bucket of water over a soldier and in the confusion managed to unfix the bayonet from the soldier's musket before fleeing. The soldier recovered his senses, grabbed his musket and shot the prisoner through the shoulder as he ran. The man died a few days later in terrible agony, and the soldier was subsequently tried for manslaughter at Huntingdon assizes; he was acquitted. In January 1798 another soldier named Lowder was in the practice of test-firing his gun when it exploded, shooting the breach pin into his forehead and almost forcing his eyes out. He died 'raving mad' a few days later.

The monument at Norman Cross.

These days, as traffic roars past the site via the nearby AI, it is difficult to envisage the events that took place here 200 years ago. The buildings were pulled down in 1816, and the only reminder of the barracks is the solitary bronze eagle, stood high atop a memorial plinth. The memorial was raised on 28 July 1914.

Upon visiting the memorial in May 2009 I was told that the actual number of deaths may have exceeded 2,000 and that there was a supposition locally that most of the inmates' bodies were buried in the fields beside what is now the AI. The graves were unmarked, and the guess is that hundreds of French skeletons lay beneath the ground hereabouts – an unnerving thought for motorists to ponder as they navigate the roundabout here at Junction 16. Furthermore, the land behind the motel at this gloomy, melancholic site is supposed to be cursed: this is where the barracks stood, and as I was told, 'They reckon it's haunted and that no one wanted to build here because its bad luck…'

OMENS OF LUCK AND LOVE

It was not all doom and gloom, however. There were certain customs that were reckoned to bring good luck in Cambridgeshire. For example, babies conceived during thunderstorms were thought to be very lucky in later life. In 1863 *Notes And Queries* observed the curious practice in Huntingdonshire of presenting a newborn baby with an egg, a pinch of salt and a penny, all for good luck. The penny was symbolic of wealth, and was for the purchase of a loaf, or 'sup o'milk', but what the egg and salt meant could only be guessed at. Perhaps they represented never going without food. The same periodical noted in 1855 of the peculiar ritual 'now dying out' of smashing a wine glass against the wall after drinking a toast. It was speculated that the frequent discovery of jugs buried beneath 'old houses in King's Parade, Trinity Street, and other sites' in Cambridge was to the same end: to procure good luck after toasting.

It is, however, perhaps not surprisingly, the area of love where there was the biggest amount of superstitious belief. For example, 'young maidens' would carry with them the empty head of the 'knot-weed' in the firm belief that if they were to encounter their future spouse the plant would blossom again within an hour. The Helpston poet John Clare wrote of such practices, 'I've heard old women, who first told it me, vow that a truer token could not be.' A similar belief was submitted to *Notes And Queries* in 1854 by Harriet Norman of Fulbourn, who explained that a piece of clover with only two leaves on it would routinely be put in the right shoe of the lovelorn young men or women of Cambridgeshire. The first member of the opposite sex that they met while walking in this fashion was their future spouse – or if not them, then someone of the same name.

Ms Porter's *Cambridgeshire Customs And Folklore* notes that in times past lovelorn young girls would often approach the village 'wise-woman' for potions and lotions to make themselves appear more attractive, or to entrance the young men of the parish. One in particular stood out as supposedly having such qualities: tea, or milk, into which was dissolved a pinch of red powder called *Dragon's Blood* which was, in fact, procured from fruit. Quite how this was supposed to work (presumably by ingestion) is unclear, since any such potion could only have acted as a placebo and not actually *physically* made people any more attractive. But Enid Porter noted how it was thought to work to a certain degree nonetheless, since chemists stored it well into the 20th century in Cambridgeshire.

Walter Henry Barrett, acknowledged as providing much of the Fenland material for Ms Porter's work, and who died in 1974, not only possessed remarkable skill as a narrator of folk tales but also had a detailed recollection of traditions long since lost. Perhaps one of the most charming rituals, which seems to have died out in the late 1800s, concerned the belief that the yarrow plant acted as 'a love herb.' Pinning small bunches of the flower to her buttonhole, a young maid would sidle up to her potential suitor, her declaration of affection clear by the plant that was displayed. If the lad ignored the gesture, then the young lady would wait until the advent of a full moon and find a patch of yarrow upon which she would walk barefoot. After this she would shut her eyes and bend to pick a random bunch of the flower, and upon returning home place the bunch under the bed. At sunrise the following day, if the yarrow still displayed

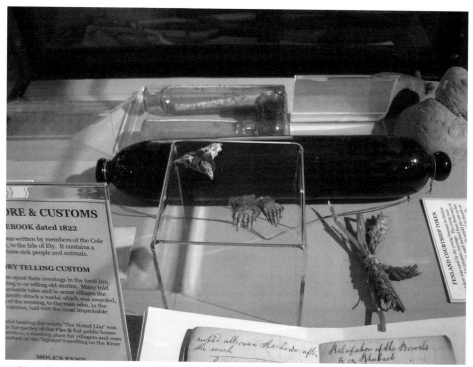

Mole's feet kept in times past as a 'lucky charm'. On the right is a Fenland courtship token, provided by lads to their sweethearts.

beads of dew then she could rest easy, as this signified that the young man who had ignored her would suddenly start to take notice thereupon. If the flowers were dry then the ritual needed to be repeated until such time as the spell began to work. I cannot help but wonder how many Fenland relationships succeeded in coming to fruition, and how many lineages exist in the region today, because generations ago someone's great-great-grandmother persisted with the midnight yarrow ritual until her beloved actually began to notice her, rather then giving up at the first failed attempt!

DEATH BELLS

Enid Porter's *Cambridgeshire Customs And Folklore* recalls the legend that in August 1845 a spontaneous, curious bell-tolling was one day heard in Guilden Morden, a spectacle that no one could explain – until some time later news reached the village that 23 former residents, who had decided to emigrate to Australia, were among the 369 lives lost when the barque *Cataraqui* was cast upon the rocks in the Bass Strait during a fearful gale. Among the dead were Amos and Fanny Pearce, and their seven children, and William and Sarah Izzard and their four children. Even as late as the 1950s there were (according to a Women's Institute meeting in 1957) still villagers who recalled hearing from their grandparents of the solemn portent that roused villagers in Guilden Morden with its supernatural tolling more than 100 years before. In February 1846 an inquiry had established that the *Cataraqui* had been destroyed at around half-past-four on 4 August (Australian time) – which villagers swore corresponded with the time they heard the mysterious bell-tolling back home in Cambridgeshire. Curiously, a local pub (which stood until some time between 1958 and 1978) near St Mary's Church was called the Six Bells, although this seems to be coincidence, since the pub was recorded as existing as far back as 1801.

Peter Underwood's *The A-Z Of British Ghosts* (1971) cites a similar phenomenon as occurring in Elm, south of Wisbech. Here, at the depressing 18th-century building called Elm Vicarage, the strange tolling of a 'death-bell' was linked to a ghost. Underwood wrote that 'some years ago' he had been in touch with the rector of the vicarage, the Revd Bradshaw, and his wife. Soon after the couple settled at Elm Vicarage, they were disturbed by footsteps thumping about the place as though an intruder were nightly walking about the place. Eventually, Mrs Bradshaw must have 'walked into' the ghost in an upstairs corridor, for the ghost announced its presence with the words, 'Do be careful.' A stunned Mrs Bradshaw asked to whom she was talking and received the reply, 'Ignatius, the bell-ringer.'

Thereafter, Ignatius appeared to Mrs Bradshaw frequently in various parts of the house. He appeared first as a fine outline, '...then gradually emerged into the figure of a man aged about 33 with "dark curly hair and thin ascetic features".' He wore an old and worn-looking brown monk's habit and sandals, and announced that he had died some 750 years earlier in a monastery that once stood on the site of Elm Vicarage. (There is evidence that a vicarage was ordained in Elm as far back as 1275, and the church itself dates to *c.*1217; there are no records, however, to indicate that a priory stood on the exact site before this, although possibly there was a building here linked to land owned by Lewes priory in neighbouring Emneth.)

Ignatius' appearances at Elm Vicarage coincided with a mysterious bell-ringing sound that appears to have been a death-knell. Underwood wrote: 'Mrs Bradshaw was the only one who heard the tolling bell, but her husband [...] would invariably hear of a death in the parish next day. This happened, I was told, 31 times in two-and-a-half years!'

CHAPTER 5

CAMBRIDGESHIRE GHOST STORIES

INTRODUCTION

Very broadly speaking, the wide-ranging phenomenon of 'ghosts' has, in the past, fallen into three general scenarios in Cambridgeshire. In the first instance, there are those ghostly encounters that, however well known, appear to be folklore and that almost conform to miniature stories with a beginning, middle and end. Perhaps the best example of this is what I consider to be Cambridgeshire's 'classic' ghostly anecdote – the well-known legend of the Black Knight of Wandlebury.

At the Iron Age hill fort known as Wandlebury Camp, just north-east of Stapleford, there is a famous legend originally written of by the scholarly Gervase of Tilbury in his expansive *Otia Imperialia* (*c.*1214). He wrote that in the diocese of Ely could be found *Wandlebiria* where 'there is a level space surrounded by entrenchments, and with a single entrance like a gate.' Gervase wrote that a generation or so ago a knight named Osbert, son of Hugh, was staying in Cambridge. It was winter, and by the fireside one supper Osbert heard from his hosts the belief that if a person were to approach the site at Wandlebury at midnight when the moon was full and shout, 'Knight to knight, come forth!' there would appear before them a fearsome spectral knight. This entity would charge out of the entrance and attempt to unhorse the brave soul who had made the bold challenge. Osbert decided to test this belief as soon as possible and subsequently made for the camp with his squire. Leaving his squire outside, Osbert passed through the ramparts and into the camp, where he shouted aloud, 'Knight to knight, come forward!' Instantly the ghostly knight materialized and charged at Osbert, who – being a skilled fighter – managed to parry the thrust of the ghostly knight (who presumably had taken 'solid' form). The spectral knight was unhorsed, and as he lay on the ground Osbert grabbed the reins of the horse and led the animal from the camp as evidence of the encounter. However, the ghostly knight managed to struggle to his feet and throw his lance at Osbert: the weapon stuck in his leg, but he managed nonetheless to get out of Wandlebury Camp while his phantom adversary dematerialised behind him. The knight and his squire led the ethereal horse – a huge, dark and spirited animal – back to Cambridge Castle where Osbert roused his hosts and bade them to come and look at the captured animal. Taking his armour off, he noticed just how bad his own injury was, although his jubilation at winning the day outweighed the pain he felt. The tethered animal was observed to be very wild, with a jet-black coat and mane, and its eyes blazed like fire. Its bridle and saddle were also observed to be as black as a moonless night. In fact, so wild was the creature that the following morning at sunrise it broke its reins and managed to escape the courtyard, thundering off into the Cambridgeshire countryside. It was never seen again, despite a huge search operation.

Every year on the night of the incident, Osbert's wound would reopen and bleed heavily. Gervase of Tilbury clearly took this story seriously, observing that the widespread repetition of the story evidenced 'proof of the truth of this.' However, not everyone was impressed. The equally scholarly Raphael Holinshed (died *c.*1580) noted in his *History Of Britaine* of Gervase's 'foolish tale' about how 'Osbert of Barnwell charg'd and unhorst the spirit, drove him away, and carrid off his black horse.' Perhaps the most telling aspect of this tale (if it has any basis in reality) is the fact that the spectral knight appears to have become solid enough to be knocked off his horse – perhaps indicating that Osbert fought a human antagonist, not a ghost. This story is one of Cambridgeshire's most enduring legends, however, and somehow seems to encapsulate the mysterious side of the county better than any other; its antiquity, the atmospheric location, the romance of myth and a supernatural encounter all make it the county's classic mysterious anecdote.

While many may have been enthralled throughout the centuries by this tale, it is likely that most regarded it as an entertaining folk story, with a question mark hanging over it as 'fact'. But a second category of ghostly tales concerns vague stories – and more specifically places – where there is a *sincere* belief (that may even persist to this day) that such a place 'is haunted' and should be avoided. These allegations may be based on foggy memories of factual events (suicides, battles, murders or accidents) that have led to a supposition (perhaps borne out by recent rumours of curious encounters there) that the site is genuinely haunted. An example of this occurred in Victorian times. *The New Monthly Magazine* recorded in 1821 the remarkable discovery of a Roman villa found by labourers digging for gravel in open fields immediately to the south of Litlington. Within the foundation walls of a quadrangular area running parallel with the north side of Ashwell Street were found Roman pottery, an ancient Romano-British coin and at least '80 bodies, some of which apparently have been buried in coffins of wood.' On the other side of the crossroads was an ancient tumulus called Limlow Hill, but the periodical noted that the site where the skeletons was discovered had been known for generations as 'Heaven's Walls', although there was no indication as to why. Sixteen years later *The Gentleman's Magazine* noted of Heaven's Walls that 'the village children were afraid to traverse it after dark. Heaven's Wall's, at "the witching time of night", were said to be frequented by beings of the supernatural order.' The magazine had been informed of this belief by the village's resident doctor, a man named Webb, who had been privy to the excavations in 1821. Prior to 1821 the site had displayed no 'walls' or other evidence of antiquity: and so (as ghost-hunter Christina Hole suggested in 1941) the name Heaven's Walls may have been derived from a long-forgotten memory of the era when the villa actually functioned around 1,700 years prior during the reign of Emperor Trajan. This was remarkable in itself; the assumption that the place was haunted probably derived from the appellation *Heaven's Walls*, which would be the type of place name to scare children. The subsequent discovery of skeletons there would have ensured this place was forever considered 'haunted'.

While impressed by such notions as folklore and superstition (I have a wishful theory that all such tales have at least a basis in fact), it is a third category of ghostly encounters that impresses the most and is in some ways the most straightforward: the type where the phenomenon is an observable, documented one, and there are numerous examples of this type that were recorded in Cambridgeshire's past as being factual events in their time.

Joseph Glanvil's *Saducismus Triumphatus* (1681), a famous study of the spirit world in Jacobean England, had an epilogue added to it by Dr Henry More called *Continuation Of Relations*. Dr More claimed to have read a letter dated 1 January 1682, penned by a trusted colleague from Cambridgeshire, that spoke of a curious incident which had occurred lately in Balsham. In that village, one Robert Churchman and his wife had fallen under the influence of a couple devoted to Quakerism, although Churchman was not convinced by the new religion since Quakers (as written at the time) 'did not acknowledge scripture for their rule.'

One day the Quaker's wife came to Robert Churchman's house but he told her to leave or there would be a falling out between their two families. The woman told him that Churchman should accept Quakerism, and to prove it was the path he would see a sign testifying as such. A few nights later a tremendous storm broke over Balsham that appeared centred directly over Churchman's house – leaving much of the rest of the village untouched – and during this some kind of entity appeared in his bedroom. It filled the room with an ethereal light and moaned at him 'Sing praises, sing praises!' without further manifesting itself. This spirit apparently took possession of Robert Churchman, and forced him to perform the most ridiculous tricks under the promise that such acts would lead him to 'the New Jerusalem.' Thus possessed, he would lick the floorboards and once he walked half a mile to his brother's house – fully naked – in an insane attempt to likewise convert his brother's family to Quakerism. He also appears to have suffered fits and to have entered into one-sided arguments with his invisible tormentor.

After this, Churchman appears to have expelled the spirit from his person somehow, for he suddenly 'spoke very orthodoxly.' However, it was not long before the evil spirit returned, invaded him again and tried to pass itself off as a 'good' spirit. By now thoroughly demented, Churchman ordered the spirit to prove it was benevolent by turning a candlestick to brass. Apparently before witnesses, 'there was a very unsavoury smell in the room, like that of a candle newly put out', but that was the best the spirit could manage and by its failure it had proved itself 'false'.

It is likely that the 'possessed man' was suffering from bouts of insanity, but he was nonetheless treated by the village physician Dr Templar, who wrote of the events in the absolute belief that they were supernatural in nature. Churchman 'was possessed by a spirit that spoke within him and used his organs in *despight* of him.'

It is clear that in the past the phenomenon of 'ghosts' in Cambridgeshire has taken many forms (just as today) and a selection of stories are noted in this chapter for the reader to ponder.

ECHOES OF THE TUDOR ERA

On the edge of the Northamptonshire border in Cambridgeshire can be found the village of Elton, and in the southern extremity of the huge Elton Park – some 3,800 acres – is the hall. Elton Hall originally dates to the reign of King Henry VII (1457–1509), but additions and renovations in the 17th, 18th and 19th centuries have produced the effect of an extraordinarily romantic building, as much Gothic castle in appearance as a stately home. C.H.M.D. Scott's poetic *Tales Of Northamptonshire* (1936) recalled a legend about the hall that he heard in his youth. This was that a page at Elton Hall was slain by a drunken Sir Guy Sapcote, one of its earliest owners. The murdered page had been a sensitive lad (some said he was Sir Guy's illegitimate son), and even some 400 years later it was still said that in the valley of the River Nene (which forms the border of Northamptonshire and the Elton estate in Cambridgeshire) there was a ghost. On summer evenings the apparition of a young lad in mediaeval clothes walked along the riverbanks, carrying flowers picked from the meadows and whom birds fluttered around.

In 2009 a former resident of Cambridge told me a story about the Olde Dolphin Inne, a Tudor tavern whose premises stretched from All Saints' churchyard to Bridge Street. In 1515 Thomas Cranmer (on his path to a clerical career) was elected to a Fellowship at Jesus College but subsequently forced to resign this when a scandal broke. Cranmer had married a woman known as Joan Black, who was a niece of the landlady of the Dolphin but derisively nicknamed Black Joan. Joan is, in fact, thought to have been the daughter of a gentleman, but pressure from Jesus College nonetheless forced Cranmer to resign and support his new wife by becoming a lecturer at Buckingham College. However, in 1516 Joan died tragically in childbirth at the Dolphin, and despite the constant slander of his enemies – who derided Cranmer as a mere 'hosteler' of the tavern – Jesus College immediately restored his Fellowship.

The unhappy demise of Joan changed the course of Thomas Cranmer's life. He followed the clerical path and rose to the heights of Archbishop of Canterbury during the reigns of King Henry VIII and Edward VI before being martyred by Queen Mary in Oxford. 'Bloody Mary' had taken her revenge for Cranmer's championing of Protestantism and his declaring her illegitimate. That was on 21 May 1556, and (as I was told) every year afterwards on this date those at the Dolphin were awoken in terror by a ghastly horrific screeching that whipped up out of nowhere: this was either Joan's heartbreak at the judicial assassination of her long-ago husband, or phantom echoes of her torment during the childbirth that claimed her life. This inn was one of the principal meeting places of 16th-century Cambridge, very popular with undergraduates, and although the story of its being haunted may be a modern supposition, it is nonetheless curious that such long-ago places, people and events are recalled in such a manner.

HAUNTED WOODCROFT MANOR

South-east of Helpston can be found (now privately owned) Woodcroft Manor, a 13th-century fortified manor-house that sometimes goes by the name of Woodcroft House or Woodcroft Castle. During the English Civil War the area around here was often the scene of violence ever since Dr Michael Hudson, a chaplain to, and supporter of, the king, had swapped his clerical garments for the garb of a humble soldier. Raising a small army of locals, he succeeded in harrying and ambushing Cromwell's men on many occasions and had many adventures.

However, on 6 June 1648 his luck ran out. Woodcroft was at this time a Royalist garrison, and a party of Roundhead soldiery entered the grounds to search Hudson out. A chaotic and bloody confrontation ensued as Hudson and his last-surviving men retreated within the house and then into its upper reaches, where they tried to defend themselves. Eventually, up on the battlements, his men dying about him, Hudson yielded to a promise of quarter and threw down his sword; however, the offer of mercy was a lie, and the soldiery advanced on him. At this point he either climbed, or was thrown, over the battlements but managed to grab hold of a spout or a projection of stone. The Roundhead cavalry's weapons hacked off his hands and he plummeted into the moat below. Upon struggling to get out of the ditch, and bleeding heavily from his severed wrists, a vicious blow to the head from the butt end of a musket finished him off. A shopkeeper from Stamford who was among the invaders cut out Hudson's tongue and ever after would carry it about with him as a keepsake, while other soldiers disembowelled the body with their bayonets.

This barbaric treatment is the reason why on June nights afterwards there could be heard the phantom echoes of invisible conflict: the clashing of weapons and screams of 'Mercy!' and 'Quarter!' – supposedly the dying words of the slain Dr Hudson.

MURDER BY GHOST

Richard Baxter's *The Certainty Of The World Of Spirits* (1692) recounts an astonishing instance of an allegedly fatal attack by a ghost upon a living person in 1662.

The incident concerned the son of a minister named Franklin, and the lad and his family lived in Ely where it appears that some kind of phantom woman had developed a kind of evil fixation with the boy. The ghost was in the 'garb and appearance of a gentlewoman' and it would seem young Franklin was fascinated by her and even encouraged her appearances: '...she and he were very free and had long been wont to disport together, even while company was in the room, and while the father [...] was sitting there.'

The boy had an apprenticeship in Cambridge and one evening the strange phantom woman appeared before him at the house of his employer in that town. The pair entered into a bizarre argument as she tried to persuade the boy to accompany her back to Ely, and when he refused the spirit 'gave him a sounding box on the ear which made him very ill.'

Young Franklin rose the following day but was extremely sick and unfit for work. At this his master decided to ride to Ely and speak to the boy's father and try and find out why this ghost had attached itself to the lad.

That afternoon, back in Cambridge, young Franklin – sitting by the fireside and in the company of his employer's wife – suddenly called out in delirium, 'O, mistress look! There's the gentlewoman!' The woman looked but saw no one, and so turned her back to the boy once more. As she did so she heard a tremendous thud and span round to see her young employee now seriously injured, his neck broken and his head lopsided. He died not long afterwards. William Drage's original mention of the incident in *Daimonomageia* (1665) noted of the boy's injury, 'He had the exact mark on his forehead, being dead, where the Spiritual Woman did hit him [when] alive.'

At the same time as this was happening, the boy's father and his employer were sat at table in Ely discussing matters when the ghostly woman appeared before them both and looked at each angrily before disappearing.

The whole saga reads as though it might be a concoction designed to cover up the murder of young Franklin, although Richard Baxter was sure it occurred exactly as he had narrated.

CAXTON GIBBET

As we have already seen, the site of the replica gibbet post at Caxton Gibbet has something of a sinister history. Long before the gibbet was erected, the route had been the setting for a brutal crime. In 1299 two rich and powerful merchants from Stamford apparently attracted three strangers as travelling companions while making their way south along *Arming-Street* (Ermine Street). After drinks at an inn in Caxton, and after sunset, the two merchants were knocked from their horses and both brutally murdered by their companions, their screams being heard by those in the church at Longstowe. When the blood-soaked robbers arrived in Royston, they were questioned about their appearance – but they escaped initial suspicion by claiming to be escapees from a bandit attack. They then fled Royston, and the crime remained unsolved; an outraged King Edward I subsequently ordered all roads in England to have their bracken and trees cut back 60ft to deny robbers hiding places. The victims, it seems, had been people of very high standing.

So this route already had a grim history, with violence stamped into the dirt of the road. An appropriate site for a gibbet, then. Apart from the multiple murderer named Atkins in 1671 and the aforementioned young highwayman named Gatward, there were many others who ended their days at this sinister spot. The traveller William Cobbett, in his *Rural Rides*, wrote of the scene one bleak January day in 1822: 'The land just about here does seem to be really bad. The face of the country is naked. The few scrubbed trees that now and then meet the eye, and even the quick-sets, are covered with a yellow moss. All is bleak and comfortless; and, just on the most dreary part of this most dreary scene, stands almost opportunely, "Caxton Gibbet", tendering its friendly one arm to the passers-by. It has recently been fresh-painted...'

The only refuge were the two or three inns hereabouts that offered hostelry for those who had come to this desolate part of Cambridgeshire to assist in the grisly process of suspending the corpse from the gibbet.

The Caxton gibbet is a later replica of the original grim landmark.

Even today, when the traffic is light at this junction where the A1198 and A428 converge, there is something lost and lonely about this place. Murderers, highwaymen and sheep stealers all ended their days swinging from this gloomy landmark in the 17th and 18th centuries, and one wonders if their skeletons still lie immured beneath what was once known as Gibbet Field on the western side of the Old North Road (A1198). There are the usual stories of felons being caged while still alive and hoisted up to die an agonisingly slow death from starvation and exposure; of travellers stopping by the roadside to use the swinging corpses as target practice with their pistols and arrows; and of glassy-eyed, skeletal corpses in tattered rags moving inside the gibbet cage to stare mournfully at passers-by on freezing, wind-lashed nights. There have been centuries for these types of stories to be generated.

But it was at the old Gibbet Inn that a now well-known incident supposedly occurred. I understand this building to have been a beerhouse that was noted in the 1850s as standing just north of the crossroads, and that later became the Caxton Gibbet Hotel in the 1930s. (However, others have told me that the inn in question stood on the site of the Yim Wah Chinese Restaurant, which itself was destroyed by an unexplained fire in 2009.) According to a famous piece of local lore the inn was the scene of a botched robbery attempt by the wayward son of the landlord, who committed his first murder when his sleeping victim awoke during the theft. Two other potential witnesses were slain in the panic over the first crime, and all three bodies were tipped down a well on the property. The crime did not remain undiscovered for long, however, and the innkeeper's son became the last person to hang in the gibbet cage that had for so long stood not so far from his parent's place of business and from which they made their trade.

The story is highly likely to be fiction, or at best a misremembering of a factual event, lacking obvious details as it does. But it is nonetheless a very familiar legend: that of the wicked innkeeper who gets his poetic just desserts on the nearby gallows. Either because of this, or any one of the *actual* instances of corpses being laid out at the inn prior to being hoisted up, the Gibbet Inn suffered much low-key paranormal disturbance over the years. Phantom footsteps thumped and clumped about the place, and are said to have come to a halt before the well on the premises.

THE EVERLASTING CLUB

The following anecdote is in all likelihood a complete fabrication, but its details are nonetheless so well known among Cambridge University students that it has become a 'sort of truth', as I was informed in June 2009 upon visiting the scene of the story, 15th-century Jesus College in Cambridge.

The College is supposed to have been founded around 1496 on the site of a former nunnery where the nuns had earned for themselves a poor reputation, but the famous legend of the Everlasting Club supposedly took place during the reign of King George II. The early Hanoverian era is synonymous with an age of casual, pitiless violence at every level of society, and during this time many 'clubs' sprang up. Some were simply mobs of rakes who wandered the night streets inflicting pointless violence on anyone they came across, but for some the drinking, gambling and Sabbath-breaking crossed the barrier into sinister spirituality and Devil worship, with all manner of dark and demonic allegations made against members. At Jesus College, the Everlasting Club was founded in secrecy and based on the Hellfire Clubs sometime in the early 18th century. From 1738 to 1743 seven students, from varying Colleges, met once every October. Although their 'entertainment' was less than sinister, the club's president insisted on the rules that bound them as a society being strictly adhered to. This included the provision that should any member not attend the yearly meeting then they would be liable to severe punishment by himself. Whether 'corporeal or incorporeal', they were members of the Everlastings.

On 2 November 1743 the club's president, Alan Dermot, was killed while duelling in Paris, and at this the Everlasting Club effectively disbanded, its remaining members graduating and leaving the University; however, bound by some perverse fear of the supernatural wrath of their dead president, the remaining members of the Everlasting Club would return to Cambridge every October for their one engagement with each other – the secretary, Witherington, recording nothing in the minutes of the meeting but the attendance of the remaining members in 1744.

Over the next 18 years the members gathered annually in the rooms of one Charles Bellasis, who had returned to the University to tutor and had taken chambers in Jesus College. By 1766 Bellasis was the sole living member of the Everlasting Club, three others having died earlier that year. The October gathering naturally went unattended, but on the night of 2 November that year there was a furious, prolonged outburst of noise from Bellasis' chambers. Swearing, laughing, singing, crashing furniture and multiple voices engaged in loud, raucous and drunken conversation boomed from Bellasis' rooms; the Master – concerned about the example his colleague was setting – dare not interrupt. At midnight, all sounds abruptly ceased.

The following morning Bellasis was found dead in his rooms, slumped on the table over the red-bound minute book of the Everlasting Society. For the first time since 1742 the names of all the members were noted as having been in attendance, and about the table were six other chairs, some overturned, as if Bellasis had been holding some kind of card party for a group of people now missing.

This story began with Sir Arthur Gray, who had it published in 1919 when Master of Jesus College, along with other short stories in a slim volume. The prose makes it clear that the story is allegedly taken from entries in the red-bound volumes of minutes, which were themselves hidden for a long time by the College to avoid scandal. Gray noted that the event supposedly occurred in a room atop a first-floor landing, and that room now stood padlocked and empty, its one window having been bricked up some 150 years ago. The story is undoubtedly fiction, although some of the participants were probably based on real Fellows and one wonders if it was inspired by College urban legends. Whether or not it was, it is clear the story is now ingrained in the lore of Jesus College. Gray wrote: '…some suspicion of the nature of the occurrences must have percolated to students and servants, for there was a long-abiding belief in the College that annually on the night of 2 November sounds of unholy revelry were heard to issue from the chamber of Charles Bellasis.'

A SPIRITED EXCUSE

When the parish constables of Wilbraham knocked on the door of the former home of the long-deceased Bishop Thomas Watson to enquire as to the cause of the riotous disturbances emanating from within, they were met with a curious excuse.

In his own lifetime, Bishop Watson was bedevilled by conflict with his ecclesiastical brothers. He was a Fellow of St John's College, Cambridge, and the rector of '*Burrough Green*, in that county', when on 26 June 1687 he was consecrated as Bishop of St David's in Pembrokeshire. This was at the order of the Archbishop of Canterbury, but at the expense of the Bishops of Rochester and Chester who had both wanted that position. In 1699 accusations were made against him of simony (paying for holy offices or positions of hierarchy in the church), and as a supporter of the deposed King James II he was a popular target for the abuse of the mob. Later that year he was convicted of the charge and a court of his religious peers cast him out of office. For some six years Watson entered in legal challenges against this, but it all came to naught and after a spell in gaol for failure to pay his legal costs he retired in disgrace to his estate in Wilbraham in 1705.

Legend had it that despite this, Watson lived a life of opulent luxury at Wilbraham, although much of his fortune was spent benevolently on various charities and causes in Cambridgeshire, East Yorkshire and Wales. The controversial ex-bishop Watson died in 1717, aged 80, at his home, still declaring himself a victim of a conspiracy.

In 1790 the *Gentleman's Magazine* reported that, some 60 years later, the bishop's old house became the scene of riotous late night partying by the then owner's servants. When the servants were questioned about their disgraceful behaviour they explained that it was because Watson's ghost haunted the property (no doubt looking for his fortune) and they dared not go to bed in their terror. All conglomerated in the same room and would drink heavily to steady their nerves! Apparently their master accepted this as genuine but a friend of his took it upon himself to perform an exorcism at the house – and thus deprived the staff of their excuse for not retiring quietly to bed at the end of the working day.

THE DRUMMER BOY OF ALCONBURY

Records show that on 2 August 1786 one Jarvis Matcham was executed at Huntingdon and hung in chains for the murder in 1780 at Alconbury of a drummer boy, Benjamin Jones, who belonged to the 49th Regiment of Foot: 'The gibbet stood in a field near the old north road, near the wood leading to Wey Bridge.'

Eighty years later, one Cuthbert Bede related to *Notes And Queries* the peculiar story of how Matcham was supposed to have been apprehended, as told to him by an elderly resident of the parish.

Matcham and the drummer boy were lodging at the White Hart Inn at Alconbury Weston while recruiting on behalf of the army. Matcham was fond of the drink, and as such had lately found himself short on funds. However, Jones, the drummer boy, kept quite a bit of money on him and the records show that on 19 August 1780 Matcham killed the lad about a mile out of Alconbury in the direction of Easton. Benjamin Jones, aged about 17, was found by the side of the road; his throat had been cut with a clasp knife. Six gold sovereigns had been stolen from the body, and no effort was spared in the hunt for the murderer as the lad had been the son of a sergeant in the Huntingdon regiment.

That it took six years to capture Matcham is perhaps down to the likelihood that he immediately fled to York and then abroad, and it is not stated by Cuthbert Bede's informant where the following event is supposed to have happened. But the fact that he was caught *at all* has been linked to a bizarre supernatural incident. Suffice to say that years later Matcham was walking with a fellow soldier in the open countryside 'when the stones began to rise up and roll afore 'em.' Matcham's companion took this bizarre event as evidence that one of them hid a dark secret, and suggested they part company. At this, Matcham commented that the dark secret was his own: he confessed to the murder, commenting that he had had no peace of mind since he had committed the killing, and was plagued by dismal supernatural encounters.

Cuthbert Bede's informant in 1866 remembered no specific talk of ghosts, '…though very likely there were; for they always put a ghost into them sort o' murders; but it weren't according to my belief; so perhaps I made no account of it.' It is no doubt the confused and total breakdown that the tortured murderer apparently suffered six years after his crime, together with his garbled confession, that forms the basis of all the subsequent ghostly anecdotes that have clung to this story, but the case is a curious one nonetheless. The earliest accounts do indeed confirm that during a thunderstorm on Salisbury Plain, Wiltshire, Matcham *did* suffer a series of terrifying hallucinations that his companion, a man named Shepherd, did not experience himself. Matcham fell on his knees, begging for mercy and demanding that Shepherd deliver him to the Mayor of Salisbury. Correspondence at the time shows that Matcham did later freely confess. Furthermore, he was positively identified by those who recalled that the suspect in the Huntingdonshire murder was missing a front tooth – as was Matcham.

Bede's informant, an 'old cottager', could in actual fact remember seeing the gibbeted corpse for himself, and in many ways his recollection of this is as interesting as the attendant ghostly legend. After his trial and execution at Huntingdon, Jarvis Matcham's corpse was suspended from a gibbet and hung in chains near Alconbury on a piece of ground belonging to the parish clerk near the river: 'He wore his regimentals, and it was them as made the red rags that flapped from the chains.' The chains bound the corpse of the executed man close round the arms, legs and forehead, and when there was a strong wind his body would be violently buffeted out at all kinds of strange angles. One can only imagine the shock that Bede's elderly informant received when he was, in his younger days, confronted with the horrific sight of Matcham's corpse standing against a tall white post near the bridge at about four in the morning, as though it had somehow climbed down from the gibbet. In fact, the swivel had been broken, and persons unknown (possibly loutish drovers who passed this way regularly) had propped Matcham's corpse up so as to frighten the subsequent travellers. Matcham's remains were finally hoisted down *c.*1830.

HEMPSALL'S GHOST

From about 1760 Upware by the River Cam had its own public house to cater for river traffic. Originally called The Black Swan, in 1806 it changed its name to the Lord Nelson, but since *c.*1850 has been popularly called 'The Five Miles From Anywhere: No Hurry' public house. Apparently, this is a truism – at one time it was *literally* five miles from anywhere, and it is said to have been the drinking spot of

Jeremiah's Tea House, Little Abington, allegedly haunted by local landowner Jeremiah Lagden. Lagden hid smuggled tea at the White Hart, leading to village rumours that he was a highwayman. He died c.1804, hanged (if you believe the stories) on the Newmarket Road.

one Joe Hempsall, whose ghost is still said to haunt Soham Mere, between Wicken and its much larger neighbour Soham.

According to folklorist Christopher Marlowe, writing in 1926, Hempsall was a belligerent farmer who lived near Soham in the early 1800s and would frequently tramp back and forth over the marshes between his home and the Black Swan for a beer. He was well known locally for having an almost photographic memory of the mere, allowing him to navigate by moonlight alone, sometimes with the aid of an old-fashioned leaping pole to cross dykes. He would even navigate the treacherous Big-Bog so as to avoid having to take the longer path route.

And so it happened that one inevitable night Joe Hempsall left the Black Swan and ventured into a blind pea-souper of a fog, refusing to heed the warning of his fellow drinkers that conditions were so bad he should take the lane. He was never seen alive again; the fog settled on the area for three whole days before clearing.

On the fourth morning, Elijah Boggers set off to Hempsall's farm to visit his friend; however, on the way there Boggers was joined by Hempsall himself, although the farmer was not his usual talkative self and, worse still, looked deathly ill. He said not a word till the pair reached the farm gate, where Hempsall said in a hollow, sepulchral tone: 'Go not in there — my body lies in Big-Bog. As I am now, so one day wilt thou be. I lost my life in Big-Bog on the first night of the fog — go to Eaudyke and there wilt thou find my body.'

Trembling with fear, Hempsall's neighbour navigated his way to Big-Bog, and there found Hempsall's drowned body caught in reeds, lying half in and half out the water and covered in clinging slime. After recovering from his utter shock, Boggers led a party of locals out to Eaudyke where they searched in vain:

the body had slid beneath the silent, filthy waters of Big-Bog. At this point Hempsall's ghost appeared again, its hoarse voice saying, 'Fear not – as I am so must ye all be. Recover my body from the west side of Big-Bog and bury me in Wicken churchyard…' The ghost then evaporated into a cloud before their very eyes. After this they grimly fished the unfortunate farmer's body out of the mere.

Marlowe wrote that ever since then it was reckoned that the farmer's ghost haunted the expanse of Soham Mere on account of the fact that he had been buried in Soham, and not Wicken as he had wished. Cries for help and moaning were also said to echo across the mere 'at certain seasons.'

OLD BUTTON CAP

Rambling, 14th-century Kingsley House in Barnack is now a private dwelling, but was at one time the village rectory. The famous novelist and historian Charles Kingsley, born in Devon in 1819, spent much of his childhood here, where he is said to have written poems and sermons at the tender age of four – the circumstance that earned Kingsley House its current name.

Charles Kinglsey grew up with the story that 'the great north room' in the rectory was haunted by the ghost of a former rector who was said to have, in life, defrauded a widow. Young Charles was told the anecdote by his grandfather. The ghost wore a flowery-design dressing gown and a cap with a button on it, and was known as 'Button Cap'. He would walk across the room, his slippers making 'flopping' noises on the floor as he searched for deeds incriminating him in the swindling of the widow. There was never any indication that a murder had occurred at the rectory, or that a skeleton had been found; Button Cap's history was concerned only with avarice and cheating.

Barnack Rectory is privately owned.

Charles was a sensitive and nervous boy, who was at one time moved into the 'Haunted Room' during an attack of brain fever. Here, he is supposed to have heard old Button Cap himself walking about the room, and the phantasm even turned over the pages of the book he was reading on some occasions. Kingsley presumed that Button Cap was looking through the pages to find the deed. Sometimes the ghost manifested itself as a kind of low rumbling noise like barrels being rolled, and for years afterwards his imagination was haunted by the weird sights and sounds he had experienced while in the room.

In later life, however, a more rationally-minded Kingsley put the phenomenon down to, among other things, rats scuttling about the old building and his own feverish mind playing tricks. He would tell his own children, when they could not sleep, that he had seen too many ghosts at Barnack to have much respect for them. He mused in 1864, '…perhaps someone had been laying phosphoric paste about, and he ate thereof and ran down to the pond, and drank till he burst!' Nonetheless, as late as 1901 a work on the life of Kingsley stated, 'Button Cap is still dreaded by some of the old parishioners…'

SKULLDUGGERY IN WHITTLESFORD

One of Cambridgeshire's most famous ghostly anecdotes concerns the excavation of three ancient tumuli, or earth barrows, between Whittlesford and Thriplow. It is said that one of the labourers engaged in levelling the tumuli found the skeleton of an ancient warrior, and at the day's end he secreted the skull away to his cottage as a souvenir. During the night he was awoken by a thunderous hammering at his door, and

looking out the window the thief was terrified to see the headless skeleton stood in the garden — and, in an ethereal voice, demanding its skull back! The labourer at once threw the skull out of the window to the phantasm.

Amazingly, this unlikely story has an element of truth in it. Around 1818, three ancient earthen burial mounds were excavated under the direction of Ebenezer Hollick, the squire of Whittlesford. On Got Moor, the three tumuli — called the Chronicle Hills — stood in a north-south line by a brook separating the two parishes of Thriplow and Whittlesford. The middle of the three was some 8ft high and 27 yards in diameter, and a remarkable number of antiquities were unearthed here: great elk antlers, remains of what may have been beaver or lemming (extinct in the UK) and four human skeletons laid on their backs. Some 100 yards to the north, there was another remarkable discovery — two more

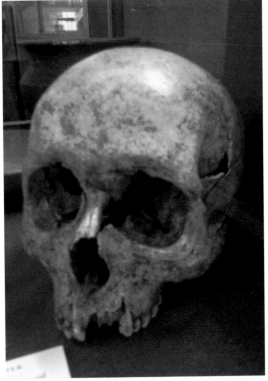

This particular skull was unearthed in 1973 near Godmanchester and is thought to have been buried in the Roman era.

sepulchres that were tentatively dated to Celtic times or earlier. The mounds here displayed nothing more than 'humps' 2ft above the ground, but underneath one of them was a small circular chamber some 8ft deep with an oak bottom. Two skeletons were found therein, one of which was in a sitting position and had on him an erect spear with a tip of iron.

The skull of the sitting skeleton was stolen upon its discovery by one of the workmen engaged in helping the squire, who took it back to his home. Almost immediately, Whittlesford was swept with the 'amusing superstition' that '...the headless skeleton of an ancient warrior knocks every night at the door of this cottage demanding the skull sacrilegiously stolen from the grave.'

GHOSTS OF THE FAMOUS

At Kimbolton, close by the Bedfordshire border, can be found Kimbolton Castle, a mediaeval castle that gradually developed into a Tudor stately home and now shares its grounds with Kimbolton School. The place is famous for being the site of the death of Catherine of Aragon, following her divorce from King Henry VIII and the elevation of Anne Boleyn to queen in her stead. Here she dwelt in retirement in a single room, in actual fact almost a prisoner, for a year and a half until her death on 7 January 1536 in what is still known as the Queen's Room.

The castle at this time was itself in a state of some disrepair and her dismal quarters may have accelerated her demise. It is famously said that as Catherine's health deteriorated she sent a humble message to the king, requesting a final interview with their daughter Mary so that she might bestow her blessing upon her; however, this simple request was denied (although supporters managed to discreetly ferry letters between mother and daughter), and perhaps this unseemly treatment is the reason why they said that Catherine's ghost haunted Kimbolton Castle's west gallery many years after her death aged 50.

There were many who believed that agents acting in connivance with Anne Boleyn poisoned Catherine to death at Kimbolton. This was apparently based on observations of the condition of her body that were made by the embalmers prior to Catherine's burial in Peterborough Cathedral. Between 1533 and 1534 the banished Catherine was also kept at Buckden Palace, the red-bricked residential seat of the Bishops of Lincoln in the village of Buckden. The mediaeval quarters that were her confines during her time here were pulled down c.1838, but before this her ghost was said to haunt the chapel there.

A later resident at Kimbolton Castle was Sir John Popham, a Speaker of the House of Commons and Lord Chief Justice who presided over many great trials of the age until his death in June 1607. He also has left a strange legacy there. To this day a portrait of the 'stern judge' hangs down from a wall in the Great Hall in the castle, and according to folklorist John Timbs in 1872 he haunts the property. He could allegedly be glimpsed sitting atop the park wall, or his shadowy figure could be seen in the shade of the great elms where he awaited 'rogues and poachers.' His ghost could also be seen atop Castle Hill, the mound within the grounds that was the site of an earlier, timber-structured Norman fort. Another less charitable allegation (almost certainly village gossip) is that during one of his sojourns to Kimbolton Castle from c.1600 onwards, he got one of the maidservants pregnant. When the child was born, Popham — enraged that it was not a boy — threw the screaming infant to its death out of an upstairs window (from the room now known as the Popham Gallery). Every so often the flagstones in the courtyard are supposed to take on a reddish hue as if a pool of blood were spreading.

Oliver Cromwell's ghost is held to haunt the lonely country lanes to the west of Wisbech, along with other places hereabouts. And during the Ely Ghost Walk I was told that (for some reason) the ghost of Nell Gwynne, the actress and mistress of King Charles II, was supposed to haunt a particular shop front on High Street.

Cambridgeshire, like almost every other county north of London, boasts associations with the most famous highwayman of the day, Dick Turpin. Many locations with Turpin links are pure folklore, however, so it is difficult to give the stories the stamp of authenticity. At Buckden, he was apparently a patron of the George Coaching Inn on High Street. In 1937, the writer George Long observed that, 'His reputed bedroom, with an ingenious emergency exit, is still shown to visitors.' Quite naturally, folklore has it that Turpin – who was executed in 1739 – rides his horse Black Bess up to the inn in spectral form; a lean figure with a pockmarked face wearing a tri-corn hat who vanishes while the horse neighs furiously. The White Horse at Eaton Socon is supposed to have also had Turpin as a guest, with one observer commenting wistfully of this belief in 1931: 'It is somewhat more stimulating to the imagination to sit in the taproom of "The White Horse" at Eaton Socon and picture Dick Turpin coming in and calling for a pot of ale or a hot toddy.'

Cambridgeshire also boasts a slightly more recent famous ghost, that of the Georgian equivalent of a rock star. By a weir at a juncture in the River Cam, between Grantchester and Trumpington, can be found

Byron's Pool at Grantchester.

the old mill pool called Byron's Pool, on account of this being a favourite swimming haunt of George Gordon Byron, 6th Baron Byron, during his undergraduate days at Trinity College, Cambridge, in the early 19th century. Lord Byron died at age 36 on 19 April 1824 of marsh fever contracted in Greece while helping the Greeks to fight for independence from the Ottoman Empire. Predictably for a poet and romantic famously described by Lady Caroline Lamb as 'mad, bad and dangerous to know', Byron's ghost is supposed to haunt the pool named after him, swimming back and forth. This belief is largely due to fellow poet Rupert Brooke, who lived at Grantchester in 1909 and wrote of Byron's Pool in his poem *The Old Vicarage*:

> *In Grantchester, in Grantchester...*
> *Still in the dawn-lit waters cool*
> *His ghostly lordship swims his pool*
> *And tries the strokes, essays the tricks*
> *Long learnt on Hellespont, or Styx.*

A GHOSTLY COMPANION

The *Census Of Hallucinations* was a remarkable survey of ghostly encounters carried out by a committee from the Society for Psychical Research. Published in 1894 in the society's *Proceedings*, it had canvassed 17,000 people and found that 1,684 had seen some form of unexplainable apparition – or, more scientifically, experienced a 'hallucinatory episode' that occurred despite no known mental health condition. The survey also indicated that certain 'ghosts' were attached to people and not places.

Margaret Verrall (d.1916) was a lecturer in classics at Newnham College, Cambridge, but was also famous in the Victorian era as a spiritualist and medium who explored the psychic phenomenon known as 'automatic writing'. She also claimed that there was a ghostly old woman who apparently followed her about. This ghost was observed by the academic not only in Brighton in 1879, but also at a house she resided in at Cambridge – having apparently followed her to the city. Mrs Verrall was able to describe the phantasm quite clearly: it wore a brooch, and seemed at first to be a normal person, not out of place at all. On closer inspection, however, a disturbing feature could be discerned. The figure wore a bonnet and within the cloth cap there was no face, merely a kind of misty void.

THE GHOST OF HINXTON CHURCH

Occasionally there come to light anecdotes that do suggest the reality of 'ghosts'. The Victorian spiritualist Frederick W.H. Myers was devoted to cataloguing believable encounters, and one of the most impressive to feature in his *Human Personality And Its Survival Of Bodily Death* (1893) comes from Cambridgeshire.

On the evening of 8 May 1885 Alfred Bard, a gardener employed at Sawston Hall, was walking back home through the grounds of St Mary's Church, Hinxton. In doing so he looked at the square, stone vault that at one time a Mr de Freville was interred in – and saw a woman who was known to him. It was de Freville's wife, and in a statement written later that year Bard confirmed: 'I saw Mrs de Freville leaning on the rails, dressed much as I had usually seen her, in a coal-scuttle bonnet, black jacket with deep crape, and black dress. She was looking full at me. Her face was very white, much whiter than usual.'

Bard had at one time been in Mrs de Freville's employ and so he idly wandered over to the stone tomb, assuming that the woman had hired the stonemason to enter the mausoleum in order to rectify some problem. Mrs de Freville's position hid the tomb entrance from view, thus preventing Bard from seeing whether the door was open and anyone inside at work. All the time Mrs de Freville said nothing, although 'Her face turned and followed me.' She was never more than five or six yards from his sight and he kept his gaze fixed on her, although Bard does not appear to have attempted communication with her. At this point he stumbled, and looking up he saw that Mrs de Freville had utterly vanished. Assuming that she had herself entered the vault, Bard walked up to it but observed that the door was locked and no key within.

The church clock told Bard that it was 9:20pm and at this point, extremely puzzled, he went home and told his wife what had happened. The following day news was brought to him by his son that Mrs de Freville had been found dead the previous day at 7:30pm, having died earlier that afternoon in her room in London. Bard later recounted his strange story to the local vicar, Revd C.T. Foster, who then informed Myers and expanded: 'My late parishioner, Mrs de Freville, was a somewhat eccentric lady, who was specially morbid on the subject of tombs.' Both Bard and his wife made sworn written statements of the event, and the vicar confirmed that in every way Mr Bard could be considered a trustworthy witness.

With no other explanation, it would seem that Mr Bard saw a ghost that strange night, with the experience all the more convincing because of its sheer pointlessness. He wrote, 'I have never had any other hallucinations whatever', and in cases like this there really is no middle ground: either Mr Bard fabricated the event for an unknown reason...or he genuinely saw a ghost.

GHOSTS IN FOLKLORE

Although the apparition witnessed in Hinxton churchyard bears all the hallmarks of an *actual* ghostly encounter, it is clear that some Cambridgeshire legends concern what appear to be 'folklore' ghosts – that is to say, stories with no real background or substance.

It is evident that in the past, 'ghosts' were referred to in a number of guises, blurring the line between sprites, imps, goblins and phantasms. *Nuts To Crack* (1834), a whimsical collection of Cambridge anecdotes, observations, jokes and half-truths, describes a ghost that terrorised the city thus:

> They said that the house in the skirts of the wood
> By a saucer-eyed ghost was infested;
> Who filled every heart with confusion and fright
> By assuming strange shapes at the dead of night,
> Shapes monstrous, foul and detested.'
> And truly they said, and the monster well knew,
> That the ghost was the greatest of evils;
> For no sooner the bell of the mansion toll'd one
> Than the frolicksome imp in a fury begun
> To caper like ten thousand devils.

A Cambridge scholar with magician's skills is supposed to have banished this sprite to the Red Sea with trickery. It is unlikely that there is any 'truth' behind this rhyme, but it does indicate the way that ghosts (as now) formed a popular theme of collective storytelling, and there are many examples of such spirits that have no real substance other then a local tradition that 'it is so'.

In other words, many ghostly anecdotes appear to be stories with no foundation in fact whatsoever. In the Victorian era, ghostly spirits and all manner of sprites were said to hold hands and dance about the ruins of Wothorpe House, just shy of the Lincolnshire border at Stamford. Here, this stately, picturesque pile was built in the early 1600s by Thomas Cecil, the Earl of Exeter, 'to retire out of the dust', meaning London; however, it fell into disrepair around the 1790s and, crumbling and isolated, must simply have been *assumed* to be haunted. Therefore, the simple story of the dancing ghosts was no doubt generated locally to 'fill the void', as it were.

Another such site, at the other extremity of the county, is written of in Ms Porter's *Cambridgeshire Customs And Folklore*. Near Great Abington, just north of the Essex border, on the land of Abington Church Farm, there was, or is, a meadow known as Sunken Church Field, so-called because of the supposition that at one time a chapel had stood there. It had fallen into disrepair and gradually its foundations were buried by the elements; however, for generations people avoided the spot at night because of the rumour that the bells could be heard pealing beneath the ground, and if one put their ear to the soil they would hear the subterranean noises of a choir singing. Quite how this story originated is unclear, although in 1851 the remains of an extensive Roman settlement were unearthed in Sunken Church Field. The British Archaeological Association noted around this time that this particular *Sunkin*-Church Field, or Church Field, was indicative of a curious phenomenon: '...the constant occurrence of Roman remains [being found] in localities known as "church fields".' Maybe the appellation was a foggy memory of the Roman era, harking back to a time when buildings actually stood hereabouts (remarkable in itself), only with time Roman villas became misremembered as 'a church' – which might then explain the myth eventually written of in 1969 by Ms Porter.

THE TRUMPINGTON STREET PORTRAIT

Around 1890 a lady was shown into a property on Trumpington Street, Cambridge, with a view to buying it. She was let in by a female servant and shown into the sitting room while the maid whisked out to fetch the owner of the house. While she waited, the prospective house buyer cast an appreciative eye round the sitting room, until her gaze fell upon a fine portrait hanging over the fire; that of a woman in a green dress wearing a singular hat with a feather in it and who glared malevolently out from the canvas above the fireplace.

At length the lady of the house walked in and then proceeded to show the potential customer about the property. The second lady was very impressed by the house, although she was somewhat perturbed when the owner confided that on occasion a phantom lady in green had been glimpsed drifting about the place. So she asked if the lady in the portrait and the rumoured 'ghost' were one and the same – to which the mistress of the house looked perplexed and asked, 'What portrait? We do not have any portraits in the sitting room.'

The two ladies returned to the sitting room and there the astonished visitor saw that there now hung above the fireplace a framed landscape – and not the chilling portrait of the glaring woman she had seen earlier.

This story has all the trappings of a Victorian urban legend, but it was included in a short-lived publication called *The Cam: A Cambridge Town Magazine* in 1927 by a man named Thorney, who had been told that it was a 'true' story by a friend. It subsequently appeared in Ms Porter's 1969 *Cambridgeshire Customs And Folklore* and is now classed as one of the city's classic ghostly anecdotes. Many can repeat the story in some broad form, and some even claim to know where this house is. While visiting the museum on Trumpington Street I was told a *version* of this story, differing mainly in the details that the house was visited by a *man* and that it remained unoccupied ever after his visit, although I find this difficult to believe and it appears to be a kind of 'new detail' added to an already familiar story.

ECHOES OF TOWN AND GOWN

These days, to stroll round Cambridge is a joy, particularly in the summer when the city really does present a fantastic, cosmopolitan façade. Hordes of students, residents and tourists compete for space among the shops, museums, street theatres and delicatessens; and European-style café culture and expensive designer clothes stores go hand-in-hand with the many traditional stores and ancient landmarks. In fact, from Castle Hill to Trumpington Street there are almost too many beautiful, historic and impossibly magnificent landmark College buildings to keep track of as one meanders through the town trying to take in the concept that the town and University are symbiotic: the two opposite walks of life somehow 'mesh' together. For example, the casual pedestrian can wander idly along Silver Street after a coffee, via the entrance of Queen's College (*c.*1448) in Queen's Lane, and then suddenly find themselves within sight of the famous 'Mathematical Bridge' that dextrously crosses the River Cam even as the punters attempt to manoeuvre under it. Bicycles are literally everywhere. Although more suitable for another book, one cannot but help be reminded of the great British luminaries who have studied at her University: the 15 alumni who went on to become Prime Minister, the 83 Nobel Laureates, Sir Isaac Newton, Professor Stephen Hawking…everyone from Lord Byron to Stephen Fry, and many, many others in between.

The students here are even now notorious and famous in equal measure for their outrageous pranks, Night Climbers, May Balls and Suicide Sundays. However, Cambridge University and its many Colleges has often, since its earliest incarnation in *c.*1209, also been the setting for drama, scandal, conflict and murder, and it is these events that are supposed to have left a supernatural imprint on many of the hallowed buildings in this most ancient and divine seat of learning. As an example, the early animosity between 'town and gown' following the arrival of Oxford students (themselves fleeing violence in *that* county) is part of Cambridge's heritage and goes to show how shaky the University's beginnings were. At Lent 1249, for instance, simmering animosity between the scholars and townsfolk erupted when a minor argument spilled into a sequence of pitched clashes. A number of properties were broken into and ransacked, and several people were killed in the violence, which led to a number of scholars fleeing to Oxford. In 1259, again at Lent, scholars managed to rescue one of their fellows from prison, where he had been incarcerated on a charge of murder. They conveyed him to a church for sanctuary, but once more a wave of violence and resentment erupted in the town. In 1261 a 'north country and a south country' scholar had an argument that ended in blows; supporters of the parties then clashed violently, and in the mêlée the townsfolk joined in. Houses were plundered and the records of the University went up in flames. There were many fatalities, not least being the 16 townsmen executed following a judicial committee set up by King Henry III. In 1322 a small army of riotous townsfolk, under the direction of the mayor, launched an assault on the Colleges, hostels and inns. They plundered books, brutally assaulted the scholars, and in the midst of the violence a parson called Walter de Skelton was murdered. 15 June 1381 saw the worst violence in years and coincided with a nation-wide 'Peasants Revolt'. Corpus Christi College and others were attacked and looted, and the populace celebrated when the documents, charters and other evidences of the University were ceremonially burned in the market place. One old woman called Margaret Starre is said to have gathered up the ashes and scattered them to the winds, crying gleefully, 'Away with the skill of the clerks, away with it!' A force of cavalry and archers headed by the Bishop of Norwich restored some order; they assaulted the town, killing and imprisoning many of the rebellious townsfolk.

Corpus Christi College entrance.

The aforementioned Corpus Christi College is the site of perhaps the University's most famous haunting. Corpus Christi was founded in 1352 when King Edward III granted a license to the aldermen and brethren of the gild of Corpus Christi and St Mary to found a College, or house of scholars. The Old Lodge was long believed haunted by the ghost of Dr Henry Butts, 23rd Master of the College and also Vice-Chancellor during a ferocious outbreak of the plague in 1631. The school gates were shut and the Colleges left desolate and empty, but Dr Butts is said to have stayed in the town and helped the abandoned populace as famine, destitution and civil unrest threatened. His charitable efforts raised awareness of Cambridge's plight and the town was spared a worse fate than might have befallen it; a year later it had all but returned to normal, but Dr Butts had become a broken man. A colleague was struck by his pale, ghostly pallor and he roamed the town in despair – his mind finally unhinged by the slander and uncharitable comments made by some members less brave than him during the crisis. Finally, the rumour swept the town on Easter Sunday that 'the Master had been found hanging in his garters in his own Lodge!'

In 1921, Arthur Grey's *Cambridge Revisited* noted that in the College Kitchen there could still be pointed out a particular cupboard where a boyfriend of the daughter of the former Master Dr Spencer (d.1693) had hidden in fear of his wrath. The young beau had become trapped and had suffocated to death, and this was another explanation for the ghost at Corpus Christi. However, Dr Butt is the favoured candidate for the ghost there.

The *Occult Review* of March 1905 ran an article concerning an instance when this ghost was clearly seen. In Easter Term 1904 an undergraduate opposite the haunted rooms had one afternoon clearly seen an unfamiliar man leaning out of one of the upper rooms opposite. The head and shoulders of the fellow were visible, and he had long hair; moreover, he glared angrily at the young student from his vantage point. Agitated, the student ran to his bedroom to get a better look but found the strange figure had withdrawn into the room and was no longer visible. He was even more agitated when he discovered that the rooms opposite had been firmly locked and empty until 6:30pm that day, and there is an eerie sensation that prior to actually seeing the mysterious figure the student had formed the subconscious opinion that something was looking at him from across the court. Apparently a subsequent attempt to exorcise the ghost produced the apparition of a 'man who seemed to be shrouded in white, and had a gash in his neck.' The exorcism failed.

Grey observed that Dr Butts' ghost was '...the most notorious of these collegiate shades', and this infers there are others that haunt the hallowed University College buildings.

CHRIST'S COLLEGE

Christ's College began life in 1439 as 'God's House', where 'twenty-four youths,' under the direction and government of a learned priest, might be there perpetually educated...' It became Christ's in 1505, and to this day – through the arch in the Fellows' Building – can be found Milton's 400-year-old mulberry tree in the Fellows' Garden, which leans sideways thanks to the elements. It is supposed to have been planted by the poet John Milton *c.*1633 following his graduation here, but despite its age it *still* bears fruit each year. This antiquity has aroused much curiosity through the ages: in the Victorian era it was an attraction worthy of much attention to ensure its preservation. It was noted in 1860 that it, '...has weathered many a tempest. Every spring it puts forth its leaves in all the vigour of youth, and in autumn nothing of the kind can be more delicious than its fruit.' It is about this famous landmark that on certain full moons the ghostly figure of a tall, stooped elderly-looking man is supposed to wander, his hands clasped behind his back as though he is deep in sombre contemplation. Jean Lindsay's *A Cambridge Scrapbook* (1955) tells us the gloomy story behind this phantasm in 'A College Tragedy' (itself derived from the transcripts of A.P. Baker in 1918). 'From the private papers of Christopher Round, formerly Fellow of Christ's College', came a 19th-century confession to a murder that had hitherto gone unsuspected. Christopher Round confessed that some 40 years prior he had watched an academic rival, Phillip Collier, stagger about the College grounds late one night before pitching head-first into the pool as though drunk. As he made to help Collier out the water, Round – in a sudden fit of madness – instead dashed Collier on the left temple with a boat-hook pole and let his rival drown. It later transpired that Collier had not been a drunkard, but had been experimenting scientifically with anaesthetics. The pair had, apart from being rivals in academia, been rivals for the affection of Mary Clifford, and Collier's clandestine experiments were an attempt to ease the pain she suffered due to a progressive medical condition. With Collier dead, the trials aborted and Mary Clifford died of her illness in distressing agony. This, they say, is why Christopher Round wanders the Fellows' Garden in silent, tortured remorse. Baker's transcripts of 1918 are highly likely to be fictitious, but not necessarily the ghost itself: a heavy and laborious step is supposedly heard *inside* the College, gloomily clumping its way up the staircase to the first floor to this very day.

of the ghost of the Lady in Black', although whether this was to encourage visitors to Woodston is unclear. On 26 October 1973 the *Peterborough Evening Telegraph* ran interviews with an elderly neighbour of the woman who had died all those years ago and who had also personally known the family said to be at the centre of events. It seemed that the panic might have stemmed from a misinterpretation of the children's belief that their mother was 'still with them' in a spiritual sense.

About this time, it was also reckoned that a ghostly Grey Lady had been observed to pass by the Queen's Head pub and along Mill Road, Harston, in the direction of nearby Haslingfield. At the little bridge that crosses the River Rhee by the mill, she was observed to throw herself into the water. The Women's Institute first recorded the belief in the Grey Lady in 1935, although astonishingly I was asked in June 2009 while in Cambridge whether I had heard of the 'woman that they say throws herself into the river out by Harston.' This I assume to be one and the same, which — for saying the anecdote (as far as I know) has not appeared in print for some 40 years (since Porter's *Cambridgeshire Customs And Folklore*) — is really quite remarkable.

Finally, in 1951 *Two Parishes — One Village* recorded the belief that the early 18th-century Manor House opposite the church at Offord Cluny was haunted by a strange 'little old lady' who would appear late at night, drift through the drawing-room and then vanish. This ghostly old lady had the distinction of being seen by each of the successive owner's wives not long after the resident family's arrival at the property.

The historic Lion Hotel at Buckden, haunted by the Grey Lady.

GRANTCHESTER OLD VICARAGE

Grantchester is now a major tourist destination thanks mainly to its associations with the afore-mentioned World War One poet Rupert Brooke, who rented a room for a while at the Old Vicarage around 1910. This place dates to 1639, and its ivy-covered façade is unlikely to have changed little since Brooke's time here. When in Berlin two years later, Brooke reminisced about the place in his famous poem *The Old Vicarage, Grantchester*, which he enigmatically described as, 'The falling house that never falls...' It is clear Brooke loved the place, writing:

> *But Grantchester! Ah, Grantchester!*
> *There's peace and holy quiet there...*
> *Ah God! To see the branches stir*
> *Across the moon at Grantchester!*

Brooke died in 1915 of an infected mosquito bite, on his way to the Battle of Gallipoli, and was buried in Greece. His prose 'If I should die think only this of me; that there's some corner of a foreign field that is forever England...' has become immortal. His death at the age of 27, together with his being famously described as, '...the handsomest man in England...' have led many to Grantchester in veneration of his heritage.

The fascination with Rupert Brooke – like so many taken before their time – is what he might have achieved had he lived a long and fruitful life beyond the startling promise of his early years. But the many who seek out the Old Vicarage may not know that it is supposed to be haunted. In the years after Brooke's death it is said that phantom footsteps were heard coming through the garden as though towards the sitting room. In 1941 the ghost expert Christina Hole speculated, quite naturally, that, '...there can be no other reason for such a haunting than his [Brooke's] love of home which is preserved for all time in his poems.' In 1971 the ghost-hunter Peter Underwood noted that the 'falling house that never falls' might refer to the 'odd little semi-ruined house at the bottom of the garden' that had experienced minor poltergeist phenomena even during a snowfall – yet

Rupert Brooke's statue stands in the grounds of the Old Vicarage.

no footsteps in the snow indicated that a trickster might have been causing the trouble. This had included 'small objects being spilled out of boxes and arranged in strange little patterns…'

THE PHANTOM HORSEMAN OF SIX MILE BOTTOM

In 1952 the Huntingdonshire folklorist C.F. Tebbutt noted that a phantom headless horseman was supposed to terrify travellers by midnight at Tidley Cross, Colne. Such horsemen are standard fare in British folklore, although the following account of a horseman elsewhere in the region is somewhat unusual.

Elliott O'Donnell's *Confessions Of A Ghost Hunter* (1928) records that the area between Burwell and Newmarket, on the Cambridgeshire/Suffolk border, was haunted by a local man named Fred Archer. In looking into this, O'Donnell was told a strange anecdote of a different ghost.

A local person was returning from a visit to Six Mile Bottom, on the Cambridgeshire side of the border, and had walked beyond (what is now) the junction between the A11 and A14. It was the small hours of the morning, and the moon shone fully overhead; it was clear to the narrator that he was alone as the road took him to the cleft in the Devil's Dyke. All of a sudden, there fell on the white road before him the clearly-defined shadow of a man on a horse, which prompted the narrator to look about him for the horseman; he had heard no hoof beats. However, he was totally alone – alone, that is, except for the sinister shadow now on the road beside him. As he walked in the direction of the Devil's Dyke the strange apparition kept pace alongside him and he had a good opportunity to look at the phenomenon by moonlight. The 'man' atop the horse could clearly be discerned that clear night, his shadowy outline presenting the impression of a rather tall fellow wearing a hat with a peak 'that might have been either what we used to call a deer-stalker, or a jockey's cap.' This apparition accompanied him as far as the Dyke, where it faded from view in the road.

The narrator brought the matter up at a later date and expressed his belief that Fred Archer's ghost had accompanied him home that eerie night. Although Fred Archer's ghost had long been reputed to haunt the area, an 80-year-old resident told the narrator that it was more likely he had seen the ghost of a highwayman. At one time, apparently, Newmarket Heath had been a notorious haunt of highwaymen, who had on numerous occasions left their victims slain by the roadside. However, the apparition might have been that of a jockey, given its appearance in proximity to the racecourse.

LATER CANTABRIGIAN GHOSTS

The 20th century saw no let-up in the urban legends concerning ghosts at Cambridge's University.

On 23 April 1839 James Wood, a scholar and subsequently Master of St John's College, died at Cambridge. His was a prodigious career, spanning 60 years – he was also Dean of Ely and an able writer on algebra – but according to collegiate folklore it is his miserable beginnings there that cause him to haunt the place. A history of the College recalled in 1907 that he lived 'as an undergraduate, in a garret in Staircase O in the Second Court, and studied in the evening by the light of the rush candle which lit the staircase, with his feet in straw, not being able to afford fire or light.' This, they now say, is the reason why his ghost haunts this staircase, not as the venerable Fellow of his later years but as an impoverished young undergraduate.

Perhaps the strangest of the University ghosts is the bizarre apparition that is now famously repeated by students to materialize within the white and black-timbered building in the grounds of St John's known

Grounds of Trinity College, Cambridge.

as Merton Hall, a small Tudor manor added to the 800-year-old School of Pythagoras. There is little evidence that Merton scholars (from Oxford, who owned the two buildings until 1959) ever used it as a place of study; however, according to Enid Porter, it was haunted by the phantasm of a large, furry, penguin-like creature. She was informed in 1966 of this mysterious thing by a Fellow of King's College, who described it thus: 'This was a furry animal that walked on its hind legs and had flipper-like front paws and a long beak.' It is telling that this monstrosity is supposed to have been originally seen by some children at the aforementioned Abbey House in the early 1900s – before later turning up at Merton Hall in subsequent years. It was apparently exorcised around 1924, although what it was is anybody's guess; however, later researchers have intelligently speculated that it was the ghost of a Tudor academic dressed in a gown and some sort of mask designed to fend off the plague. The bizarre nature of this entity has meant that it has imprinted itself firmly in collegiate urban legend.

It is at Trinity College where there are better instances of ghostly phenomena, including encounters in the 20th century. Trinity College was founded in 1546 during the reign of King Henry VIII, and in the 1800s the College was visited by the parents of the famous poet William Wordsworth (d.1850) – who himself received a degree at St John's in 1791. Wordsworth's parents, however, had been visiting their *other* son Christopher who had risen to become a Master of Trinity College, a position he held till 1841. Christopher, without doubt a learned and divine Master, related to his parents that on numerous occasions students had been known to pack up and abandon certain comfortable chambers at Trinity that they were using as accommodation. Dr Wordsworth was curious of the phenomenon, particularly the suggestion that the evacuated rooms were 'haunted', and so he undertook a rather uncharitable experiment using the next student who arrived at Trinity looking for lodgings. This student was placed in the 'haunted' rooms and some days later Dr Wordsworth approached the young man and enquired as to how he was finding his accommodation. The student responded that, although the rooms were very convenient, he would be leaving forthwith: every night his sleep was disturbed by an unnerving supernatural incident. He would awake to be confronted by the sight of a child (the assumption was that it was a boy) who wandered about the rooms, moaning and holding his small hands out before him, palms upwards. That the apparition was a ghost was clear: the doors were securely locked night after night, but still the strange child found his way in to pitifully roam the chambers in the half-gloom.

T.C. Lethbridge's *Ghost And Ghoul* (1962) recounts a personal experience the author had at Trinity College in 1922, when he clearly saw late one evening a man in a top hat open the door to rooms in New Court where he was talking with a friend. The strange fellow in the top hat strode purposefully into the middle of the room and placed his hands on the table there, and Lethbridge had assumed that his friend had received a visit from one of the College porters. As it was late, he left the chambers but the following morning asked his friend what the porter had wanted. His friend had seen no one enter the room, nor open the door, or anything, and 40 years later Lethbridge was still baffled by the event, having seemingly witnessed a ghost *that had opened the door*. Maybe the door that opened was itself part of a 'spectral replay' of an entirely mundane incident that somehow now supernaturally repeated itself. Furthermore, having

King's College Chapel.

witnessed the fellow clearly, Lethbridge formed the retrospective opinion that it was only the top hat that had presented the appearance of a porter; in other respects the man had looked as though he were in hunting garb.

As we have seen, unexpected outbreaks of violence and tragedy in the Colleges of Cambridge's world-renowned University have sometimes left a curious psychic imprint there, and it is somehow strange to associate such deeds with the hallowed, venerable Cambridge of today. But violent crime can happen here, as it can anywhere: for example, at an assizes held at Cambridge Castle on 18 March 1540, a scholar named Metcalfe of St John's College was convicted and executed for the slaying of a burgess named William Lankyn. After his death, Metcalfe's possessions were the subject of some squabbling between two factions – the 'corporation and the University' – including who should get his 'long gowne with a *whood* faced with Russels.'

There have been numerous shooting incidents as well. In 1791 two students of Pembroke College fought a duel over some trifling dispute near Newmarket, with one of the combatants being so seriously wounded that he died two days later. The University felt scandalized by this episode, and the Vice-Chancellor immediately made it clear that any students even caught firing pistols in target practice would be severely dealt with. This was a rule that one Cantabrigian character, the poet and writer Walter Savage Landor, ignored in 1794 when he discharged his weapon at a window in Trinity College behind which a hated Tory adversary was holding a political roister. Long before this, however, pistols had been unloaded by four students at St John's to force a moaning spectre that resided in a dwelling opposite the College to keep quiet. This was in 1706, and one suspects that – since the threat apparently worked – the moaning might have been less than spiritual. Even the iconic, statuesque and Gothic King's College – often described as the most magnificent of all the Colleges – has seen bloody violence, as late as 1930. On 4 June that year, Alexander 'Sandy' Wollaston – a former scholar in medicine who had become a tutor here after an adventurous life – died aged 55 after being shot in his rooms by a crazed student named Potts. Potts was being questioned about possession of a firearm at the time, and he then fatally turned the gun on an unfortunate police officer named Willis who was questioning him before shooting himself. There are supposed to be supernatural echoes of this last event: mysterious 'bangs' that seem to crack near one's ear from no discernible source, so I understand, although I suspect this to be an urban legend.

Finally, the 26 October 2007 edition of *Varsity* (the famed independent College student newsletter) reminded its readership of a traditional phantasm worth including here by virtue of its sheer absurdity. At Sidney Sussex, in 1841 and again in 1967, a gruesome floating 'purple eye' was reported, with the 1967 sighting being the spur for a widespread debate on the supernatural. Even in the realm of the paranormal, some things are *truly* inexplicable.

SCRIMSHAW'S POLTERGEIST

It is easy to believe the Fenland of Cambridgeshire is a haunted region. Here, in this strangely primeval landscape, they say that phantom Roman auxiliaries have been witnessed marching out of the mist in silent formation. Stories such as the one collected by ghost hunter Peter Underwood in 1980's *This Haunted Isle* seem more believable in this dank, remote and gloomy part of the county. He was told how, decades earlier, a member of the resident Fuller family had lashed out with a whip at a 'vague ghostly form' in the vicinity of Wicken. The whip hit nothing, and the shape melted into the dusk. Out here, such stories not only seem plausible but probable: it is not a place where it is comfortable to be lost come nightfall. The phantom dog Black Shuck patrols these roads at night, and even now – a thousand years on – it is easy to conjure up vivid images of Hereward the Wake, sword in hand, crashing through the woodland during some vicious attack.

On a particularly overcast day it is also not difficult to imagine the poltergeists that they say have periodically bedevilled the lonely farmsteads that dot this part of the county. The 8 May 1897 copy of the *Peterborough Advertiser*, for instance, published a lengthy account of the poltergeist that had lately invaded a house at Tick Fen in the depressing middle-of-nowhere east of Ramsey, and caused havoc the previous month. The so-designated 'Haunted House' was subject to a terrifying series of crashes and knocking noises that emanated from nowhere, and these terrorized the family living there so much that a posse of Fenlanders began to keep a nightly watch both inside and outside the property for the supernatural presence. Still the tremendous noises plagued the house, and as the writer W.T. Stead observed, 'No timid ghost was this, for the pulsations continued with Vulcan thud, and reverberated o'er the stillness of the Level.'

However, the county's most famous poltergeist is undoubtedly 'Scrimshaw's Poltergeist'.

In the Fenland extremes of the county of Cambridgeshire, nestled just shy of Lincolnshire's border to the west and Norfolk's to the east, is the pleasant little village of Gorefield. Westward of the village, at a house along the roadway known as Turnover Bank, lived a fruit farmer named Joseph Scrimshaw.

The entity that invaded Scrimshaw's property on 12 February 1923 did so at a time when the family was in some turmoil; the farmer's wife had left him, taking one of the children with her. He was left with his 16-year-old daughter Olive and his 82-year-old mother, who also resided at the property, being attended to daily by a domestic called Harriet Ward.

When it started that afternoon, the phenomena took the rather mundane form of oil lamps that refused to light. Olive was sent out for some candles, and they too refused to be lit with the result being that Joe Scrimshaw found himself eating his supper in the gloom and in a foul mood. However, this was rapidly followed by a random sequence of altogether more worrying – and clearly supernatural – poltergeist-like events. First, Granny Scrimshaw's lace cap was observed to rise from her head, followed by a frightening prolonged outbreak of objects crashing noisily to the floor and smashing to pieces: a wash stand, books, dishes, a water filter, crockery. Perhaps most amazing of all, a 400lb piano was observed to move from place to place about the room before tipping itself over in a violent, noisily-discordant heap on the floor. The family were plagued throughout the night. The one constant, it was noted, was Olive, who was always present during the disturbances, and so subsequently she was sent to lodge with relatives – although this apparently failed to stem the entity's violent trouble causing. Word quickly spread in this isolated Fenland village that Scrimshaw's house had been invaded by a poltergeist. Neighbours were called, who witnessed the 'poltergeist' for themselves: John Fennelow, T. Marrick, W. Maxey, G.T. Ward and even a local police officer named Hudson saw some of the disaster being wreaked in the household.

Very soon, the media got hold of the event, and on 21 February 1923 the *Isle Of Ely And Wisbech Advertiser* screamed, 'HAUNTED GOREFIELD HOUSE' at its readership, and for over three weeks the local – and then national – media had a field day. Sir Arthur Conan Doyle, creator of Sherlock Holmes, was impressed enough by the believability of the story to send Scrimshaw a letter advising that he ventilate the house, also suggesting that Olive Scrimshaw might have some connection to the events.

Harriet Holmes' grave in Gorefield.

There was a sequel to these events, in many ways even more bizarre, that has ensured this story has entered local legend. Before long a local 'wise woman' was brought to the house on Turnover Bank to exorcise the property. Here she practised an archaic ritual utilising a small medicine bottle filled with hair and nail clippings, pins and apple pips. This was plugged and thrown on the hearth; no one was allowed in the room until the heat of the flames had shattered the bottle – a circumstance that according to the rite lifted the curse from the property. Not long after, on 6 March, this woman – Harriet Mary Holmes – was found dead in a few inches of water in one of the dykes that criss-cross the Fens. It was not clear what had happened, but there was speculation that she had suffered a convulsive fit and died during the episode. At the time there were curious rumours that there was one final, furious outbreak of poltergeist activity in the Scrimshaw household that was, with hindsight, found to have coincided with the supposed time of Mrs Holmes' strange demise. A coroner declined to hold an inquest into her death, perhaps now anxious for the reputation Gorefield was earning for itself to be nipped in the bud. But after Mrs Holmes' death the Scrimshaw household was forever at peace. Despite the question mark over Mrs Holmes' death, the exorcism she had performed had apparently worked.

Charles Fort, the compiler of all things out-of-place, noted of the suggestions that the whole episode was a hoax: '...the damage to the furniture amounted to about £140.00' – no small sum in those days. But for me the most intriguing aspect of the case concerns Harriet Holmes, the 'wise woman'. Early in 2009 I visited the plot where she lies buried next to her husband John in the grounds of St Paul's Church. Here, behind the modern-looking, flint-and-stone fronted church, I found her gravestone bedecked with floral offerings. She was the wife of a humble farmer, and she died the best part of a century ago; yet there are clearly those who still venerate the memory of this curious character, of whom Fort notes (unfairly), '...sometime before, had been accused of witchcraft.'

GHOST HUNTING AT THE OLD FERRY BOAT INN

Perhaps the most famously haunted place in the former county of Huntingdonshire – no mean feat in itself – is the Old Ferry Boat Inn at the tiny hamlet of Holywell. Situated by the edge of the Great Ouse, the place is allegedly England's oldest inn. Although the building as it now stands is probably of late 16th-century origin, it is supposed to have foundations that date back to the mid-seventh century, or possibly even as far back as AD 560. There is even a legend of Hereward the Wake escaping the Normans across the river and seeking sanctuary at the Old Ferry Boat Inn.

Whatever its true age, this ancient public house – till recently *Ye Olde Ferry Boat Inne* – is now universally famous for the story of Juliet.

Sometime around the advent of the Norman Invasion, it is said that a young local girl called Juliet Tewsley fell in love with a rough young reed-cutter called Thomas Zoul; however, her attentions went unheeded and eventually the gentle-hearted Juliet donned her favourite pink dress and hanged herself from a willow tree by the River Great Ouse. Because she had killed herself, Juliet was not buried in consecrated ground and as such was placed under a grim unmarked stone slab by the side of the river. Some 500 years later, what became Ye Olde Holywell Inne was constructed on the site of the old tavern and the builder incorporated the site of Juliet's gravestone into the granite flooring. For centuries afterwards, Juliet's ghost was supposed to rise from this gravestone, and in her pink dress she would sadly drift from the inn and out towards the river's edge.

That this simple story has endured for so long is due in part to the physical evidence of the gravestone. It is extremely curious to consider that the remains of this tragic figure are (supposedly) just beneath one's feet, and framed newspaper cuttings nearby are a testament to the fascination with which generations have held this legend. 17 March is known as 'Juliet's Day', or 'Juliet's Eve', since this is supposed to have been the day on which she took her life, and sporadically on this

Juliet's grave in the public house. Framed newspaper clippings concerning the ghost are on the pillar.

date every year professional ghost-hunters and the curious alike have gathered to spend the night here to watch for spectral activity. These meetings reached a pitch in the 1950s when literally hundreds of people would arrive at the inn in hope of seeing Juliet; however, ghost expert Peter Underwood, writing in 1971, noted that Juliet was a ghost, 'that everyone knows about but few have seen', although he was told by the landlord in 1965 that the pet dog would not go anywhere near the gravestone, and some local women refused to come anywhere near the inn on 17 March.

In 1966 the then manager, pointing to the grave, told the *National Geographic Society*, 'The stone from her grave is here, partly under that settee in the lounge floor.' And today (2009) a brown-leather upholstered settee still backs gingerly onto Juliet's grave – just as one did 45 years ago. Knowing this lends this small part of the inn an odd sensation of having become 'trapped in time'. It is almost as if there has been a subconscious effort to not disturb Juliet too much...

HAUNTED HANNATH HALL

Hannath Hall is another place that attracted the attention of ghost hunters in the 1950s. The hall itself is a gloomy-looking Elizabethan pile, nestled away in the lonely and somewhat removed countryside between Tydd Gote and Tydd St Giles, just shy of the southern Lincolnshire border. Originally called 'Sparrow's Nest', the hall subsequently became the property of the Hannath family, and it changed name in 1812 when Joseph Hannath purchased the place for just under £8,000. It is said that when Hannath's wife died in the mid-1800s he had her corpse placed in an open coffin in a bedroom on the top floor of the north wing, to which the servants were ordered to take meals three times a day. This grim ritual continued for some six or seven weeks until Joseph ordered his wife's remains taken out into the front garden and buried underneath a horse chestnut tree.

Joseph Hannath himself died in 1868 and willed the hall to his late sister's children. The hall changed hands over the next century, and in the late 1950s attracted the attention of the Society for Psychical Research (SPR).

The events that followed the residency of two women, Mrs Page and Mrs Halls (mother and daughter), in August 1957 are outlined fully in ghost-hunter Andrew Mackenzie's *Frontiers Of The Unknown: The Insights Of Psychical Research* (1968). Shortly after moving in, the tenants were terrified by crashing noises against a bedroom door – the so-called 'haunted bedroom' where Mrs Hannath had been laid out – as well as rapping noises in other rooms and sinister groaning noises. Many of the noises occurred in the very early morning, but strangely they did not appear to be associated with the late Mrs Hannath. This was established after the SPR were called in: on one occasion at half-past one in the morning the SPR heard the noises themselves and managed to 'talk' to the entity using a simple system of one knock for 'yes' and two for 'no'. This engineered scenario led the SPR to deduce that that entity was the phantasm of a woman who had been slain in the house sometime at the turn of the century when the hall was in the possession of the Williams family. One of the residents began to suffer such horrific nightmares that they eventually fled the hall.

The phenomenon continued, however. In April 1959 the then tenant's wife saw the apparition of a little boy, aged about six and with fair hair, stood on the threshold of a small room in Hannath Hall. This strange young boy looked about the room and then utterly vanished, but seemingly he re-appeared some months later at the same time of day and in the same part of the house. This time he was observed to be wearing what looked like white, frilly-necked nightclothes and furthermore his fair hair was seen to be curled and long.

In October 1957 Dr Alan Gauld and Mr A.D. Cornell of the SPR became the first paranormal investigators to visit the house seeking for a rational explanation. They largely discounted the possibility of some kind of subterranean water activity welling up and causing the disturbances.

The case is a curious one, not readily associable with the event (the death of Mrs Hannath) that one would assume made the hall 'haunted'. Village folklore now has it that the place is also haunted by one of the maids, who killed herself after being forced to take food to the corpse in the upstairs bedroom in the Victorian era. By 1961, the hall was still being visited regularly by investigators, but although the disturbances gradually died away the legacy of this place is still, apparently, well known. At the Tydd Gote Inn in January 2006, while looking for the hall, I was met with some bemusement until someone said, 'Oh, you mean the *haunted house*, don't you…'

Hannath Hall is privately owned, although a small store by the house sells fruit and vegetables to the public in the summer.

SPINNEY PRIORY

In the no-man's-land along Stretham Road between Soham Mere and the preserved wetlands of Wicken Fen can be found a large Georgian farmstead called Spinney Abbey that at the time of writing also functions as a bed-and-breakfast. The heritage of this place is remarkable, and it is no wonder that it has long had the reputation of being haunted.

At one time had stood here Spinney Priory, a building that owed its foundation to the daughter of the lord of the manor, Beatrice, and her husband Hugh Malebisse around 1228. On 12 May 1403 there was bloodshed there when the prior of 13 years, William de Lode, was brutally stabbed in the priory church by two canons named Catesson and Smyth; the prior managed to barricade himself into the priory hall but the two attackers, accompanied by another canon called Hall, broke down the door. De Lode was killed with Smyth's dagger, but although the three attackers were convicted of murder at Cambridge Castle that July, the Bishop of Ely, John Fordham, declared the culprits subject to clerical law – and that is the last that is heard of the matter. The implication is that the murderers were 'sprung' by the clergy, their ultimate fate unknown.

The murder may have been due to internal squabbling concerning the roles of canons at the parish church. De Lode may have been trying to stop his canons from serving the villagers at the church, although there is something of a question mark over the event that can never be resolved now. As time passed the Augustinian priory gradually fell under the ownership of Ely, before finally ending its days for good in 1540 under the Dissolution of the Monasteries.

In 1664 Oliver Cromwell's son Henry and his wife Elizabeth settled at the Spinney Abbey estate. Henry Cromwell had lately been Lord Lieutenant of Ireland but had lost his position with the return of the royal Stuart line. In 1669 Henry suffered the indignity of a stopover by King Charles II, who was returning from Newmarket with his retinue. One of the king's men is supposed to have picked up a pitchfork and arrogantly carried it aloft before Cromwell, an insulting parody of the fact that Henry Cromwell had been mace-bearer before his fortunes changed. Prior to this intrusion upon his property, Henry is said to have been farming contentedly; one can only wonder at the words that Henry Cromwell (a highly-regarded figure still in Wicken) would have said to Charles had he not refrained.

Henry's son – another Henry – was forced by debt to sell Spinney to Admiral Edward Russell in 1692, and the resultant Spinney Abbey farmstead obliterated most traces of the old priory with the exception of the cellars and some of the woodwork. In the late Victorian era it is said that Chambers Waddelow Golding, the eccentric son of the then owners, once took a horse indoors and rode it up the stairs. He drank himself to death sometime around 1900. A number of skeletons were unearthed under the house in 1935, their positions suggesting they had suffered a non-Christian burial and naturally generating speculation that at least three of them belonged to the missing murderers of 1403.

The earliest references to Spinney Abbey being haunted date back to at least 1873. But S. Leslie's *Ghost Book* (1956) brought the weird occurrences fully to the public's attention. The resident Fuller family at Spinney were baffled by supernatural noises, including a particular Sunday when old Robert Fuller and five others (including his son Thomas) heard unexplained monastic chanting in the western part of the house. Faint music actually accompanied the sombre Latin strains, and Fuller had previously heard such sounds when by himself in the farm's stack-yard: the phantom sounds came from some 15ft above ground where the priory chapel had once stood.

Years later the ghost-hunter Peter Underwood visited Spinney Abbey and talked to Robert Fuller's son Tom. At the property Underwood was shown the cellars, which he observed were: '…remnants of the old building with reputed secret tunnels.' He also wrote of '…seeing the remains of a grating and the attachments for primitive handcuffs showing that the cellars were used as dungeons.' In his definitive *A-Z Of British Ghosts* (1971) Underwood explains that Tom Fuller claimed to have seen the spectral figure of a monk drift slowly up the garden path only to vanish at a corner of the house. The figure wore a hood that hid its face, and apparently its footfalls could be heard when sometimes the ghost walked about Spinney Abbey itself.

An experiment that Underwood carried out at the place provided a curious result. He placed 'delicate thermometers' at certain points in Spinney Abbey, among them a part of the enclosure in the piggery where, for some unknown reason, the normally placid pigs would begin to scrap, as well as the area where the strange chanting had been heard and the area where the ghostly monk was thought to walk. This last thermometer on the night dropped inexplicably by seven degrees at 2.10am, although the others did not imitate this despite being no more or less exposed. At this time, the horses in nearby stables became extremely agitated for 10 minutes before quieting down as the thermometer rose once again to its expected temperature. Underwood wrote, '…perhaps some shade of a ghost passed near me that night.'

CROMWELL'S GHOST

In January 1661, upon the restoration of the monarchy, Oliver Cromwell's corpse was exhumed from its resting place in Westminster Abbey and subjected to the grim ritual of a posthumous execution. The body was hanged 'in a green seare cloth' (it had been excellently preserved through embalming) for a full day before being taken down and cruelly decapitated. The head was stuck on a pike outside the abbey for a quarter of a century. At some point around 1684 Cromwell's skull was either taken from its pole or blown off during a gale, and it was passed around for almost three centuries before finally being buried in secret at Sidney Sussex College, Cambridge, in 1960. What happened to the rest of the corpse has forever been speculation. Some said the remains of the protector had ended up in a 9ft-deep grave at the site of his most famous military victory at Naseby, Northamptonshire; one correspondent to *Notes And Queries*, Mr

Markland, explained that he had been told that the Lord Protector's remains had ended up in an unmarked grave in the family plot in Northborough, Peterborough. This was apparently common knowledge locally.

The same periodical published a very detailed description of Cromwell's head in 1859, as it passed through a succession of families and as observed by a correspondent. At the time it was in the possession of the Hon. Mr Wilkinson, an ex-MP for Buckingham and Bromley, and was displayed by Wilkinson's daughter for the curiosity of a parson and the correspondent at the time. Remarkably, the head (having been embalmed) was in a good state of preservation, and it was described rather ghoulishly as being not a 'skull' and almost entire: 'The flesh is black and sunken, but the features are near perfect,

Oliver Cromwell's statue in St Ives.

the hair still remaining, and even the large wart over one of the eyes [...] is yet perfectly visible. The pike which was thrust through the neck still remains, the lower wooden part in splinters, showing that it was broken by some act of violence.'

This, they say, is the gruesome, yellowed phantasm that has been seen floating by itself about Sidney Sussex ever since the head was finally interred there on 25 March 1960. The *exact* location where the head rests, near the antechapel, is kept a firm secret, although guides will direct the attention of the curious to the plaque that merely states:

Near to this place was buried on 25 March 1960 the head of OLIVER CROMWELL Lord Protector of the Commonwealth of England, Scotland and Ireland, fellow commoner of this College 1616–17.

The head is apparently still confined in the oaken box that the Wilkinson family stored it in, which is itself within an airtight container. Until this relic is allowed to be displayed in public, we can only guess at what it must be like to behold; although the article in *Notes And Queries* gives us the scantest idea of the sense of enormity that sight of the head might produce. The witness observed in the 1850s: 'When it is raised from its hiding place, and held in one's hand, what a world of thought is suggested!'

Unsurprisingly for a region with such connections to the Lord Protector, it is said that his ghost haunts other locations hereabouts as well, Naseby and the remote Fenland lanes near Wisbech among them. Between 1631 and 1636 Oliver Cromwell lived with his family in St Ives, and on Market Hill – opposite

Cromwell House, Ely, accommodated the Lord Protector and his family between 1636–47. In the 'haunted bedroom', there is alleged to be a supernatural presence that most believe is Cromwell himself.

the great statue of the man himself – can be found the proud façade of the three-storey Golden Lion Hotel. Its frontage even advertises itself with a golden lion on a plinth protruding from the third-storey wall. Here I learned that Room 13 is haunted by the ghost of the warrior-politician himself as well as a mistress! The story I was told was that at some point Room 13 was superstitiously renamed Room 12, perhaps to rid itself of the association of being haunted. Here we find what is still known as the Cromwell Room on account of the story that Cromwell supposedly had a district HQ set up there. The haunting is a debateable one, since when he *lived* in St Ives in the 1630s Cromwell actually resided at Wood Farm near the now-demolished Slepe Hall, although the Golden Lion would appear to be old enough to accommodate such phantoms. Although it has a Regency-style appearance, I am told that its foundations are actually Tudor in origin and it functioned as an important posting inn from the 1600s onwards. Nonetheless, in 1970 the place was so badly bedevilled by poltergeist activity that the Cambridge Society for Psychical Research was called in to investigate. Andrew Green's *Ghosts Of Today* (1980) explains that around this time the phantom of a Roundhead-era soldier was glimpsed on the premises gliding through a wall into Room 15 by a chambermaid; seconds later the occupant of the room ran out into the corridor saying he had seen a man in 'Royalist uniform' who had simply vanished. Could this have been Cromwell? Most likely it was not, as I understand that a ghost that is actually *recognisable* as Cromwell himself has not been seen since the late 1800s.

Around this time in the long-haunted Room 12 an occupant is supposed to have seen a spectral lady dressed in green, who I assume might have been the mysterious 'mistress' long suspected to haunt this place that I was told of.

A SUPERNATURAL ATTACK

As we have seen, Elm Vicarage (now a private residence) was not so very long ago found by Peter Underwood to be haunted by a ghostly monk named Ignatius. This apparition was seen many times by the wife of the rector, Mrs Bradshaw, who (after her initial shock) actually managed to strike up a conversation with Ignatius. From this she learned that Ignatius had been the bell-ringer stationed on the site of the present rectory whose job it had been to warn his fellows of imminent danger. Some 700 years earlier, he had fallen asleep on duty, and there had been extensive flooding that claimed the lives of several of his brothers: because of this, he was destined to haunt the vicarage, in his old and worn monk's habit, in penance. Underwood's authoritative work *The A-Z Of British Ghosts* (1971) recounts how Mrs Bradshaw claimed a remarkable – not to say unique – paranormal occurrence during the height of the haunting.

One September night, as she retired to sleep in a box room usually reserved for visitors, Mrs Bradshaw found that the family dog would not stay in that room and had to be forcibly shut in with her. During the night she awoke to feel something wrapping itself around her throat. Wide awake now, she found it to be the green tendril of the wisteria that grew on the wall outside the bedroom. Somehow it had snaked in through the open window and was now slowly throttling her. She ripped the plant away from her throat, but the instant she did this the bedclothes were thrown off and she was violently knocked across the bed. Slowly, the invisible entity that had invaded the bedroom began to take form, and Mrs Bradshaw could make out a black shape looming before her, and two hazy, gnarled hands that were reaching for her throat.

Underwood was told that these phantom hands succeeded in *physically* choking the woman. At this point Ignatius the ghostly monk entered the room, and in some kind of supernatural mêlée managed to un-grip the hands that were strangling Mrs Bradshaw. As she scrambled, exhausted, for the door handle to escape she saw the creature that had attacked her, for now the dog was on the bed barking at a 'horrible vague creature' with 'a huge head and a red face.' Mrs Bradshaw's husband confirmed that his wife had come into *his* bedroom in a state of extreme distress and that vicious bruising remained about her neck for days afterwards.

When Ignatius next appeared before Mrs Bradshaw he explained that she had been attacked by the phantasm of a murdered man, but that because he, Ignatius, had saved her life he had gone some way to completing his penance and would not be seen so often from that time. Quite what the truth is behind this story is unknown; it is fantastic even for a story about the paranormal, but Peter Underwood – a world-renowned expert on such phenomena – appears to have had no reason to doubt Mrs Bradshaw's sincerity.

NUN'S BRIDGE

One of the county's most notorious ghosts is said to haunt the ancient bridge that crosses Alconbury Brook, near Hinchingbrooke House. This bridge is historically called Nun's Bridge, on account of the fact that Hinchingbrooke House was built around a Benedictine nunnery that dated to the time of William the Conqueror, and which itself had replaced an even older priory. This was until it fell under the ownership of the Cromwell family in 1538 following the Dissolution of the Monasteries. This spot is well known for being haunted by a phantom wearing the black-and-white vestments of a young Benedictine nun, and the shock she causes means that she can be fatal to encounter. As far back as 1966, Harry Ludlam wrote of her in *The Mummy Of Birchin Bower And Other True Ghost Stories*: 'Several cars have swerved and hit the side of the bridge. There have also been fatal accidents at the spot, which rumour has blamed on the nun.' The story is that she is the ghost of a mediaeval nun who broke her holy vows and took a monk as a lover, although they were both later killed by their brethren for this transgression. Perhaps the ghost is pathetically trying to show today's motorists where her remains lie buried.

On the morning of 22 January 1830, during the ownership of the seventh Earl, Hinchingbrooke suffered a disastrous fire that started in the Great Bow Room. Although the pictures and furniture were saved, the incident caused the place to be rebuilt and improved in the Elizabethan style. During the renovation work two years later, builders found two 13th-century stone coffins bearing the skeletal remains of two prioresses buried beneath the foot of the stairs by the library. Hinchingbrooke House is to this day said to be haunted by a ghostly prioress; perhaps she is the earthbound soul of one of the venerable ladies whose tombs were disturbed all those years ago. (These remains are still at Hinchingbrooke, under the stairs and collectively called the Nun's Bones.) In 1970 the building became part of Hinchingbrooke School and home to hundreds of sixth form students: perhaps unsurprisingly, there are now many urban legends of ghostly monks, nuns and distressed children at this historic place.

THE BOY WHO WANTED HIS MUMMY

An unnerving haunting in 1966 was considered credible enough to be taken seriously by the famous Society for Psychical Research, and details of the incident can be found in the SPR's *Item Notes V.53-55* (1985).

A Mrs Herbert, formerly a resident of Australia, had lately come to England to reside at Vicarage Farm, in the charming village of Waresley, south-east of St Neots. Two days after arriving in the country, and on her very first night at Vicarage Farm, Mrs Herbert had a very frightening experience.

During the night she found herself unaccountably awake, and, turning her head, she saw the apparition of a little boy kneeling at her bedside. The figure had a 'thin, drawn face' and looked very distressed. Even more distressing, she felt his little fingers on her arm and knew instinctively that he was missing his mother. After a stunned silence that seemed like an age, Mrs Herbert said the word 'Mummy', and at this the frightened little boy at her bedside disappeared from view.

It is worth considering that this kind of encounter appears a distinct category again from other types of 'ghostly' encounters such as poltergeist outbreaks, 'tape-recording'-type ghosts etc. The incident appears almost cross-dimensional. Possibly, then, at some point decades ago maybe a little boy had opened a familiar door and somehow found himself looking at a woman sleeping in a bed in an unfamiliar room – a circumstance that was in fact his own ghostly vision of the room in the future…

PETERBOROUGH MUSEUM

It might be thought that Peterborough Cathedral is the most haunted place in this city. This is not the case, although it does have ghosts: I recall being told during the Peterborough Ghost Walk some years ago the stories of this magnificent place being haunted by phantom chanting and a monk who appears to stumble as though mortally wounded. The most fascinating piece of folklore concerns a mysterious flickering candle-like light that is supposed to sometimes be glimpsed behind the upper reaches of the stained windows which adorn the West Front of the cathedral. The story is that during the founding of the cathedral's present incarnation (*c.*1118), a mason (or glazier) working at night by candlelight fell from the scaffolding and was killed upon the flagstones.

However, the most famously haunted place is Peterborough Museum and Art Gallery on Priestgate. This building was founded in 1816 and 40 years later the 3rd Earl Fitzwilliam granted it its status as the city's first hospital, the Public Dispensary, Infirmary and Fever Hospital. The building then became a museum in 1931 and now finds itself, along with the cathedral, the premier tourist attraction in the city, housing over 200,000 artefacts largely gathered from Peterborough's own history.

This striking Georgian building has been haunted almost since it began functioning as a museum. The *Peterborough Citizen* reported in May the following year that the wife and daughter of the caretaker were disturbed by curious footsteps they heard walking about the Norman Cross Room (formerly the Women's Surgical Ward) between 8 and 9:30pm. In December 1931 the caretaker's wife, Mrs Yarrow, had caught sight of the ghost in a corridor, briefly seeing a man in a light grey or greenish suit who vanished inexplicably. She could make out no features, since the man's face glowed with a strange kind of ethereal light, although he appeared to be young – in his 30s – and had darker, brown-coloured hair visible against the phosphorous glow of his face.

The Yarrows nicknamed the ghost 'Thomas', since when he was first spotted it had been the evening of the feast day of St Thomas, 21 December. Thomas's activity was supposed to be heightened when the moon was a waning crescent, and despite the unnaturally loud footsteps he was believed responsible for, he was also observed to drift as though floating. The publicity in the *Citizen* led many during these moon phases to stand and gawp at the upper windows of the building in hope of catching sight of him.

There is supposed to be a tradition of phantom footsteps echoing through the building long before it became a museum, however, and the place is now so famously haunted that the Peterborough Ghost Walk actually starts there. It would seem that along the way Peterborough Museum has collected ghosts in much the same way it has collected historical artefacts, with someone on the tour telling me that there were at least eight supernatural entities there! Perhaps the most familiar is the phantom whose presence is still felt on the stairs and first-floor corridor: this trapped spirit is believed to be that of Sergeant Thomas Hunter, a soldier of the Australian and New Zealand Corps. He was so seriously injured in the fighting of World War One that he died at the hospital (as the building was then) on 31 July 1916, aged 36. Hunter was originally from County Durham but emigrated to Australia in 1910. After being wounded during the Somme offensive, he was invalided back to Britain and put on a train to Yorkshire, where there was a military hospital. However, his injuries were so bad that the train halted at Peterborough and he was rushed there for emergency treatment. For a few days he was semi-conscious before dying, and the death of this man – so far away from home – gripped and saddened Peterborough at the time.

His grave can still be sought out in Broadway Cemetery, where there is an enormous stone cross. It is bedecked in the national flags of Australia and the United Kingdom, and it is a very popular site of pilgrimage on ANZAC day – 25 April – to this day. The ghost at the museum is commonly called the 'Lonely ANZAC' and the *Northern Echo* reported on 24 April 2003 of the monumental efforts to trace Sgt Hunter's history by a former north-east soldier, John Harvey, who told the newspaper: 'Some of the museum staff are convinced his ghost is stalking the corridors. Furniture has been moved around and, in the room where he died, the temperature is known to suddenly drop.'

I cannot help but think that it is a curious coincidence that *two* ghosts at the museum have the moniker 'Thomas'. Perhaps the original spectre in 1931 in the light suit was, in fact, Thomas Hunter. The appearances of 'Thomas Hunter, the Lonely ANZAC' had their heyday in the 1970s; however, ghostly apparitions, unexplained lights, temperature drops, Roman soldiers, poltergeists, malevolent entities...all allegedly reside within the walls of the museum these days. Whatever the truth, Peterborough Museum and Art Gallery is now so famously haunted that it is a regular site for 'ghostly sleepovers' and even attracted the attention of TV's *Most Haunted* team in April 2005.

A FORLORN YOUNG WOMAN

As far as churches go, St Mark's on Barton Road, Newnham, is a relatively modern one. Newnham was a rather isolated village until it was swallowed up by an expanding Cambridge, and its church only dates to 1901, replacing a small wooden one nearby which had itself only existed since 1870. The church's curious design and red-bricked façade reflect its modernity, and it is the vicarage here (also on Barton Road) where there are alleged to be ghosts.

Three vicars in succession reported varying supernatural phenomena here, with the first hearing unnerving crashing sounds during the night prior to his wife glimpsing a semi-transparent young girl stood by the bed. The vicar's successor found that minor poltergeist activity pestered the property, including – for all its banality – the mysterious arrangement of doilies *beneath* the glass of a dressing table. In 1997 the then incumbent vicar told ITV's *Signs And Wonders* show that she had also seen the ghostly entity that resided at the vicarage.

Just prior to moving into the property in March 1996 she had spotted what she described as 'a forlorn young woman' staring sadly out of a window, and since moving in she had repeatedly caught the scent of strong tobacco smoke in the air.

EXORCISMS AT PETERHOUSE

Even today, Cambridge University is still bedevilled by ghosts. In fact, in December 1997 it was widely reported that the oldest (and smallest) College, Peterhouse, might have to be exorcised after two staff members reported seeing a ghost in 18th-century clothing drift across the floor of the ancient oak-panelled chamber known as the Combination Room (linked to the Fellows dining room). It was reported that the Dean of Peterhouse was *considering* an exorcism, since some of the kitchen staff were reluctant to enter the 'haunted' room. The ghost is thought to be that of Francis Dawes, the Senior Fellow and Bursar, who hanged himself in the 'old tower' on 29 September 1789. When he was found that afternoon (as his dinner guests sat waiting for him to make an appearance), his corpse was observed to be quite cold to the touch. His actions baffled many; it was thought that his politics during the election of a new Master the previous year had made his life at Peterhouse too uncomfortable, a circumstance that might have had a bearing on his otherwise inexplicable suicide.

Dawes' suicide is all the more curious when taken in conjunction with another urban legend at Peterhouse. Adjacent to the College, off Little St Mary's Lane, can be found the Church of St Mary the Less, with its secluded wild garden area. A stone gate here protects the old cemetery, and for some 250 years there were rumours that some dark presence, supernaturally evil, lurked atop the stonemasonry. It apparently glared malevolently at Peterhouse, and it was said that students whose dorm windows overlooked the graveyard were prone to suicide. Who — or what — this entity was is not clear, although some thought it the vengeful spirit of the Puritan militant William Dowsing. In the 1640s, Dowsing was responsible for the desecration of the interior of Little St Mary's.

An exorcism performed by the Dean of Peterhouse in the 1960s allegedly banished this malicious spirit. And, if the newspaper reports are to be believed, another such exorcism was being considered 30 years later in Peterhouse itself. Does the apparent consideration of such a course of action in such a hallowed seat of learning lend credibility to the ghostly phenomenon in Cambridge? You'll have to make up your own minds. But *The Independent* newspaper reported on 20 December 1997 that 'no less an eminent figure' than the Senior Bursar had seen the ghost that November. The paper quoted him as describing the encounter thus: 'It was wearing a wide collar, like a pilgrim, and seemed to be holding a large hat. I moved closer to get a better look. I wasn't frightened in the slightest; I was more concerned about frightening it away. It was very benign. After a few seconds, it quietly disappeared. The room was very cold, although a fire was still burning in the grate…'

WHOSE VOICE?

In today's age of technology, there are occasionally instances where such technology apparently serves to provide evidence of the supernatural. In 2000, *Fortean Times No. 139* ran a letter from a correspondent in Wisbech illustrating this.

The correspondent had recently purchased a telephone answering machine with a chip and not a cassette. One evening he missed the phone as it rung but managed to pick up the receiver as the caller was leaving a message. He told the magazine: 'Later that evening as I was about to erase the start of that message, I picked up what sounded like another voice in the tiny gap between the end of my pre-recorded message and the start of the caller speaking.'

Turning up the volume, the correspondent observed the mysterious voice talked in a very low and menacing manner. The start of what it was saying could not be deciphered, but during the short speech the words 'crash' and 'stupid' could be made out before the caller of the evening started recording their message and obscured any more of the sinister talking that there might have been.

The correspondent to *FT* maintained that he found this completely inexplicable, although 'I have actually always maintained that there was a presence in the caller's house (having been a baby-sitter previously), and wonder if my answer machine has picked up someone/something residing there.' This is not entirely unique: I have myself heard first-hand accounts of mobile phones being called and displaying the telephone number of someone deceased, and also urban legends of telephone booths on street corners that, when misdialled, provide eerie, frightening messages.

MODERN HAUNTS

The market town of Wisbech has an impressive history of ghosts. At one time an inn called the Old Talbot had stood in the town, and in 1898 it was observed to be haunted. This was thought to be on account of an incident 'many years ago' when a human skeleton was discovered by builders embedded in the wall.

In the mid-1960s, it seems that there was much excitement in Wisbech, for the town had two simultaneous hauntings at different locations. I recall being told years ago during a visit to Wisbech that the Bowling Green public house, on Lynn Road, 'has a poltergeist.' This activity supposedly stemmed from an incident in the middle 1960s when the then landlady saw the apparition of a man in the distinctive clothes of an 18th-century Quaker – wide-brimmed hat, white neckerchief and long black coat – slowly making his way down the staircase of the pub. As he descended, he awkwardly manoeuvred a coffin behind him and I remember it being said that the landlady is actually supposed to have physically moved out of his way to allow the Quaker to pass.

Around the same time, in December 1965, the paranormal investigator Tony Cornell paid a visit to a shoe shop in the same town bedevilled by strange events. In his book *Investigating The Paranormal* (2002) he details how he observed a remarkable phenomenon at this place of business. In an empty storeroom at the top of the property, Cornell saw a line of footprints in the dust on the bare floorboards leading from the window to the fireplace. There were no other footprints thereabouts to indicate that someone living had entered the room by any normal means, and of the footprints themselves there was merely a line of seven or so. Stranger still, all appeared to be of a naked, *right* foot. Random electrical failures, doors slamming, door handles being depressed and mysterious footsteps clumping about the place also plagued the property, and the *Eastern Daily Press* covered the strange events at the time.

What these last instances example is that ghosts, in whatever guise they choose to materialize, can appear in the most mundane of places. It is also clear that the phenomenon is here to stay. It appears self-evident that, these days, it is just as likely to be commercial premises that are haunted as stately homes, castles, churches and lonely lanes; however, above all it indicates that in Cambridgeshire, some things never change, and one of them is the love of ghostly stories (and even the sincere belief in ghosts themselves). And, as in the previous two instances, the local media are always intrigued.

In October 2005 the *Cambridge Evening News* carried a story about the Unicorn Steak and Ale House on Church Lane, Trumpington. Here, the landlord had complained that some mysterious poltergeist-like force had emptied the clubs out of his golf bag, and ashtrays had moved with no explanation. The public house was built around 1858. There was some suggestion that events were linked to the sighting of a little girl dressed in Victorian clothing who had recently been glimpsed running through the bar.

In February 2007, the *Ely Standard* reported how a series of unexplained events prompted the proprietors of the Soham Lodge Hotel on Qua Fen Common, Soham, to call in a professional medium. The outbreaks involved low-key poltergeist activity at first, such as pointlessly moving stationary about, and a tap suddenly turning itself on and soaking a staff member. In Room 11, guests were complaining of feeling uncomfortable, or not sleeping well. The bar cage would rattle and shake violently, and it appears from the newspaper account that gradually the disturbances were becoming more sinister – a cleaner heard the footsteps of someone invisible following them down a corridor, accompanied by a whispering noise. When a clock hurled itself off the wall, a medium was called in who identified no less than three unhappy spirits on the property.

On 13 May 2009 the *Telegraph* reported how a recent fire – blamed on an electrical fault – had forced 10 occupants, including three guests, to flee the historic George Hotel on High Street, Ramsey at 3:40am. A curious aspect of this was that the 400-year-old hotel was supposedly haunted by the ghost of a former landlady called Mary, who had died in a fire: tradition held that 'Mary' was responsible for poltergeist tricks that seem associated with this. The paper was told, 'Mary hates fire so much she steals people's lighters and blows out candles. It is strange that the fire was contained to that one room and did not spread.' The room where the blaze started was supposedly the very room long-haunted by Mary's earthbound spirit, although quite which fire this lady herself is supposed to have died in is unclear. The George Hotel dates to c.1630, and in August 1636 'fifteen commoning tenements' were destroyed in a fire that broke out along Great Whyte. A great part of High Street was burnt to the ground in May 1731 in another fire that lasted several days, although the George Hotel apparently survived this unscathed.

A SMALL CONCLUSION

And so it goes on. The New Inn, an old posting inn on High Street, St Neots, is said to be haunted by the phantom of Henry Rich, 1st Earl of Holland, who was either apprehended here or incarcerated here following the Battle of St Neots in 1648. And at the prestigious Bull Hotel on Westgate, Peterborough, whose origins began as a 17th-century coaching inn, staff will tell you that the place is haunted by phantom footsteps and the mysterious jingling of a ring of keys. One is left with the feeling that Cambridgeshire is a haunted county, and that ghosts – or rumours of ghosts – are quite literally everywhere. If I have one overriding impression about ghosts as a whole it is that they are only seen by certain people who often judge themselves 'sensitive'; on the other hand people who set out to 'look for' ghosts seem to be the least likely to find them, whereas those who claim to have seen one ghost often claim more than one supernatural experience; however, the intangible nature of ghosts themselves takes many forms, as we have seen, and so this theory is not a truism in every case outlined in this compilation. Whatever the truth, from the ghostly folk-tales of old to more modern and credible accounts of random supernatural phenomena, it might be possible for this chapter to continue indefinitely. Our fascination with ghosts will never leave us, it seems. This is abundantly clear from the numerous regional ghost-hunting concerns nowadays, as well as the many popular town ghost walks (the Cambridge Ghost Walk is very highly regarded), and localised studies of the ghostly phenomenon in such works as Doughty and Haynes' widely respected *Haunted Ely* (2003). Many commercial premises such as pubs and restaurants actively promote the fact that they are haunted on their online websites now.

Currently attracting the attention of ghost-hunters and the curious alike is Wansford Railway Station, since 1845 the HQ of the Nene Valley Railway that runs for nearly eight miles between the Peterborough Nene Valley and Yarwell Junction. It can be found between Stibbington and Water Newton. The original Georgian-style station building on Platform 3 is said to be haunted by a phantom passenger who is responsible for making doors swing open (and who, legend has it, has been caught on CCTV), and in January 2008 it was reported that a team of paranormal investigators had opted to spend the night there in hopes that the ghost might manifest itself. The ghost of a Victorian-era stationmaster supposedly haunts Wansford Tunnel; the unlikely-sounding story is, apparently, that he ventured into the tunnel to entice his pet cat out, but was struck and killed by a locomotive. I also understand that the cat itself haunts the tunnel and glows brightly in an ethereal light, mewing pathetically.

As to the eternal, unanswerable question of what such 'ghosts' as this might be, the simple suggestion that they are trapped, earthbound souls seems as good an explanation as any. As a Huntingdonshire contributor to *Notes And Queries* (1st Series, v.364) humbly observed: 'An unbaptized child was buried, [and] a neighbour expressed great sorrow for the mother because "No bell had been rung over the corpse". The reason she gave [for her concern] was, "...because when anyone died, the soul *never left the body* until the church bell was rung".'

CHAPTER 7

THE WEIRD ANIMAL KINGDOM

INTRODUCTION

Occasionally, unexpected deposits of animal remains from eons ago that are found here remind us that at one time the British Isles were the habitat of some remarkably exotic animals. In some instances such finds afford an amazing glimpse into the natural history of this region: an 1851 gazetteer of Cambridgeshire observed how not many years previously the part-skeleton of an elephant had been discovered 10ft below the ground near Chatteris by workmen digging for gravel. The jaws and teeth of an extinct species of elephant (*Elephaus Primigenius*) were similarly discovered near Whittlesey around the same period.

However, some finds were rather more enigmatic. In January 1850, when workmen were excavating soil near Woodwalton to provide materials for the Great Northern Railway, they made an exciting discovery at a depth of between 20 and 30ft. The jumbled bones of both land and sea animals were found deposited in the strata at the same site, it being commented at the time, '...judging from the large size of the former, and their peculiar form, it is probable that they belonged to an extinct race.' The exact nature of the phenomenon that dumped them here (or, indeed, what type of animals they were) is not clear. Perhaps oddest was the find recorded in the *History Of Wisbech* (1834): the Tudor-era antiquary Sir Robert Cotton had discovered the 'petrified skeleton of a large sea-fish, nearly 20ft in length' at a depth of a mere 6ft while digging a pool 'near Connington Downs, Hunts.'

Vertebrae, flipper and tooth of a Plesiosaur that were found in Huntingdonshire.

In the Norris Museum in St Ives there can be seen such relics as Plesiosaur remains, mammoth tusks and an almighty ammonite fossil the size of a seat – all found in the historic county of Huntingdonshire.

Such finds, while not being 'mysterious', are still nonetheless remarkably curious since they bring into sharp focus the change in the natural landscape that this region has witnessed over several millennia. At the very least they remind us that no way of life stays the same forever. Excavations at the tumuli called the Chronicle Hills, Got Moor, Whittlesford, in 1818 turned up a large deposit of the bones of some small quadruped, '…the most singular circumstance is that there is no living animal now in the country to which these bones, thus deposited by millions, may be anatomically referred.' It was supposed the remains belonged to the Arctic lemming, a colony of which had presumably been hemmed in by some disastrous flood eons ago and drowned.

However, this chapter is concerned not so much with historical curiosities as it is with the folklore and legends of Cambridgeshire's animal kingdom. Strange animal stories always intrigue us, and there is a never-ending source of such tales in the area.

Some of the legends about animals appear to be fables. The well-known story of Cromwell being abducted by a monkey is, one assumes, an allegory – another of those tall tales designed to impress upon people that he would always be spared by divine intervention to lead Britain to greatness. Daniel Wilson's 1848 autobiography of Cromwell, *Oliver Cromwell And The Protectorate*, is one of the many books that considered the tradition worthy of inclusion. Following his baptism at the parish church of St John's, Huntingdon (in the presence of his uncle Oliver, afterwards Sir Oliver Cromwell of Hinchingbrooke, 'whose name he received'), the infant Oliver Cromwell was conveyed to 'the noble old mansion of Hinchinbrooke' nearby. As he lay slumbering in his cot in the furthest reaches of the house, a monkey snatched the unattended babe, took him out the window and scaled Hinchingbrooke onto the roof. The terrified family rushed outside with every blanket, bedspread and feather bed, ringing the house in the expectation that at any point the monkey would drop young Oliver to the ground. But, 'the sagacious animal brought the fortune of England down in safety: so narrow an escape had he, who was doomed to be the conqueror and sovereign magistrate of three mighty nations, from the paws of a monkey.' All one is left wondering is where on earth a monkey came from in Huntingdon in 1599 and whether this story has even the barest basis in fact. Now, there is no way to prove or disprove it conclusively, although it is assumed to be a myth…

Some animal beliefs seem curiously ill-informed for such a rural county as Cambridgeshire. For example, it used to be thought that three months after their birth cuckoos changed into hawks. However, some observations of animal behaviour belong to the world of reality and are mysterious by virtue of their total inexplicability. In 1909 there was recorded a mysterious plague in Hughes' almanac *Cambridgeshire*: 'The brown rat has become a source of great loss from its voracious appetite and skilful burrowing. For some unexplained reason multitudes of these rats have recently appeared in this and the adjoining counties. More than 5,000 were lately killed on a single farm in one season.' This almost sounds like a rodent mass migration.

Even stranger, on 18 December 1920 the *Evening News* pondered the reason why some 30 widely-separated flocks of sheep in Cambridgeshire spontaneously broke out of confinement and fled in all directions, with some jumping their hurdles in panic. The sheep had been observed to be restless the previous day, and W. Varney Webb, the Chief Constable of Cambridgeshire, speculated that the sheep were panic-stricken by meteors and the Northern Lights, which were strikingly brilliant on that particular evening. It was also suggested that – somehow – the sheep had scattered upon 'sensing' the vibrations from the Great Earthquake of Haiyuan, China, that killed an estimated 240,000 people. Whatever caused the incident, it apparently only affected sheep in the Cambridgeshire region, although a folkloric observation was made that sheep jumping hurdles was a sure sign of coming bad weather.

Some animal tales merely force us to suspend disbelief and question previous eras. Daniel Dawson, for example, might very well be the only person in the UK to have ever suffered capital punishment for 'murdering' horses. Dawson was a tout at Newmarket, and was paid by bookmakers in 1809 to put out of action a horse named Pirouette who was expected to win the Claret Stakes. This he attempted to do by poisoning the horse's water trough with arsenic. Four horses, including Pirouette, died in distressing agony, and it was sheer chance that none of the stable-boys also died, as they often drank from the same trough. Dawson was sentenced to death in August 1812, the *Newgate Calendar* observing: 'At twelve o'clock he was led to the platform on the top of Cambridge Castle, and was *turned off* amidst an immense concourse of spectators, it being market day. He died without a struggle.'

And so in this chapter, we look at the beliefs and legends surrounding animals, their curious and humorous behaviour…and even instances where there appears to be a supernatural or paranormal explanation for their very appearance.

A FISHY STORY FROM CAMBRIDGE

In November 1807 it was noted that a young salmon was caught in the Cam near Jesus Green sluice. This was considered quite remarkable at the time, since it was said to have been the first ever caught so high up the river; however, the following tall tale is of interest to others beside professional anglers, the only question being: how much of it is true?

The famous story of the so-called 'Book-Fish' was first described in a 1627 tract titled *Vox Piscis: Or, The Book-Fish Contayning Three Treatises Which Were Found In The Belly Of A Cod-Fish In Cambridge Market...* We are told that on Midsummer Eve 1626 a codfish that was brought to Cambridge market was found to contain, when gutted, '…wrapped in a piece of canvas, a booke [that was] much soyled, and defaced, and covered over with a kind of slime and congealed matter. This book was then beheld by many then and there with admiration.' The book contained three treatises on religious matters, and Benjamin Prime, 'the Bachelor's Bedel', who had been present at the marvellous discovery, managed to obtain it and had it conveyed to the Vice-Chancellor of Cambridge University. The leaves of the book, whose outer binding was wrapped with a canvas, were found to be in poor condition, and it was assumed that the 'voracious fish' had swallowed the book after it had been lost by a shipwrecked seaman. It was supposed to have rested a lengthy time in the gut of the codfish before providence revealed the marvel at Cambridge market. One of the three religious treatises that the brittle pages contained was *A Mirror Or Glasse To Know Thy Selfe. Being A Treatise Made By John Frith While Hee Was A Prisoner In The Tower Of London.*

Robert Chambers' *Book Of Days* noted of this John Frith that: 'Strange to say, he had long been confined in a fish cellar at Oxford where many of his fellow prisoners died from the impure exhalations of unsound salt fish. He was removed from thence to the Tower, and in 1533 was burned at the stake for his adherence to the reformed religion.' That his work, then, should later turn up in the gut of a codfish makes the whole affair even more remarkable, and there were those that thought the whole incident a skilfully manipulated joke, despite the wonder having the backing of many learned men of Cambridge as being a genuine event. A Mr Mead of Christ Church, Cambridge, wrote, 'I saw all with mine own eyes, the fish, the maw, the sailcloth, the book, and observed all I have written; only I saw not the opening of the fish, which not many did, being upon the fish-woman's stall in the market, who first cut off his head, to which the maw hanging, and seeming much stuffed with somewhat, it was searched, and all found as aforesaid. He that had his nose as near as I yester morning, would have been persuaded that there was no imposture here without witness. The fish came from Lynn.' Some others less scientifically minded saw it as a grave portent of forthcoming disaster, and it appears that the event helped many to find religion. However, the wags of Cambridge clearly did not take it so seriously and had a great time with this, one writing, 'If fishes do bring us books…then we may hope to equal Bodlyes Library…'

HUNTINGDONSHIRE STURGEONS, ETC

The River Great Ouse meanders its way westwards, and at Huntingdon takes a turn southwards. Long ago, there is supposed to have been an incident at this turn that gave rise to the peculiar regional insults of 'Huntingdon sturgeons' and 'Godmanchester black hogs'.

View from Godmanchester looking out on the Ouse Valley Way.

Following a period of heavy rain the river was greatly swelled and at a certain point on the bend the inhabitants of Huntingdon, Godmanchester and Brampton all congregated to ponder a mystery. Up the river, away in the distance, a large dark shape could just be observed in the water floating towards them and bets were taken as to what it was. The people of Huntingdon believed it to be a great sturgeon; those of Godmanchester thought it a black hog, and the inhabitants of Brampton thought it a donkey.

Presently the dark object floated nearer and revealed itself to be the bloated, drowned carcass of a donkey. The villagers of Brampton had proved themselves correct, and in jubilation they declared the folk of Huntingdon to be 'sturgeons' and the people of Godmanchester to be 'black hogs'. These insults stuck and became used more and more arbitrarily, often the cause of many a violent fracas between parties from the respective communities.

In fact, this abuse may not have stemmed from community rivalry, but from an enigmatic note of an incident in 1624 when it was observed that, '…the *bailiffes* and York, the constable of Huntingdon, seized Sir Robert Osborne's *nagged colt for a sturgeon*.' Quite what this means is unclear.

A PATRIOTIC DOG

In May 1804 two French prisoners-of-war managed to escape from the barracks at Norman Cross. On getting as far as the perimeter of the barracks they split up in different directions, with one of them managing to get clean away.

The other headed in a vague easterly direction, soon quitting the public road and charging frantically through the flat landscape east of Peterborough. After a few miles he came to a stile and climbed over it, whereby he found himself in a field confronted by a shepherd's dog 'of the ordinary, and true English breed' which simply would not let the Frenchman pass any further. The Frenchman tried to shoo the dog away, and then became more threatening; it was to no avail, and whichever way he went the dog manoeuvred in his path and stopped him going any further. Eventually the fugitive turned back to the stile but the dog then caught him by the heel and refused to let him go. By this point a group of locals, attracted by the commotion, were running towards the conflict, and the prisoner surrendered. He was afterwards marched back to Norman Cross and was re-incarcerated, his spirited escape foiled by a dog who – somehow – appeared to recognise that he was an enemy of England.

HOPS AND NIGHTINGALES

A curious belief concerning bird behaviour was recorded in T.F. Thiselton-Dyer's *English Folk-Lore* (1878). There was a widespread belief that some mysterious connection existed between the nightingale and hop fields, a connection that drew them to migrate and settle near such fields. The nature of the connection was unknown, but was assumed to be in the manner of the way a cat is drawn to catnip. The tradition was centuries old; the nightingale was supposed to have introduced itself to South Yorkshire upon the planting of hops near Doncaster – and then deserted that county when the hop fields ceased to exist.

However, in Huntingdonshire it was observed that there was an area by the Great North Road that had once been renowned for its hop fields to such an extent that the scholarly William of Malmesbury had described the county as 'the garden of England.' From those times, centuries ago, the

[…] still exhibited a very high degree of palpitation, or muscular motion, though separated from the rest of the body.'

T.F. Thiselton-Dyer's *English Folk-Lore* (1878) makes reference to a man who not so many years prior apparently made a similar living in Cambridge itself. He would sit upon the steps of the Gothic and iconic 15th-century King's College Chapel hawking live snakes – which he would offer to skin for his customers for their use in headache remedies (the skins usually being wrapped round the forehead). Perhaps such a trade had been going on for a long time; a study by the Cambridge Philosophical Journal in 1830 entitled *Transactions* learned that recently a man had been admitted to Addenbrooke's Hospital after being mysteriously bitten by a venomous snake suspected to be a viper at the back of Queen's College.

By the late Victorian era the viper was almost unheard of in Cambridgeshire. But a story from the neighbouring county of Northamptonshire provides skin-crawling evidence that snakes were, apparently, much more frequently seen in this part of Britain than they are nowadays. A county newspaper reported in March 1760 that a man had been digging at the roots of an old tree in woodland near Northampton when he and a companion discovered the slimy, writhing lair of 'near 100 snakes of diverse colours and a bed of birds' wings and feathers, among which they secured a serpent nine inches round the middle and *five feet* in length.'

Folklorist Edwin Radford wrote in 1949 that even during his own lifetime he could recall a Cambridge man known as 'the Duke of York' who would sit on the steps of King's College (one wonders if he was a relative of the previous trader) who made a living showing visitors live specimens of English snakes he had captured. He, like his predecessor, also had a sideline in selling snakeskins as a cure for various ailments, particularly of the head.

Nearer our own time, those with a congenital fear of snakes might like to avoid thinking about the reason behind the following riddle. In March 2007 it was widely reported that staff at a garage on Histon Road, Cambridge, had found a dead 3ft-long python behind the instrument panel of a Vauxhall Astra they were tuning. How it got there was a mystery; although it was assumed to be some kind of bizarre joke, or an escaped pet that had somehow found its way into the car.

A CABINET OF CURIOSITIES

At one time – before it was presented to the Museum of Garden History in London – a remarkable antiquity graced the collection of a learned Cambridgeshire doctor. This was a specimen of a Tartarian Lamb, better known as the Vegetable Lamb of Tartary – a bizarre thing that was supposedly both an animal and plant simultaneously. The exhibit's label read that it was a 'vegetable, called the Tartarian Lamb, from its resemblance to the shape of that animal.' Looking like some sort of deformed quadruped, the vegetable lamb was covered with a sort of downy fur and despite being a plant was still possessed of bones and blood. It tasted of fish, and its blood of honey, and folklore had it that those who tried the bones were granted the gift of prophecy, provided that they uttered the correct incantations. It would reportedly 'suffer no vegetable to grow within a certain distance of its seat.' The origin of the specimen remained unclear; a journey to Asia in search of this fabled plant-animal in 1715 had not managed to locate one in its natural environment, and there was a suspicion that the occasional specimens that did turn up were – like this one – segments of tree fern that had been manufactured to resemble animals by the people of southern China.

Gonville and Caius College, Cambridge: Dr Clarke's lecture here astounded his class in 1818.

More in keeping with what we know about the natural world in Cambridgeshire – although in many ways more bizarre – were the instances where regional newspapers occasionally reported freakish (though natural) births among the animal kingdom. Just over the Peterborough border in Stamford, Lincolnshire, there was a great buzz around a cat belonging to Mrs Pollard that was reported by the *Stamford News* in April 1802 to have given birth to a curiosity. This kitten had two distinct and perfectly formed heads, although joined to the same body. The poor animal also had eight legs and two tails. The truly astounding thing was that it was the *second* such kitten to be born to this particular cat, since it had birthed a previous kitten with two heads 'some time since.' In Molesworth, there was another freak of nature observed in 1942. Here, a duckling was born with a second set of eyes in the back of its head, as well as a beak. It also sported four legs and four wings.

However, perhaps the most amazing curiosity formed the basis of a lecture given by Dr Edward D. Clarke at the University of Cambridge in February 1818. Clarke was a geologist, and, as he explained to his astonished audience, he had made a breathtaking discovery while digging for fossils in a friend's chalk quarry (where is not said). At a depth of 270ft Clarke had discovered, among the fossils of sea urchins, a number of fossilised newts. Three of them appeared excellently preserved and so Dr Clarke carefully extracted them from the rock and gently put their solid form upon a sheet of paper in the sun. Then, in absolute amazement, Clarke, his friend and the hired workmen all watched as the little forms began to stir. Two of the newts did not last very long, and after a while were clearly dead; but the third thrived so

142

vibrantly that Clarke took it to a pond — where it managed to escape his fingers and disappear. The doctor then set about collecting specimens of the other fossilised newts, but the phenomenon did not repeat itself.

Even more remarkable was that this species of newt was unknown to science and was presumed to be from a long-extinct family. The mystery came to light in the correspondence of a Revd Cobbold, who had attended the lecture at Gonville and Caius College. How on earth they survived nearly 300ft down, entombed in rock, for millennia is unknown and there were those throughout the 1800s that considered stories such as this absolutely preposterous. The matter prompted furious debate in Victorian Britain and has never really been resolved: the supposition being that some amphibians, under certain circumstances, were possessed of a phenomenal longevity that almost defies belief.

True or not, this mystery has its modern equivalent. It was reported in April 2004 that a packet of stir-fry vegetables, upon being emptied into a wok in a home in Huntington, contained a *live* little brown frog with bright red feet! Again in Huntingdon in 2007 a natterjack toad was found wriggling about in a packet of salad by a surprised woman unpacking her groceries. In both instances, the amphibians had somehow survived the packing process and the sealing of the packets, and quite how they got in there was something of a mystery.

HOMING INSTINCTS

Sometimes it has been the *behaviour* of an animal that has proved newsworthy. On 5 January 1801 an escaped bullock nosed its way into a passage of the 16th-century Royal Oak public house on Crown Street, St Ives, and from there proceeded to clamber awkwardly up the stairs into the dining room. There, bellowing nonsensically, it charged at the front window ('which was a sash') with such ferocity that it — and the entire window frame — crashed violently out of the building and dropped 20ft into the street. Apparently unharmed, the bullock manoeuvred itself to its hooves and then ran towards the bridge. As wary townsfolk attempted to corner the beast it threw itself clumsily over the bridge and into the Great River Ouse where the current carried it away so rapidly that this was the last that was seen of it.

Particularly fascinating are the stories of 'homing animals'. In a letter to the *Daily Telegraph* printed on 15 October 2006 a reader observed: 'In his youth, my father-in-law worked on a farm in the Cambridgeshire Fens, and told of unharnessing the horses after working in the fields, often a long way from the farm, and leaving them to make their own way home.' On 28 February 2008 it was reported that Barney the cat been found alive, although in some distress, in a back garden in Babraham — having vanished *two years* earlier from his family's home in Whittlesford. Naturally the family had given him up for dead, but once back home he settled back into the normal routine as though nothing out the ordinary had happened. Such odd stories always delight us, although perhaps the award for the most outlandish goes to the following anecdote.

Fortean investigators Mitchell and Rickard's book *Unexplained Phenomena* (2000) notes the astonishing behaviour of a pet rabbit called Robert. This animal was purchased in 1978 for a six-year-old girl in Cambridge, and proved not a little unruly; Robert, a large white red-eyed rabbit, ended up being taken out into a walled back yard to be re-hutched — where he promptly disappeared off, having escaped somehow. Later on that year, however, a scratching at the gate announced that Robert had returned.

Robert, it seems, had the run of the house much like a dog or cat, although he was very badly behaved. He gnawed books and interrupted his owners' sleeping patterns by getting onto beds where he would 'bounce' to wake them up. When the family grandmother, who lived in Suffolk, offered to take the rabbit off their hands, she found him so bad-tempered that she let him into the wild before long. But three days later he turned up back at her house and in exasperation she gave the animal back to her granddaughter in Cambridge. In desperation Robert was taken to the Gog Magog Hills and set free once again. However – amazingly – two years later a familiar scratching at the family gate in Cambridge told them that *somehow* he had managed to find his way back home again. Robert the rabbit died in 1982 during a scrap with a large rat.

BIG GAME HUNTING: THE FEN TIGER AND OTHERS

In September 1979 the local media reported the bizarre spectacle of a small troupe of monkeys that had allegedly been observed swinging through trees near Stamford on the Lincolnshire/Peterborough border. They were supposed to have escaped from a 'travelling circus', although quite where said circus was based is unclear.

Such sightings are never really properly explained; it is as though the animals have just 'turned up' in the county. But monkeys aside, the evidence for some kind of giant panther-like animal prowling the Cambridgeshire countryside seems to grow every year. This is a mystery that refuses to go away.

There can be few today that are not at least aware that the county is supposedly the stalking ground for a large feline-like animal nicknamed the Fen Tiger – although it might be more accurate to use the plural *animals* since there are surely more than one of these beasts, given that it/they appear to have been on the prowl here for decades now, as well as in Cambridgeshire's neighbouring counties. The numerous names that the animal(s) goes by is testament to the fact that it cannot be pinned down to a specific locale: the Beast of Bretton, the Fen Tiger, the Beast of St Neots, the Beast of Castor and so forth.

Urban legends of 'alien big cats', or ABCs, in the county go back at least to the 1950s, although it is generally agreed that the first credible sighting of such an animal in Cambridgeshire occurred in 1982 at Cottenham, north of Cambridge. Eight years later in 1990 a mysterious panther-like animal was supposedly haunting Castor Hanglands, a natural reserve of grassland, woodland and wetland west of Peterborough, according to the *Peterborough Evening Telegraph* in December 2003. However, much in line with the large panther-like animals of neighbouring counties, the Fen Tiger (and his other mysterious feline cousins) really became a celebrity in the mid-1990s.

The animal originally seen in 1982 had been a large, Labrador-sized feline-like creature (the appellation 'Fen Tiger' was a slightly-misleading nod to the nickname of Fenland folk in former centuries). By 1993 it was rumoured that a huge cat-like beast haunted the wetland wilderness of Wicken Fen, although it was to the area of drifts and fields about Cottenham that the Tiger (or a different one) returned the following year – and his appearance here created a sensation.

The incident, in early June 1994, may have opened the floodgates for all future sightings. It was widely reported that in that month a Mr William Rooker managed to snatch a two-minute piece of video footage that showed a large, black leopard-like creature moving stealthily on its haunches through a field adjacent to Oakington Road between Cottenham and Westwick, north of Cambridge. Mr Rooker described the animal – which he originally considered a dog – as flat-faced, and this incident was highly publicised at the time. In fact, so well known has it become that the British Big Cats Society website now considers the footage (which although of the usual ill-focussed video type) to offer possibly the best evidence for a panther-like creature anywhere in the UK; they describe the video as being 'almost certainly [of] a large, cat-like animal.' The footage was taken in the early evening, and it shows the mysterious animal first sitting in the field some 150 yards away from the tripod-steady camera that Mr Rooker had *originally* set up to take rural shots. When the animal bounds away, it is in smooth, feline-like movements; its long tail is clearly visible and the creature has been judged to be a black puma, a panther, or possibly a dark-coated leopard.

By 1995 the mysterious animal had returned to (or still resided in) the area; two police traffic officers alleged that they spotted it near Westwick Hall in the hamlet of Westwick, again by Oakington Road. Perhaps it was staking out the crossroads known as Lambs Cross!

The local media regularly have a field day with the puns this story generates. But jokes aside, the suggestion is that there is more than one big cat out there, although it would be self-defeating and tedious to note every report of a big cat in Cambridgeshire. In the late 20th century and early 21st century it has been seen in virtually every part of the county. Suffice to say that some encounters with the Fen Tiger do stand out as bearing standard aspects. In February 1996, for instance, it was reported that a motorist had narrowly avoided colliding with a large cat-like animal near Willingham. The shocked motorist afterwards commented, 'I've lived in the country all my life and I've never seen anything like this thing. It just stopped in the road and watched me – I had to swerve to miss it.' But, curiously, this would appear to be a different animal to the Westwick Fen Tiger: for it was described as being *tan-coloured*, larger than a greyhound and with the distinctive long thick tail of a big cat.

However, the stereotypical description of the big cat is that reported by the *Cambridge Evening News* on 18 May 2006, as quoted by a lorry driver: 'I thought it was a big dog at first, but I've got a two-year-old golden retriever and it was bigger than that. It seemed to be a puma – it definitely wasn't a fox. It just ran straight across about 20ft in front of me and took me totally by surprise. It was black and looked to be going at a good speed across the road.' This was in the late afternoon as he drove along the A505 between Whittlesford and Duxford.

The 'physical evidence' for big cats is in some ways slightly more substantial (and by definition more convincing) in Cambridgeshire than in other parts of Britain. As we have already seen, the Fen Tiger obligingly allowed itself to be filmed at Cottenham, and when desperate it would seem that the animals actually attack livestock. It is occasionally blamed for making off with calves, or for slaughtering poultry, or – in 2003 – for killing a lamb and making off with its leg near Oakington. There is also a muddled report of a dead cow that was found lying in the road near Godmanchester on 30 November 2004, a circumstance upon which the farmer blamed the animal being attacked and possibly dragged by a large black puma. On 4 October 2004 a veterinarian called out to inspect the mauled carcasses of two sheep (and a further injured sheep) in fields at St Ives attributed the bloody mess to nothing less than an attack by some sort of large, predatory cat. In May 2008 a *Cambs Times* reader who lived in Chatteris contacted the newspaper to inform them that his veterinary surgeon thought it possible that his pet greyhound had been mauled to death by a large cat. Most recently I understand that a dog walker has found the carcass of a recently-slain muntjac deer in open fields near Longstanton. The deer had been brought down by something large biting at its throat. It had then been partially devoured – an attack not in keeping with the *normal* behaviour of, say, a dog, one has to admit.

Frustratingly ambiguous evidence continues to be forthcoming. On 26 August 2007 the *Cambridge Evening News* published an indistinct photograph of a black feline-like animal taken from a property in Snailwell, on the fringes of Chippenham Park. The person who took the photograph described the mysterious animal as about 5ft long and 3ft from the ground, and this is another of those instances where the witness confirms themselves now to be an avid believer in the phenomenon of the big cats, despite previously being somewhat sceptical. The so-called Beast of Bretton is supposed to have been responsible for vicious marks observed in the bark of trees near Wansford in September 2008, as if some large animal had been sharpening its claws. Photographs of the two trees, the bark rent and scratched from them, appeared in the *Peterborough Evening Telegraph*.

One wonders how close we have come to recovering the carcass of one of these big cats. Given the amount of times that they are spotted by drivers who, at night, almost collide with them, it is remarkable that they have not yet ended up as roadkill.

Or have they? In September 2004 a large black animal, possibly a panther, was supposedly seen stretched out as though dead on the central reservation of the M11 at Grantchester. I personally have fleetingly glimpsed the carcasses of very large animals laid out by the roadsides of rural Cambridgeshire on several occasions, usually on some windy stretch of thin country road that is, at that time, unaccountably traffic-heavy. Such roads usually present no safe parking place anywhere nearby by which one might make their way safely back on foot on the grass bank to see what the mammal might have been. In fact, herein lies another minor enigma: as at Grantchester, what seem to be carcasses of large animals that look as though they might be the Fen Tiger are subsequently found to have vanished when an inquisitive driver makes his way back later to investigate. Some people have suggested that this is evidence of a governmental conspiracy by the Department for the Environment, Food and Rural Affairs (DEFRA, formerly MAFF) to remove carcasses of big cats in order cover up the phenomenon.

Photos, footprints and alleged carcasses aside, quite often it is the simple sincerity of the witness that is the most convincing evidence for the Fen Tiger and his ilk. It is often the very banality of the witnesses' reports that appear to convince, the lack of sensationalism somehow creating a weird paradox that makes the testimony more credible. The witness is inevitably, naturally nonplussed and frequently unnerved, but the big cat does not ever seem to growl, pounce or give chase. The *Cambridge Evening News* of 21 August 2007 reported just such a convincingly typical, fleeting encounter. A female dog-walker had been making her way along the railway line and thence into a field at Shepreth when the sighting took place, and the newspaper quoted her as saying: 'I spotted a large black cat sitting in the middle of the path. It was about 100 yards from us. I was a little scared and turned around to walk back but did not for fear the cat would run after us. As we walked back I kept looking to see if it was following – and it was not. But when we were 50 yards from the railway line I saw out of the corner of my eye the cat was coming slowly up the field beside us. By this time, I panicked and decided to run the last 50 yards and the cat did not follow us over the railway line.'

THE NATURE OF THE BIG CATS

And so it goes on, and one cannot help but make some fascinating observations at this juncture. The case of the Cambridgeshire ABCs presents no coherent structure: masses of evidence and yet no absolute proof, and a genuine uncertainty as to the number, location and even the species of the elusive beasts. The traditional picture painted of the animal is that it is large ('as big as an Alsatian' is often the standard quote, together with, 'It definitely wasn't a dog of any kind.'), with short, black shiny hair and a small panther-like head. It moves stealthily on its muscular haunches through a field and its thick powerful tail usually catches the attention of the witness.

But this description is not always a truism, which further confuses this entire picture. For instance, in November 2004 the *Cambridge News* reported that footprints 'the size of a clenched fist' had been found in the fields about Rampton on numerous occasions. Each print was observed to be 4.5in wide, with a stride of 22in and a width of 10in apart as they trekked through the wet grass; furthermore, the creature had been glimpsed once or twice; however, it was no muscular, stealthy black panther but an animal more akin to an African wildcat – larger than a fox, sandy coloured and with a tail displaying dark rings. The animal spotted earlier that year by a motorist near Landbeach Pit was described as having bluish-green eyes and resembling an ocelot, a leopard-coloured wildcat from South America. Such an animal appears to be distinct from the 'black panther-type' animal.

'Explanations' for the sightings, such as they are, are consistently trotted out, yet the phenomenon remains a mystery that is tantalizingly out of reach. Some link the big cats to UFOs, claiming the beasts are displaced animals that have been 'abducted' from their natural habitat only to be mistakenly returned to the wrong country. Or else they were released by their owners. They escaped from circuses. They have always been there. They do not exist... Some believe that they are a resurgent population of the native British wildcat, although where they have been hiding for two centuries is unclear: as long ago as 1827 the wildcat was considered extinct in Cambridgeshire, with a natural history journal remarking, 'Among the Carnivora, we have to note the entire absence of the Wild Cat (*Felis Catus*)...' Native species can linger for some time after being thought extinct; the large, ground-dwelling bird called the Bustard supposedly became extinct in the UK *c.*1832, yet a solitary specimen was observed to haunt Burwell Fen as late as March 1856. Locals taking pot shots at it eventually drove it away. But in the case of the Fen Tiger, the native British wildcat would seem to have been a distinct, separate and (most importantly) very extinct animal that cannot be responsible for most of the current sightings.

Some things can be tentatively regarded as 'definite', however, and that is that unless every single witness is either hallucinating, mistaken or lying then some kind of gigantic cat, or cats (for there are surely more than one), prowls the Cambridgeshire countryside.

In February 2009 it was reported that Shepreth Wildlife Park, north of Melbourn, would be positioning motion-sensing cameras on private properties and had the facility to humanely trap any ABC that was picked up. But animals like this continue to split opinion in Cambridgeshire. The police and wildlife experts have on occasion speculated that it is at least *possible* for such an animal to exist in the Cambridgeshire wilds – but fundamental objections exist. There would seem to be more than one species; but if one were to take a single species, such as the traditional black panther, then there must be more than one animal, perhaps small colonies of them. Any less and there would not seem to be a viable breeding population; any more, and one would assume they would be seen more frequently and their existence proved beyond reasonable doubt. At the moment, however, we are in a kind of limbo in our knowledge of this phenomenon. The Fen Tiger (despite the evidence of 1994) and just like all the other panthers, will never be caught or *conclusively* photographed or filmed; although we will be tempted to imagine that it might *just* be true by a few almost-convincing seconds of blurred footage, or a fuzzy, indistinct black-and-white photograph. A few footprints may be found, although these will be contentious. There will, however, be much reliable witness testimony. The legend will also be dubiously fed by stories that appear to be outright urban legends: people will tell you that 'a friend of a friend' says that one of these animals meandered calmly into the house of the aunt of someone they know. Or that they know *for a fact* that decimated livestock has been hound hanging from a sturdy tree branch somewhere; blood dropping onto someone passing by underneath alerted them to the ravaged carcass hanging over their head.

And after the flap has died away in a particular part of Cambridgeshire, the big cat will vanish into history, only to appear somewhere else in the county some years later, and it cannot help but be noticed that in this respect these animals are phantoms not too dissimilar to Black Shuck himself.

Although this generation lives by the internet, the DVD and mobile phones — and likes to think itself less superstitious than generations gone by — this is modern folklore in the making, happening now to people who you probably know or live near. Yet these animals appear almost supernatural somehow. It is certainly curious that quite often, when the location of a big cat sighting is pinpointed on an OS map it can be seen to have been in the vicinity of an ancient tumulus, a moat or another antiquity — a circumstance that would appear to add to it a kind of supernatural status. Take Rampton, for example, where Giant's Hill can be found. Or Chippenham Park, where three tumuli can be found either side of the A11. If Black Shuck were a spiritual, ethereal hound, could it be that these animals are his modern incarnation? Until one of the big cats *is* caught, who can tell? For now, a letter to the *Folklore Society News (No. 52)* seems to sum the situation up. In 2006, in response to being told that a large black felid had been spotted prowling the partly-wooded grounds of Girton College, a correspondent observed: 'There have been earlier cases of big black felids being seen, and even videoed, in Cambridgeshire. But according to our greengrocer, a local countryman and farmer, so has Black Shuck, who also fits the above description. So what is it that people are seeing? Natural history and folklore seem to be overlapping here.'

The Fen Tiger is now a firm favourite with the local, regional and national media, and his existence is a standard talking point up and down the county. At the time of writing in 2009, he has most recently been glimpsed lurking about the spinneys, copses and downs that border the fringes of Abbotsley Golf and Country Club, south-east of St Neots. Here, the animal was observed to be beige-coloured, extremely agile and looked as though it was chasing something. In respect of the colour, again the animal appears distinct from the traditional 'black' panther — although the stunned golfer who observed it was convinced it *was* a puma-like animal. It was seen at 7:30 in the morning by a golfer on the 11th Fairway of the Cromwell Course, according to the *Cambridge News*. Paw prints and a viciously mutilated badger discovered in the snow earlier that year had already raised suspicions that a larger-than-average predatory 'something' was residing hereabouts. Here at Abbotsley there *are* places for such an animal to hide, but much of the countryside is also wide open and one wonders what these animals live on. They must be exceptionally adaptable. And in certain places like Abbotsley, they must almost be hiding 'in plain sight' — in the patches of woodland that are seen from the roads and passed by every day by unsuspecting motorists and cyclists.

Perhaps the mysterious animal seen at Abbotsley was merely 'passing through'. But the Fen Tiger, in his many guises, has been witnessed, with varying degrees of reliability, in every corner of the county over the last 15 years or so. Everyone seems to know someone who has seen him. And one is left with the feeling that, out of all the phenomena discussed in this book, this is the one that the average person is most likely to encounter in Cambridgeshire.

the chancel.' Tom is said to have been born in Marshland St James, and the 19th-century archaeological *Journal* records in 1879: 'Another mound, close to the Smeeth Street Station, between Lynn and Wisbech, has also a traditional interest. It is called the Giant's Grave, and the inhabitants relate that there lie the remains of the giant slain by Hickathrift, with the cartwheel and axle-tree. The mound has not been examined. It lies in the corner of the field, with a slight depression round it, and has now only an elevation of a few feet. A cross was erected upon it, and is to be seen in the neighbouring churchyard of Terrington St Johns, bearing the singular name of Hickathrift's Candlestick.' At the junction of Smeeth Road with School Road and Walton Road can be found Hickathrift House, which stands on the former site of the huge earthen embankment referred to as Hickathrift's Wash-basin. There is also a cul-de-sac off Smeeth Road named Hickathrift Field after the supposition that he inhabited this area. Today the village sign at Marshland St James displays a depiction of Sir Tom Hickathrift and the tinker Henry Nonsuch – the only man to outwit him in combat and ever after the giant's closest companion.

The story is – I assume – largely a fairy tale, although I have always felt that such folk tales have a basis in genuine events, or at least *rumours* of a genuine event. *The English Works Of Sir Henry Spelman* (1727) noted that one *Hikifric* was reckoned to have taken part in an ancient clash between a lord of the manor and residents of Tilney, armed with an axle and a wheel. When the legend of Tom Hickathrift *the giant* gained currency in the 1600s, one early element of the tale is that he kills two highwaymen during an altercation, which seems curiously ordinary compared to his later exploits. Maybe these actual events spawned exaggerated tales of his heroic deeds – and more importantly his stature as a 'giant' – over the centuries. Nonetheless, it is tempting to speculate how place names such as Hickathrift Field come to be. Generations must just simply have 'known' that this is where the giant Tom Hickathrift was born.

But there are many other stories of strange and fantastic creatures from this county: griffins, supernatural creatures, and werewolves. One might also wonder under what circumstances these tales came to exist, unless – somehow – they had a genesis in factual events…

THE GRIFFINS OF LITTLE RAVELEY

Surely one of the strangest tales ever marketed as 'fact' occurred in Raveley (whether Great Raveley or Little Raveley is not clear) in 1662. In that year a farmer called John Leech, prior to setting out for the Whittlesey fair one morning, decided to have a few ales beforehand with a neighbour at the local inn. At length, heavily refreshed, Leech stated to his friend: 'Let the Devil take him who goeth out of this house today!'

However, later on he had a change of heart and left the inn. As he rode his horse to Whittlesey he remembered his rash oath and began to regret having uttered it. The more he thought about it, the more Leech began to think he ought to return to the inn, lest the Devil come and take him, and in a state of complete indecision he spurred his horse first one way and then the other, until gradually night fell. At around two in the morning he suddenly found before him in the road two monstrous creatures 'in the likeness of griffins.' The griffin was a mythical creature, with the powerful body of a lion and the face of an eagle. Enormous wings adorned its back and its feathered forelegs had the talons of an eagle while its hindquarters were that of the lion. It had ears that resembled those of a horse. As such it was part terrestrial beast and part aerial, a huge flying animal that was written of at least 700 years earlier as being a real creature by Irish chroniclers. The two griffins grabbed Leech with their talons and took him into the air,

Stone representation of a griffin on the church at Kimbolton.

where their beaks tore at his clothes, before dropping him 'a sad spectacle, all bloody and goared' into a farmyard just outside the village of Doddington.

It was in this state that Leech was discovered and gently carried to the home of a gentleman, where as he lay in bed recovering he told his bizarre story. Before long, however, he began to take a turn for the worse; his ordeal had evidently sent him half-insane, and although he was well cared for, those looking after him became afraid to enter his bedchamber. Presently, the gentleman of the house called for the local parson. Upon entering the bedchamber Leech became so violent that the servants had to physically rescue the parson, and they were then forced to tie Leech to the bedposts while they decided what to do next.

The following morning the household could hear nothing from the afflicted man's room and so assumed that he had quietened down somewhat. Upon entering, however, they found Leech dead upon the bed, 'with his neck broke, his tongue out of his mouth, and his body as black as a shoe, all swelled, and every bone in his body out of joint.' Apparently Satan had managed to claim him after all.

Were it not for the impressive-sounding testimony to the series of events, this story would undoubtedly have been classed as a work of fiction about the evils of drink. But 'six sufficient men of the town' stated that every word was the truth, and 10 days later a tract telling the '*Strange and True Relation of one Mr. John Leech: Who lived in Huntington-Shire, at a place called Ravely, not farre distant from Huntington Town, who was (about ten dayes agoe) carried twelve miles in the ayre, by two finnes, and also of his sad and lamentable death*' was produced. Those looking for an explanation might speculate that Leech was attacked by robbers taking advantage of his drunken state, that he concocted the story of the griffins for reasons best known to himself and that he was subsequently killed in the struggle to rescue the parson. For their part, blaming satanic wrath for his death would certainly have been less trouble than admitting manslaughter for all concerned.

THE LITTLE PEOPLE

For some reason, Cambridgeshire appears not to have the depth and wealth of fairy lore that some of the adjoining counties do, such as Northamptonshire and especially Lincolnshire. But nonetheless there is some small evidence that the 'little people' once inhabited this county. Folklorist Enid Porter did observe the scarcity of such stories, but managed to obtain from W.H. Bartlett a belief that circulated in the Littleport Fens to the effect that some cows – by natural design – had three normal-sized teats and one very small one. This last was reserved for the fairy folk and should a human attempt to milk it they would find their hand covered in warts as punishment.

The Northamptonshire folklorist Thomas Sternberg recorded in 1851 that he had heard certain ponds were designated 'fairy ponds' by the peasantry. There was apparently one such place near the village of Brington, near the Northamptonshire border, where, 'a few years ago they might be seen rollicking on the surface, and gambolling among the water-plants which lined the edges.' Further south can be found the defunct hamlet of Shingay, remarkable for being the base of an order of knights called the Hospitallers during Crusading times. Although the chapter at Shingay was a small one – overseen by two knights and three priests – it was by its nature exempt from every ban imposed on other parishes. This meant that during the reign of King John (1199–1216), when a law banned the rites of burial (and corpses often lay decomposing where they fell), Shingay was a haven for those who wished a decent burial for their deceased friends and relatives. Here, mass continued to be said and bodies could be laid in hallowed earth. The Revd W.E. Conybeare found in 1910 that there were still villagers who recalled hearing how in the dim and distant past 'fairy-carts' were supposed to spirit corpses away in the dead of night to the parish of Shingay to ensure they received a proper burial. Shingay and its church have ceased to exist, its population absorbed into the neighbouring village of Wendy to form the parish of Shingay-cum-Wendy. This is a shame; it would be interesting to have seen how full Shingay's churchyard was compared with larger, surrounding villages.

In 1926 it was observed that fairies were supposed to dance in Fenland meadows on the nights of the full moon. But although the little people are seldom seen these days perhaps they are still there: the Helpston poet John Clare (d.1864) wrote:

'Now in the corn-fields, now in the new-mown hay.
One almost fancies that such happy things,
With coloured hoods and richly burnished wings,
Are fairy folk, in splendid masquerade
Disguised, as if of mortal folk afraid,
Keeping their joyous pranks a mystery still,
Lest glaring day should do their secrets ill.'

THE SHAG FOAL

John Clare, the famous 'Northamptonshire Peasant Poet', was born on 13 July 1793 at Helpston – now a village in the Soke of Peterborough, but at the time part of Northamptonshire. His poems depicted images of rural England that showed a loving appreciation of nature; some, such as *The Village Minstrel, and Other Poems* (1820), focussed upon the folklore he had grown up with in the early 1800s. Of particular interest is his reference to '…offsprings of "Old Ball"…a shagg'd foal [which] would fright the early-rising swain.'

The Hills and Holes, Barnack, haunted by a strange bear-like phantasm.

Clare explained this cryptic reference for the benefit of his readership. An 'Old Ball', he said, merely meant the foal of a mare. But the 'shagg'd foal' was something entirely different – a sinister, supernatural entity widely thought to haunt the country lanes and primitive highways and byways of this part of Britain: 'It's a common tradition in villages that the devil often appears in the form of a shagg'd foal; and a man in our parish [Helpston] firmly believes that he saw him in that character one morning early in harvest.'

Despite the assumption by Clare that the 'shagg'd foal' was a demon in disguise, the creature's true nature was something of a supernatural mystery. Across the region there was a consensus of opinion that this scruffy-looking young horse with blazing eyes was some form of trickster spirit: a goblin, or boggart, or a bogie beast which had taken the form of a dilapidated, insane animal to commit the kind of mischievous trickery on the road that farm-dwelling bogies played from the safety of the cellar.

Folklorist Thomas Sternberg, three decades later, understood that the Shag Foal was a 'mischievous goblin who prowls about the county in the guise of a shaggy foal.' In watery areas to the north of the county the tricks of the Shag Foal were potentially lethal. It would lure lost travellers into watery marshland using its soft whinny and glowing eyes. When the traveller found himself waist-deep in filthy water, and lost in the undergrowth in the dead of night, the Shag Foal would drift away through the woodland, its whinny replaced by a horrific, distorted half-human laugh. Sternberg noted that this creature was reckoned to delude people into mounting it, '…and then vanishing with a shout of fiendish laughter' – presumably after depositing the unfortunate traveller somewhere dank, wet and inhospitable. The extensive drainage projects of the 17th and 18th centuries regularly disinterred ancient human remains, boats and weapons (in 1829 a 'very antique sword was found, in a high state of preservation' while deepening the river at Ely), a circumstance that no doubt fuelled the rumours that those so discovered had been 'led there' by some malicious hobgoblin.

This creature was one of the most famous rural supernatural entities of the 17–1800s, although belief in it was on the wane by the end of the 19th century – perhaps because drainage, improved transport facilities and road systems, and bigger towns had robbed it of its playground. Nonetheless, belief in the creature lingered on in the Midlands into the 20th century; although seemingly only in the form of an entity that grandparents used to be fearful of. As late as 1902 natural historian George A. Morton was told stories of a Shag Foal that supposedly haunted the region around Barnack by a woman whose family had lived there for generations. In days gone by, this entity took the form of a large, black, scruffy-looking bear-like animal.

A FENLAND WEREWOLF LEGEND

The scholarly Gervase of Tilbury noted in his *Otia Imperialia* (*c.*1214) that werewolves were common in England in his time. Christopher Marlowe's *Legends Of The Fenland People* (1926) wrote that the Fens were the ideal location for those who wished to perform the secret and mystical rites that allowed them to change into a were-creature: 'Now the conditions favourable to transformation were to be found in their entirety in the wild district between the Isle of Ely and the shores of the North Sea – more especially in the days before the land was drained. Here were the thinly populated swamps and fens, the silent meres and rank vegetation that spirits were supposed to haunt.'

Marlowe wrote of a rumoured incident that had taken place in a hamlet near Crowland in the late 19th century. A lady artist, a good-looking girl in her mid-20s from London, had taken herself off to a small Fenland railway station to make sketches of the banks and windmills. She was staying with a farming family two miles distant, and on her way home in the dusk she encountered the farmstead's live-in helper – herself a young, attractive widow – in the lane. Although unsure of why this young domestic would be out in so wild a place at such a time, the London artist was nonetheless glad of the company on the lonely walk back to the hamlet; however, the widow acted strangely and gradually fell behind the lady artist, who turned to peer into the gloom for her mysterious companion. What she saw was the young widow drop onto all fours and transform into a terrifying wolf-like creature, which now bounded towards her and leapt at her throat. The lady artist shone a 'pocket torch' at the monster's eyes, at which point it shrivelled up in smoke and vanished instantly.

When she eventually arrived back at the farmstead the lady artist found that the young domestic had apparently never left the building, but had been found by the farmer and his wife writhing on the floor screaming that lightning had blinded her. A doctor was called for but could make no sense of the servant girl's injuries and confined her to bed, her burned retinas shielded from sunlight by bandages. The doctor noticed that the lady artist very quickly returned to London in a state of some agitation after these events, and so he tracked her down and was told the bizarre story of the 'werewolf attack'. When the young serving girl around whom this mystery revolved eventually recovered, she also left the farmstead and was not heard of again.

Marlowe suggested that the widow was somehow telepathically 'projecting' herself from the farmstead in the form of a wolf to attack the lady artist, but to what end he could not say. Nearer our own time, it is often repeated of Hinchingbrooke House, Huntingdon (particularly so since it began housing sixth formers in 1970) that the 9th Earl of Sandwich, George Montagu, performed a very curious ritualistic act. The earl, who died in 1962, fearfully ordered the entire west wing pulled down in 1947 – allegedly because he believed it had become home to a werewolf. The wing had been built in the late 1800s to accommodate servant quarters, but lately it had stood derelict and falling slowly into disrepair. Mournful howling from the surrounding countryside troubled the earl so much that he went to the trouble of demolishing the west wing to deny this gruesome creature its hiding place. At least, that it what they say…

THE SHUG MONKEY

Not so very long ago it was whispered that the road between West Wratting and Balsham (now the B1052) was haunted by a strange, loping creature that almost defies categorisation. It was referred to as the 'Shug Monkey', and it was a large rough-coated animal with big, blazing bright eyes.

Sometimes this strange creature would walk upright, although awkwardly, on its hind legs but it could apparently move fastest when it whizzed about on all fours. Its existence was first recorded by author James Wentworth Day, who was told in the 1950s of a creature said to 'haunt an overgrown and little-used lane called Slough Hill in the parish of West Wratting.' Children would avoid the place after dark in the early 1900s, but quite what this shaggy-haired monstrosity's exact status was is unclear; it does not appear to have been thought of as an animal such as a Yeti-type creature, or even an escaped primate. The Shug Monkey appears to have been considered supernatural, like Black Shuck himself or the 'shagg'd foal' mentioned earlier, or even the form of some sort of demon or were-creature.

Whatever it was, it is long gone now. For those who think such unnatural entities are nothing more than tales to frighten children, it should be stated that there is a school of thought that even considers these creatures inter-dimensional…

This road in West Wratting was allegedly haunted by a bizarre thing called a 'Shug Monkey'.

FRESHWATER MERMAIDS

Although Cambridgeshire is nowadays landlocked this was not always the case, and it is curious to note that the county does have legends of mermaids. It was written in 1853 that, 'The mermaids were in former times considered as the agents of witches [...] the term is derived from *Mere*, a lake, water or sea. For instance, there is Whittlesea-Mere in Cambridge...'

Drainage of the Fens appears to have left the strangest legacy in this part of the world: rumours of mermaids trapped in deep pools, unable to even get to the rivers to make their way back out to sea. Even as far inland as Fordham, not far from the Suffolk border, there were stories that 'something' haunted a large pond found in the countryside. In 1864, the poet J.R. Withers based his work *The Pond In The Meadow* on these fantastic stories:

> *Play not, my dear boys, near the pond in the meadow;*
> *The mermaid is waiting to pull you beneath;*
> *Climb not for a bird's nest, the bough it may sliver;*
> *And the mermaid will drag you to darkness and death...*

For all its briefness, the poem paints an atmospheric picture of Withers himself as a boy, fearing the old rumours of the evil mermaid lurking in the great, dark ponds of the Fordham countryside. Upon visiting the site again as an adult he noted progression appeared to have robbed the creature of its home: 'And children now fearless the buttercups gather; for the pond is fill'd up and the mermaid is gone.'

Charles Harper's *The Cambridge, Ely And King's Lynn Road: The Great Fenland Causeway* (1902) makes fleeting reference to a bizarre creature that supposedly haunted the River Great Ouse. This is the fourth-longest river in the UK, and it rises in Northamptonshire, flowing through Bedfordshire, Huntingdon and the Cambridgeshire Fens before entering the Wash at King's Lynn, Norfolk. Harper recorded that the Fenland stretches were feared by local men, who believed there to be an abominable creature lurking about the banks of the Ouse Washes. Harper described this monstrosity as 'a half-amphibious creature, something between a water-sprite and a sewer man, muddy from head to toe.'

Morley Adams' *In The Footsteps Of Borrow And Fitzgerald* (1913) tells an even weirder story. These landlocked freshwater mermaids not only appeared to be more brutal than the tempting sirens of seafaring legend but they also seemed to have colonised (or inter-bred) with the folk of small Fenland communities. It was suggested that every now and then the mermaid gene would produce 'web-footed children'. These were generally girls or women, very beautiful, and unless their bare feet could be observed it was nigh-on impossible to recognise them for what they were: '…either a witch or a fairy, with a strong homicidal tendency. She generally drowns her victims in the dykes among the marshes.'

Adams wrote that he knew a 'score of fen-folk' that would repeat this same belief. At such places as Gildenburgh Water, with its proximity to the River Nene, and henceforth the great bay of the Wash – and *Whittlesea-Mere* – maybe the scuba divers of today ought to be very cautious when swimming among the carp.

WHAT SLITHERS BENEATH DENNY ABBEY?

Imposing and solid-looking, Denny (or Denney) Abbey near Waterbeach looks as though it ought to have ghosts. It has swapped hands many times: it housed Benedictine monks until their possessions became the property of the Knights Templar. This order being dissolved in 1312, Denny fell under the ownership of the Knights Hospitallers who re-granted it to King Edward II. Edward's son and successor bestowed it upon Mary de St Paul, Countess of Pembroke, who founded a nunnery before dying in 1376. In 1838, however, Denny was recorded as being now a 'spacious dwelling house. The transept of the chapel still remains, and, with the refectory, is used as a barn.'

The stories of ghosts here are vague: Ms Porter heard that to walk seven times round nearby Soldier's Hill produced phantom monastic chanting. The area hereabouts was frequently waterlogged, but there are nonetheless many stories of underground passages that radiate out from beneath the abbey. John Harries' *Ghost Hunter's Road Book* (1968) writes of this: 'At Denny Abbey there are traces of underground workings which cannot be regarded as cellar. Such inexplicable man-made excavations are now full of water and produce weird turbulences and noises.' Harries noted that these subterranean noises were believed by locals to be caused by 'enormous eels' that lived in the flooded tunnels and had grown to gargantuan proportions after being 'trapped for centuries with a fishy banquet alongside.' The 'fishy banquet' was the constant supply of monks and others who fell victim to the Fenland environment…

CHAPTER 9
AERIAL PHENOMENA

INTRODUCTION

Ever since time immemorial our ancestors have looked to the heavens on lonely, silent nights and made strange and wonderful observations of incredible aerial phenomena. Many such sightings seen in the sky over Cambridgeshire are what science fiction writer Arthur C. Clarke dubbed 'mysteries of the first kind': the kind of astronomical – but natural – oddity that filled our forebears with amazement and, quite often, portentous terror, but for which we now have a scientific explanation.

One can imagine the excitement that a total eclipse of the sun would generate if witnessed over the Fens even in this day and age. Therefore we can easily guess at the magnified sense of doom and terror that the eclipse of 1715 generated in the hardy and superstitious Fenland peoples of that era. This occurred on 22 April that year and was visible to most in the southern half of Britain; totality was observed at around 9:15 in the morning, where the central line of the moon's shadow ran through the Fen district, midway between Holbeach and Wisbech. One scientifically-minded observer commented, 'I thought it not improper to give the publick an account thereof, that the suddain darkness, wherein the starrs will be visible about the sun, may give no surprise to the people, who would if unadvertised, be apt to look upon it as Ominous and to interpret it as portending evil to our King George and his government, which God preserve. Hereby they will see that there is nothing in it more than natural...' I should imagine that in this part of Cambridgeshire the phenomenon was virtually unheard of, and that the good scientist's words went largely unheeded in a wave of panic that swept the Fens. In the defence of Fenlanders, however, it is clear that they took delight in the more familiar heavenly wonders, as *The History Of Wisbech* (1834) picturesquely explains: 'The Aurora Borealis is sometimes seen casting forth its streaming light; the clouds are tinted with the beautiful shades of the setting sun, and assume all their wild and gigantic features...and the rainbow, that gracious token of promise, with its expansive arch is stretched out from horizon to horizon. These are glorious scenes which the inhabitants of the Fens can partake of.' Such phenomena, while being explainable, are still nonetheless exceptionally wondrous to the modern observer: who has not felt the need to point out a rainbow to someone at some point in their life, or tell their children that there is gold buried at the end of it?

Thus it is easy to see how the awe of the sky at night was reflected in Cambridgeshire folk belief. In 1866 it was observed, for example, that it was deemed unlucky in Huntingdonshire to count, or even point at, the stars. T.F. Thiselton-Dyer's 1878 *English Folk-Lore* refers to a number of beliefs in the same region concerning the moon. The observance of a moonless sky, otherwise known as 'Dark Christmas', promised a good harvest. Another proverb promised that however many days old the moon was on Michaelmas Day was an indicator of how many floods the region would experience afterwards. Even the Helpston poet John Clare referred in his piece *The Woodman* to a curious haziness sometimes observed around the moon, as though cosmic fog had blanketed it. This was referred to as the moon being 'burred', and *The Woodman* has a line:

> *And burred moons foretell great storms at night;*
> *In such-like things the woodman took great delight.*

The steeple of All Saints' Church, St Ives, was destroyed in a plane collision during World War One.

Perhaps the strangest belief was the one recorded by Northamptonshire folklorist Thomas Sternberg in 1851. This held that a Sabbath-breaker sat alone on the moon awaiting death, having been whisked up there for some offence on a Sunday – and that he gazed back at the Earth even as those in Cambridgeshire gazed up at him on his lonely prison in the heavens.

With folklore in mind, aerial enigmas sometimes cross the boundaries into the world of the supernatural. At St Ives, the phantom echo of a small plane losing altitude appears to have been heard over All Saints' Church, where on 23 March 1918 a small British aeroplane clumsily crashed into the steeple, part-destroying it and sending the body of the pilot – and the wreckage of his craft – crashing through the roof. Records indicate that immediately afterwards, there was a second air crash, although this one caused less damage and did not have fatal consequences. In 2009 I was told by a fellow visitor there that some people are supposed to have heard a zooming noise accompanied by a 'phut-phut-phut' sound as though a struggling aeroplane was flying by overhead; the sound apparently vanishes as it reaches the restored steeple, although those that look skyward cannot see anything. It is as though the doomed kite-like fighter plane is caught in some sort of time-loop, heard in the years since the tragic accident by those 'sensitive' enough to catch the unnerving noise.

But the modern generation is more familiar with the enigma of Unidentified Flying Objects (or, to be more up-to-date, Unidentified Aerial Phenomena). Although much in space is explained, it still carries (and always will carry) the awe-inspiring wonder of other galaxies, other universes and limitless cosmic possibilities. With this in mind, a glimpse at the recently released Ministry of Defence archives reveals what a wealth of strange things have been reported in our skies that could not be identified. So while this chapter is concerned with all manner of what would appear to be inexplicable *natural* phenomena, it is also concerned with Cambridgeshire's own *X-Files* – which do indeed suggest something truly out of this world.

THE EVENT OF 1646

According to the 17th-century *Thomason Collection Of Civil War Tracts* there was a prodigious event witnessed in the skies above Cambridgeshire, Suffolk and Norfolk on 21 May 1646.

In Newmarket, on the Cambridgeshire border, a pillar of cloud was observed to ascend from the earth 'with the bright hilt of a sword towards the bottom.' The pillar of cloud took the form of a pyramidal spire, or steeple-like shape and rose into the sky 'with diverse swords set around it'. As it soared higher something like a sword or lance with a sharply defined point descended *out* of the sky and was seen to intercept it. Another of these sharply pointed lances was also visible in the sky but it did not interfere with the spectacle. George Thomason (d.1666) also recorded the amazing observation from Newmarket that, '…there were seen by diverse honest, sober and civill persons, and men of good credit, *three men in the ayre*, striving, struggling and tugging together, one of them having a drawn sword in his hand.' An ominous rumbling, as of drums beating, was also heard from the sky about this time.

One wonders what to make of all this; on the face of it, it appears totally inexplicable, and the spire-like cloud rising from the ground sounds almost like a rocket taking off. Bizarrely, a similar phenomenon – or maybe the same one – was observed from The Hague, Netherlands, on the same day. The Thomason Tracts also recorded numerous other weird aerial oddities (three suns being seen over the north-west of England in 1650, for instance), and it is worth remembering that this war-divided period in England's history was beset by portents and superstitious marvels. But the strange scene was witnessed by 'diverse and severall persons of credit from Norfolk, Suffolk and Cambridgeshire' – who despite the era, are unlikely to have made such a fuss if the event was (as some speculated) a comet and a clap of thunder that chanced to happen together.

SPECTRAL SKY ARMIES

W.H. Bernard Saunders' *Legends And traditions Of Huntingdonshire* (1888) mentions tantalisingly that, 'It may be that the atmosphere of the county of Huntingdon has reflective qualities peculiarly its own, for it is stated in the *Peterborough Advertiser*, that a mirage was witnessed at Fletton, in 1885.' Perhaps this is the explanation for the Stuart and Jacobean-era phenomenon of 'sky battles' – wondrous apparitions of armies marching in the sky, or even clashing violently. But perhaps the most amazing observance of a 'phantom' sky army was the one collected by Saunders in 1888.

Unfortunately Saunders was unable to glean much information about this remarkable occurrence, other than that it was observed in the sky somewhere near St Neots in 1820. Hearing of it indirectly, he took it that the vision had constituted a kind of phantom army, a troop of horsemen riding along in formation that was visible for some time. He ascribed the vision, however, not to the supernatural but to a *Fata Morgana* – the kind of mirage seen at sea that accounted for 'ghost ships', only in this instance it had been seen on land.

But what to make of the bizarre experience of a Victorian policeman in Harlton, south-west of Cambridge, who feared that a battle was occurring somewhere? It was 3 January 1869, and the officer reported hearing the booming of what sounded like cannon – six or seven times there was the report of heavy weaponry that came from the horizon. The publication *Nature* took the report seriously enough to investigate, observing that there had been no earth tremor or anything else that could have accounted for the atmospheric 'booms'.

THE PHANTOM SCARESHIPS

In the early 1900s Cambridgeshire, along with other parts of the British Isles, was menaced by phantom airships, or dirigibles, of unknown origin. It is a mystery that even today raises more questions than it answers.

The phantom 'scareship' enigma first gained public attention across the Atlantic in 1896. The first shaky test flights by airships in Europe were some way off, but in the Autumn of that year people in San Francisco, California, were reporting that huge cigar-shaped objects with bright lights were being spotted floating through the sky. In 1897, with genuine airship activity still some months away, another wave of mysterious 'phantom airship' sightings was reported across the western and mid-western states. Rival newspapers speculated wildly as to what was going on, and unknown, unnamed 'eccentric inventors' claimed the airships were their handiwork. But the sightings died away.

The puzzling sightings proved to be a bizarre forerunner of what was to come in other parts of the world. For, in 1909, mysterious phantom Zeppelin invasions were reported in New Zealand, Australia and, in particular, the UK.

In the early days, this bizarre airborne horror that so fascinated the imaginations of the Edwardian public seemed to favour the region where the borders of Northamptonshire, Lincolnshire and Cambridgeshire all converge. The first major sighting of a 'scareship' in Britain occurred in the early hours of 23 March 1909, when PC Kettle's ears were alerted to the steady buzz of a high-powered engine while he patrolled Cromwell Road, Peterborough. Looking skyward he was utterly dumbfounded – and not a little unnerved – to see a gigantic 'object, somewhat oblong and narrow in shape, carrying a powerful light' that sailed speedily through the star-lit sky. PC Kettle told the *Peterborough Advertiser* this, and although the sighting was at first dismissed as nonsense by his red-faced superiors, it was followed by reports of giant airships from all over the British Isles in the months that followed.

On 5 May the mysterious sky-borne object was sighted again in the region. A Mr C.W. Allen was motoring through the village of Kelmarsh, Northamptonshire, accompanied by some friends. All heard a loud 'bang' in the night-time sky and looked up. They heard a 'tock-tock-tock' noise as of a motor engine and saw above them a 100ft-long torpedo-shaped object with bright lights at either end sailing swiftly through the heavens. Although the sky was dark, they could make out a platform suspended beneath the object where figures appeared to be visible. Once again, the strange object sailed in the direction of Peterborough. The bemused Mr Allen and his companions, who had slowed down their car to look at the object, thought it must be the product of an 'English inventor.' Their account appeared in the *Daily Express* a week later.

On 9 May the phantom airship was seen over Burghley House at about 11 o'clock at night – when it appeared to be shining a bright searchlight into the woodland on the edge of Burghley Park. The object had apparently found something that interested it in this extreme south-western part of Lincolnshire. The searchlight, attached to a giant, dark cigar-shaped object in the sky, rose and fell into the woodland some eight times before the object turned and sailed south-east in the direction of Peterborough.

Also on 9 May, reports came in not only from Burghley House, but also Wisbech and Northampton, where another PC reported that he had seen mysterious lights sailing through the sky at around 9:30pm. Apart from the constable, hundreds apparently stood in the town and watched this bizarre airborne object silhouetted against the blanket of stars. It was even seen in Southend that night (20 minutes before being seen in Stamford, Lincolnshire), over the county of Essex, making it possible to give the 'scareship' an approximate speed of 210mph.

By this time, PC Kettle's original account had been dismissed: the luckless constable, the public was assured, had been the victim of a practical jape, as had the people of Northampton. Pranksters had sent up a kite with a lantern tied to it and the wind had given it the appearance of movement; the motor-noise that drew the constable's attention was the 'motor which goes all night in the Cobden Street bakery.' This was according to the Chief Constable of Northampton, Frederick H. Mardlin. Charles Fort, the compiler of all that did not appear to make sense, commented of this supposed hoaxer that he '…could not have been a very *practical* joker. He must have been fond of travel. There were other reports from various places in England and Wales. There were reports from places far apart.' In July an eccentric English inventor claimed that the airships had been his secret project but this was also dismissed as nonsense.

However, by this time, sightings of the objects had been reported almost daily across the south-east of England, and a man walking along a lonely road over Caerphilly Mountain, Wales, claimed that he had stumbled across one of these objects at about 11pm on 18 May, after it had touched down. Two men in thick fur coats and fur caps were stood by the roadside, studying something in depth. But the Welshman's arrival spooked them and, jabbering furiously in an unknown tongue, they clambered aboard a carriage swinging beneath a 'long tube-shaped affair', at which point the whole contraption rose clumsily in a zigzagging fashion. Newspapermen who visited the site found flattened grass, newspaper clippings and assorted random debris. Witnesses in Cardiff independently confirmed the sighting of the airship that night.

The occupants of these carriages, or 'swinging boats', beneath the airship were variously described nationwide as Germans, or Orientals. Or else they were clean-shaven Americans, or rude Frenchmen. They were foreign agents spying on strategic locations and were paving the way for an invasion. Or they were all hoaxes. Some even thought the clumsy contraptions contained men from the Moon, or Mars; however, as Fort recorded in *LO!* (1931) 'The stoppage [of sightings] was abrupt. Or the stoppage of publication of reports was abrupt.'

So who sent the scareships? Given the tense build-up to World War One, the first and most obvious answer is that they were, indeed, German Zeppelins on reconnaissance missions. But by 1909 there were only three working dirigibles in Germany, owing to financial difficulties and a series of crashes. Only two were in the hands of the German army, neither of which was thought technologically capable of travelling as far as the British Isles, nor of undertaking the complicated manoeuvres the British scareships had done. Perhaps, then, the scareships were prototype British army airships? Again, this is unlikely, as the army's two airships – the *Nulli Secundus I* and the *Nulli Secundus II* – had been dismantled by 1909.

So if the technology and capability had simply not been there in 1909, and no nation was prepared to admit responsibility, then what were the scareships that frightened the inhabitants of the East Midlands during this time, and seemed – always – to sail away in the direction of Peterborough?

WONDROUS METEORS

The afore-mentioned Cambridgeshire event of 1646 may in actual fact have been a meteorite sighting; this in itself would possibly have caused much excitement and subsequent elaboration. I myself recall to this day being amazed by the sight of what I can only describe as a 'green fireball' sweeping through the clear starlit sky on 3 December 2006. When such things are observed and then followed by another dramatic event, there is sometimes – even today – a suspicion that one somehow heralds the other. On 6 February 1818 the people of Cambridge and elsewhere observed a large luminous meteor in daylight that preceded a minor earthquake later that day. Indeed, the earthquake of 27 February 2008, which was centred on the

Lincolnshire Wolds but which also rattled Cambridgeshire, was apparently preceded by mysterious lightning flashes in the sky and ball lightning.

In 1897 a meteor witnessed over Doddington was estimated to be travelling at 19mph and to be 34 miles up in the sky, but occasionally fragments of these flash through the earth's upper atmosphere and actually strike the earth. On 5 May 1991 Arthur Pettifor was tending onions in the garden of his home in Glatton when his attention was suddenly arrested by a loud 'whooshing' sound. Something winged the top of a tree and then shot through a conifer bush just 20ft from where he was stood. Mr Pettifor called on a neighbour, and together they began a search for what the mysterious object might have been. They soon found a shallow crater that contained – incredibly – a piece of stone that was still warm to the touch. This piece of stone was sent to the Natural History Museum to be scientifically analysed, where it was identified for what it was: a 17lb meteorite! One can only wonder at the remarkable escape Mr Pettifor had; if he had been standing a few feet to the left, he might have actually been *struck* by this piece of cosmic flotsam that fell to earth. It would certainly have killed him outright, making him possibly the only person in the UK ever to have been struck and killed by a falling piece of space debris.

A SMILE IN THE SKY

On 14 September 2008, an amazing sight was observed over Cambridge, and captured on camera. At 16:45 what is known as a circumzenithal arc was displayed – a phenomenon that creates an *upside-down* rainbow. This kind of atmospheric oddity is caused by sunlight that is being filtered through ice crystals in the upper atmosphere, and is exceptionally rare outside the Poles. The atmospheric conditions have to be just right for these types of rainbow to appear, and they are phenomenally rare in the UK itself, let alone Cambridgeshire. Luckily a Cambridge astronomer managed to snap this amazing sight and following its appearance on the *Cambridge News* website the image flashed around the world via the internet, with the national media also quickly becoming fascinated with the wondrous photograph. Many newspapers charmingly referred to the event as the sky smiling.

STRANGE RAIN

One can only imagine the devastation that was caused in 1465. On 24 August that year hailstones were recorded as falling on St Neots that were a phenomenal *eighteen inches* in circumference. Although a remarkable natural wonder, such events do remind us that on rare occasions the sky throws something at us on the ground that we can only marvel at.

On 18 August 1874 it rained ants. Huge clouds of winged ants were seen to swarm up near Sawston, only to be deposited *en masse* on Cambridge. The insects were observed to be largely the *formica fusca*, or small winged male ant, although in among it all there were two other types: one of a different species of winged ant, and – bizarrely – a large variety *without* any wings at all. How had they been swept up in the swarm? It was a question that bemused the readers of the *Cambridge Chronicle and University Journal*, who reported the strange event.

On January 2002 it was reported that a resident of Histon, north of Cambridge, had found a goldfish struggling and flapping on her lawn. Presumably a bird of some kind had dropped the fish, although none was observed, and if a bird *was* responsible then, strangely, it had not tried to recover its prize.

THE EMERGENCE OF UFO LORE

It was in 1947 that weird objects witnessed in the sky became synonymous with visitations by beings from another planet, following Kenneth Arnold's highly publicised sighting of nine flying saucers over Washington. There are today those that still dimly recollect the urban legend that a UFO is supposed to have crashed in the Fens in early 1964. This, I assume, is based on a report submitted by a member of the public to the Meteorological Office in Cambridge on 5 January that year concerning an object that appeared to display a curved surface plummeting to earth somewhere in the vicinity of Horse Moor near March. The Ministry of Defence was alerted, and in turn a patrol car was sent out but no sign of the 'thing' was observed: the final guess was that the object had been some piece that fell from an aircraft – although no such accidents were reported. For 30 years this odd mystery stayed buried in the MoD files under the Thirty Year Ruling until it was declassified, and the 11-page report can now be found within two open documents held by the National Archives at Kew (*UFO Reports (1964-1965) AIR 2/17526* and *AIR 2/17527*). The mystery of what actually hit the Fens all those years ago is open to suggestion: a large meteorite and a UFO being the predictably popular public suppositions. It is certainly curious that nothing was found during the search, given that the land is so flat hereabouts. Or, at least, nothing was *allegedly* found, and to true-believers this incident remains either a cover-up, or, even more fantastically, some believe the remains of a small alien scouting craft lies submerged and hidden somewhere beneath the murky water of a Fenland waterway called the Sixteen Foot Drain!

Such is the stuff of UFO folklore. During many visits to the Fens I heard this vague belief repeated time and again, although there were never any specifics. I wonder if, like ghosts, it has something to do with the primeval landscape of the gloomy and empty Fenland of Cambridgeshire. It almost seems to be the

Part-remains of a disused runway at RAF Waterbeach.

type of place where mysterious missiles ought to come soaring out of the sky to be lost in the vastness of the Fenland. The world-renowned export on the UFO phenomenon Jenny Randles may have experienced this sort of myth-making to a certain extent herself. In her collaboration *The Complete Book Of UFOs* (1995) there appears an account of the famous RAF Lakenheath Incident over East Anglia on the night of 13 August 1956. This was when a US Air Force alert led to RAF Venom fighters being scrambled to intercept mysterious 'blips' of light spotted on radar that were apparently reconnoitring the region. The invaders appeared to be capable of performing manoeuvres that were (and still officially are) impossible for conventional aircraft. The saga continued throughout the night, and into the next day, with a number of Venom fighters being scrambled from RAF Waterbeach to engage whatever it was that was being picked up by radar operators on the ground. But they engaged nothing, and although the affair caused a furore at Whitehall it has never really been properly explained. During the chaos, however, one Venom fighter lost one of its fuel tanks over Cambridgeshire, which crashed into a field, and was forced to return to Waterbeach. Ms Randles wrote in 1995 of this strange night, 'We have also tracked down and talked to civilians in Cambridgeshire who apparently saw the Venom streak overhead with the UFO in hot pursuit near Ely and Lakenheath!'

UFO folklore has it that in late 1977 a curious object that could not be identified was observed from the ground speeding towards Cambridge City Airport (now Marshall Airport Cambridge UK), far faster than any plane; it shot over the small regional airport, then performed a U-turn on itself before zooming off in another direction. The UFO had well and truly arrived in Cambridgeshire, if this near landing on the concrete of the 2,000 metre runway between Cambridge and Teversham is anything to go by.

THE UFO PHENOMENON IN CAMBRIDGESHIRE

1977 was the year that Spielberg's *Close Encounters Of The Third Kind* was released to universal acclaim, and in the run-up to its premiere in New York in November, fiction apparently mirrored 'fact'. For the previous month the *Cambridge News* had covered the reports of UFOs on the Cambridgeshire/Essex border. The police in Saffron Walden received two reports of an amazing spectacle in the sky thereabouts: two large headlamp-like lights that merged to form a kind of 'star shape the size of a double-decker bus.' This then transformed into a shuttlecock shape and red beams shot from each end. This wonder was observed to perform the same ritual some six times. The following night a driver reported a bright amber light that appeared to be following an aircraft before losing interest, hovering for a moment and shooting off in a different direction. This weirdness came on the back of multiple sightings of strange bright lights in the skies above this part of Cambridgeshire.

Maybe the first 'UFO' was the 'ball of light' reported by the *Bury Post* on 28 August 1783. This was observed in the borderland between Norfolk and Cambridgeshire, flying through the sky between nine and 10 in the evening. Thirty seconds after appearing it fragmented into three separate glowing balls, each reliably considered to be equal in size to the original. They were quickly obscured by the horizon, but a couple of minutes later a low, threatening, rumbling noise was heard, and it appeared after the fact that the curious lights had preceded a minor earth tremor.

As we have seen already, weird sky phenomena, usually assumed to be some kind of natural atmospheric oddity, has allegedly preceded earthquakes even in our own time, so this might not have been a UFO as such. But it is somehow indicative of the pattern of UFO 'behaviour' in Cambridgeshire. For some reason,

CHAPTER 10

INEXPLICABLE INCIDENTS, BIZARRE BEHAVIOUR AND PECULIAR PLACES

INTRODUCTION

In his book *The Link: The Extraordinary Gifts Of A Teenage Psychic* (1974) the now-world famous psychic healer Matthew Manning wrote of the bizarre supernatural encounters he had as a teenager with a ghost at the family home in the village of Linton near the Essex border in southern Cambridgeshire.

Minor disturbances had previously been observed at the first family home in Cambridge. They had begun at that house in February 1967, when Matthew was 11 years old. These incidents were nothing startling, just puzzling displacements of everyday household objects that could not be accounted for. But the phenomenon was so persistent that it led Matthew's father to contact the Cambridge Psychical Research Society, an undergraduate society that was started during the second term in Cambridge early in 1879 and had gone on to investigate many instances of the paranormal and supernatural over the decades. Dr A.R.G. Owen (a recognised expert on poltergeists) visited the family and proclaimed that they did, indeed, harbour a poltergeist and it was likely to be centred on Matthew. *The Link* explains that by this time the situation was getting worse: apart from the displacement of mainly lightweight objects, there had now begun constant knocking, thuds, small clatters at window panes and creaks in all parts of the house at all times of day.

In the autumn of 1968 the family moved to Queen's House in Linton, a beautiful little Queen Anne house with half an acre of garden and a prominent staircase. But the relocation made no difference; the mysterious force that plagued them simply followed. It had been observed that the force had dissipated when the three Manning children were sent to stay with relatives. But upon the return of Matthew Manning, it began once more, with heavier objects than before not only being moved about but physically tipped over. A lull in the unnerving activity at the bedevilled house in Linton coincided with a spell that Matthew spent at boarding school – but when he returned, it began once again: and this time with a vengeance.

The poltergeist appeared to be simultaneously trying to 'get through' to Matthew and, apparently, to manifest itself in physical form. One Christmas the boy heard furious scratching behind the wood panelling in his bedroom, and footsteps crunching outside as though someone were beneath his window. Throughout 1970 and 1971 it became inescapably obvious that it was Matthew who was the focus of all this, since weird phenomena had now begun to follow him to Oakham School, the prestigious boarding school in Rutland. (At one point the school matron recorded how, during Matthew's time there, it was typical for her room to suddenly become freezing cold and for showers of pebbles or small wood chippings to be deposited in her lap while reading or listing to the radio.)

But the strangest incidents occurred whenever Matthew was back at Linton. In July 1970 Matthew suffered a frightening experience. One night, after he had gone to bed, a sinister scratching noise from behind the wardrobe forced him to switch on the lamp. As he watched in heart-pounding fear, he, '…saw to my horror that the cupboard was inching out from the wall towards me. When it halted it had advanced about 18in. I switched off the light and almost simultaneously my bed started to rock back and forth.' When the bed lifted itself several inches off the floor and moved to a different part of the room the petrified lad found the courage to escape the bedroom and run to his parents' room. The following morning, virtually every room on the ground floor looked as though a bomb had exploded within, despite no noise being heard during the night. Pictures had been flicked off the wall, furniture was piled in untidy heaps, tables were tipped over…

Around this time the plague that had been visited upon this family appears to have taken a new direction, into a wholly different dimension of the supernatural. Coinciding with the random poltergeist outbreaks came the depositing of small objects that no one could account for, as if they had appeared from a vortex. Mysterious pools of water welled up from nowhere, and other objects were observed to dance in the air and make 90-degree turns. More unnervingly, childish scrawling began to appear spontaneously on the walls, with one message apparently reading 'Matthew Beware'.

Over time the house became literally defaced with this supernatural graffiti, and Matthew himself now found that he was increasingly being visited by what he initially took for a real person. A second book by Matthew in 1978, *The Strangers*, explains that while still only 16 he first encountered the spirit of one Robert Webbe near the staircase in 1971. Webbe, Matthew gradually discovered, had in life added the front portion of Queen's House in 1730, and he had died there three years later. Matthew wrote that he wore a Georgian wig and '…a green frock coat with frilled cuffs and a cream cravat'. 'Webbe' walked with the aid of two sticks and complained about gout-type pains that riddled his legs, an ailment that may (it was later speculated) have ultimately caused his death. In one remarkable incident, that appears almost cross dimensional, Matthew found he was able to present the 'ghost' of Robert Webbe with an obviously solid toy doll's wooden clog – which Webbe then placed in his coat pocket. He then faded away in the traditional manner of a ghost – the clog also disappearing. The entity that had revealed itself as Webbe was blamed for more than 500 scrawled names and dates that appeared on walls in the house over a six-day period in July 1971.

But Matthew Manning's story is more than a ghost story. One is left feeling that were it not for Matthew himself, none of it would have occurred. There is a powerful suggestion that the 'spirit' of Webbe, and perhaps others from the Webbe family, manifested largely because of Matthew's own paranormal, psychic abilities – and in effect helped him to re-channel the poltergeist-energy that he was either generating unconsciously or had 'attached itself' to him somehow. Matthew began to undertake experiments in automatic writing (what some believe is a channelling of supernatural energy through one's own hand to create the signature works of long-deceased artistes or simply ordinary people like Robert Webbe) and then extended this to delicate artwork. A phenomenal amount has been written about this remarkable man over the past four decades, ascribing to him virtually every kind of psychic human achievement: accurately predicting the Grand National outcome, recreating the masterpieces of the great artists, spoon-bending in the style of Uri Geller, and (in one show-stopping piece) his mere appearance somehow creating havoc with the electricity supply during a TV interview with David Frost in 1974. Such was his status by 1980 that a guidebook to English villages actually quoted Linton as being noteworthy as the town with 'claims to modern fame as the home of the remarkable psychic Matthew Manning.'

Matthew Manning's abilities have continually withstood many a scientific test, but in the early 1980s he distanced himself from the idea that his pictures might have been due to communication from the spirits of long-deceased master artists; he has now largely moved on from the sensationally publicized events of his Cambridgeshire upbringing. He is now a household name in his own right, however, for another spiritual trait: he has travelled to many parts of the globe to focus on marvellous 'psychic healing' – an art in which he is a recognised expert practitioner, although surely he cannot have much competition.

Matthew Manning's is a story where several dimensions of the supernatural and paranormal seem to overlap, and whatever the truth is behind his bizarre experiences he is not the only person from our county to display these paranormal 'abilities', if one wishes to call them that. His is a story that leaves one scratching their head and almost afraid to ask the bigger questions and speculate on the bigger picture – since it might, just maybe, force us to question everything we think we know about life. In many ways, his tale is representative of this final chapter, which focuses on the things that have been observed in Cambridgeshire that do not make sense in any kind of conventional way. Phenomenal and paranormal human abilities, the sometimes baffling natural marvels of the Cambridgeshire landscape, whimsical anecdotes of exploding socks and all other manner of head-scratching enigmas that do not fit the perceived order of things are laid out here for the reader to ponder.

AUTOMATIC WRITING

Long before Matthew Manning, leading spiritualists of the Society for Psychical Research were undertaking experiments with clairvoyance and telepathy at Cambridge University. The tests often involved those who considered themselves to have the 'gift' of mediumship, and typical was the series of controlled experiments carried out at Emmanuel College that commenced on 12 November 1892. Here, at 2:00pm, an 'operator' named Mr Green attempted to 'read' and answer a number of questions that were hidden from his sight, written down and sealed in envelopes – but which others called 'agents' had read and would try to communicate telepathically to him. Throughout the tests, sometimes this silent, subliminal channelling apparently worked for often Mr Green would immediately write down the correct answers to the questions that were hidden in the envelope; although sometimes he merely wrote gibberish and claimed to be 'tired.' However, even limited success in this field still has to be counted as some sort of success, and the spiritualist Frederick W.H. Myers wrote of one remarkable occurrence that astounded all in the room: 'One of the company [Myers wrote] then attempted to get the name on a visiting card transmitted [psychically, to Mr Green], and the question was written, "Write name on card." Mr Green did not know that this experiment was about to be tried, and the card was picked from a pile at random. The name was John B. Bourne. A sentence was (unconsciously and automatically) written by Mr Green, which proved to be, "Think of one letter at a time and then see what will happen".' The agents did so, collectively and deliberately thinking of J for Jerusalem, O for Omri, H for Honey, N for Nothing etc. As they did so Mr Green wrote down 'John Bou…' before apparently losing the psychic connection. In short, he seemed to have somehow telepathically 'received' the greater part of the name on the card by concentrating on what the others were thinking.

In August 1921 a man named William S. Packenham-Walsh contacted a medium in the south of England named Mrs Clegg, on account of an overwhelming passion he had developed with the life story of King Henry VIII's executed queen Anne Boleyn. Mrs Clegg was employed so that Packenham-Walsh could 'connect' with the spirit of the long-dead queen. He had developed an all-consuming interest in the queen after reading an autobiography of her while doing missionary work in China, and the story is all the more remarkable in that Packenham-Walsh was a member of the clergy and later a canon of Peterborough Cathedral. In one remarkable incident 'Anne Boleyn' – through Mrs Clegg – told the clergyman that 'You will be offered a parish with the snowdrops and you will go to it with the daffodils.' Quite what this meant was unclear until Packenham-Walsh was offered the parish of Sulgrave, Northamptonshire, on Christmas Day 1921. He visited the parish in early January 1922 and found that the vicarage grounds 'were white with snowdrops', but when he actually moved there in March the gardens were found now to be ablaze with daffodils. This was a circumstance that the groundskeeper of 40 years had never known, and Packenham-Walsh wrote, 'In that "Snowdrop Parish" we remained for over 30 years until I retired aged 87 in 1954.'

In November 1922 the clergyman entered into correspondence with another woman who possessed the 'psychic gift' named Eleanor Kelly, and she relayed messages from Ann Boleyn via the medium of automatic writing for Packenham-Walsh's benefit. In June 1924 the clergyman took the opportunity to pray at Catherine of Aragon's shrine in Peterborough Cathedral, and thereafter learned from Ms Kelly that she had been contacted by the spirit of Catherine, who imparted: 'Anne [Boleyn] is beside me as I write and sends her greetings to thee and to that one she hath charge of in her earthly pilgrimage [Packenham-Walsh]…'

The whole story of Packenham-Walsh's otherworldly contacts with Anne Boleyn were told in his work *Tudor Story* (1963).

ASTRAL PROJECTION

Spiritualism and experimentation with psychic abilities were very fashionable in Victorian Britain. Frederick W. H. Myers' authoritative *Human Personality & Its Survival Of Bodily Death* notes an incredible instance of so-called 'astral projection' that occurred in the house of one Sarah Hall, at Wansford. The Hall family house, Sibberton Lodge, was a converted church, and in the winter months of 1863 Mrs Hall and her husband were paid a visit by a cousin and her husband. One evening all four were sat round the dining table having supper, when there suddenly appeared a solid-looking figure by the sideboard. The group could only stare in amazement, for the apparition was of Mrs Hall herself, even as she sat there looking at it. She wrote that her doppelganger wore: 'a spotted light Muslin summer dress' of a type that she herself did not even possess. As her husband stammered, 'It is Sarah!' and pointed, the apparition simply vanished. There is no suggestion that the group were experimenting with – or even talking about – spiritualism; Mrs Hall wrote, 'The apparition seemed utterly apart from myself and my feelings, as a picture or a statue.' The most bizarre feature of this already weird experience is the detail that the phantom Mrs Hall wore a dress that the real Mrs Hall did not own.

SELF-HYPNOTISM

In early July 2008 a number of national newspapers picked up on a modern story of a strange human attribute. On 7 July a 67-year-old woman from March was reported as self-hypnotising herself so that she would feel no pain during a complicated one-hour knee operation that involved drilling into her knee and inserting a tiny camera into her leg to see what might have been causing a persistent knee ailment she was suffering.

The lady in question was a former nurse who had moved to Cambridgeshire 40 years before, and for the past 15 years she had been a trained hypnotist. During her operation at the Orthopaedics and Spine Specialist Hospital in Peterborough she remained fully conscious, and left the same day following the operation. What was even more remarkable, however, was that in the past 10 years she had been operated on twice before for foot problems without anaesthetic, after hypnotising herself in this way on those occasions as well. Remaining awake throughout her operations, the lady in question was the only person to have been operated on in this way at the hospital.

THE 'GIGANTIC BOY' OF WILLINGHAM

Down the centuries, there have been many people whose prodigious stature has marked them out in folklore. Born at St Neots on 28 August 1795 was James Toller, a boy later displayed in London as the Young English Giant. By the time of his death in 1819 aged about 24 he had attained the incredible height of 8ft 6in. Conversely, in 1787 one Richard Whitelamb of Wisbech was exhibited at a travelling fair; born in 1763 he was a mere 34in high by his 23rd year. The publicity posters are a sad indication of how such people were exploited, with the hoardings reading, 'This wonderful prodigy of nature will wait upon ladies, or gentlemen, at their own houses, at the shortest notice.'

But the wonder of the mid-1700s in Cambridgeshire was the birth of Thomas Hale, who went on to become widely known as 'the Gigantic Boy of Willingham'.

Thomas was born to a father of small stature, Thomas Snr, and an averagely tall mother, Margaret. The mother had been a servant and Thomas was her second child: and for the first three quarters of a year the boy grew 'wonderfully' despite having only his mother's sustenance. When she died shortly afterwards it was predictably supposed that she died by 'his drawing away her vital nourishment.' The boy grew exceptionally quickly and was observed at the age of 2 years and 11 months to be 3ft 9in high, with his entire body in proportion. He was able to overpower other children twice his age in wrestling. Not only this, but his intelligence appeared accelerated as well: he was reckoned to have the understanding of a boy of five or six years old.

He also weighed above four stone, and was very strong. On one occasion he picked up and threw a blacksmith's hammer weighing 17lb, and in other respects he appeared even more developed. Although not yet three, his voice was like a man's, 'very coarse', and his 'anatomy' was scientifically observed to be as developed as someone 10 years his age. Although all this sounds highly unlikely, testimonials were provided by the Revd Mr Almon, minister of the parish, and Mr Thomas Dawkes, a surgeon at Huntingdon, to the effect that, '…this child, Tho. Hale, was born on Oct. 31, 1741. Between Aug. 28 and Nov. 30, 1744, this child grew 2 and a half inches, i.e. from (just over) 3 feet 8 inches to 3 feet and 11 inches.' By the age of four, a contributor to the *Gentleman's Magazine* wrote in January 1745, Thomas Hale was 'to all outward appearances…nearly arrived to a state of manhood.'

When he died on 3 September 1747 poor Thomas was not yet six but was 4ft 6in in height and weighed seven stone. His visage gave the appearance of a decrepit old man; he was balding, and as one Victorian writer described it: 'He, in fact, passed through several stages of childhood, youth, manhood and old age in a space of about 70 months. He died of extreme old age…'

Thomas Hale was buried in St Mary and All Saints' Church, Willingham, where his tombstone bore an inscription in Latin, which in part read:

Stop, traveller, and wondering know;
Here buried lie the remains of Thomas...
Who not one year old had signs of manhood...
Before six died as it were of an advanced old age.

'SUFFERINGS OF ELIZABETH WOODCOCK'

The following incident is remarkable, in that it is the kind of survival story usually associated with the Australian outback, the Brazilian jungle or the Arctic tundra...not the countryside outside Cambridge.

In the winter of early February 1799, one Mrs Elizabeth Woodcock was making her way home on horseback northwards from market at Cambridge when for some reason she chose to dismount (possibly to pour herself liquor from a flask). Others say more romantically that the horse reared at the strange sight of a blazing meteorite shooting through the early evening sky, at which Elizabeth herself commented, 'Good God, what can this be!' At any rate her horse promptly ran off and poor Elizabeth, with little idea what to do next as darkness crept in, opted to find the most sheltered position, which was under foliage in the fields by the roadside, and wait for some passing traveller to assist her. It was bitterly cold, and in the evening it began to snow. It snowed heavily, and before long Elizabeth and the thicket she was sheltering under resembled an Arctic snowdrift; it was all she could do to find the strength to attach a handkerchief

to a stick and plant it atop the mountain of snow that was building about her and the thicket she hid under. By morning it was heaped to a height of 2ft above her head, and the little flag she had made was not visible in the blanket of white that had settled on the Cambridgeshire countryside.

Frozen almost solid in a crouched sitting position, Elizabeth slipped into a state of suspended animation, unable to speak or move – but yet still barely conscious. She heard about her church bells, and as once more night succeeded day she even fancied that she occasionally heard the voices of villagers in conversation as their horses passed by her. For four full days she remained trapped in this white hell, only kept alive by the fact that her frozen hands held before her nose a single pinch of snuff that contrived to act as a poor substitute for sustenance.

Remains of the memorial stone that once marked the site of Elizabeth's ordeal.

On the fifth day the snow began to melt but by now Elizabeth was so ill with frostbite and weak with hunger that she could not lift herself. She remained a further three days beneath the thicket in the melting snow and freezing winds until a party of villagers spotted her by-now visible handkerchief on its stick signalling her hideaway. Calling out, Elizabeth's rescuer received the stammered reply from the frozen woman, 'Dear John Stittle, I know your voice. For God's sake, help me out!' Unbelievably she had not been that far away from her home in Impington, north of Cambridge, when her remarkable experience had occurred. Had the night been merely cold – and not freezing and snowing – she could simply have walked home. Instead she lost an entire week to the elements in a snow-blanketed landscape that had lost all its landmarks.

As incredible as this sounds, the experience of the celebrated traveller Dr Edward Clark bears the remarkable event out. His *Travels In Various Countries Of Scandinavia* evidences that he was no stranger to weather extremes. Yet it was in Cambridgeshire in 1818 that he nearly died when the stupefying, freezing cold led him to fall by the roadside while his horse ambled off. Were it not for a passing stranger he would have frozen to death. Elizabeth Woodcock escaped this fate due to her frozen state slowing down her metabolism, and were it not for being packed in snow she would have died. Unfortunately she lived but half a year more, however. The villagers did not know how to treat the frostbite she had received and eventually she died from its effects in July at the age of 43. This was combined with the ill effects of alcohol presented to her by well-wishers and those seeking to help her numb the pain of her frostbite.

A memorial stone for a long time marked the site of the incident; this can now be found in the Cambridge and County Folk Museum, along with a picture of poor Elizabeth: in her shawl and bonnet, and burrowed away in the mountain of snow that almost became her tomb.

HUMAN CURIOSITIES

W.H. Bernard Saunders' *Legends And Traditions Of Huntingdonshire* (1888) notes a couple of instances of human marvels. In April 1853 there was puzzlement when a married woman named Wilkinson fell down some stairs at Eynesbury with a terrific thump on the head. She had been completely blind for the past 20 years – but 'the shock caused to the system' by this tumble resulted in her eyesight fully returning. Little more are we told about this miracle.

In January 1838 'a Cambridge paper' recorded a strange instance of a 'Sleeping Beauty' in Needingworth, east of St Ives. Twelve days prior, an 18-year-old girl had fallen 'in a trance asleep.' It was observed of her that 'she keeps quite warm, except her feet and they are cold and stiff' and none could rouse her. Her father carried her downstairs and laid her out by the fire in hopes that its heat might rouse her but it had no effect – although she clearly still showed signs of life. One Monday, however, she opened her eyes and groggily asked for something to drink 'which being given her, she became convulsed for a time, and then sank into her former state of torpor, in which she has continued ever since.'

One wonders what became of this young girl, and if she was, in fact, being poisoned. But the next story reads almost like an urban legend – until you realise that it not only happened, but that it happened in our own time. On New Year's Day 1996 a doctor was called to a family farm at Stonely at around two in the morning, where he sadly pronounced the death of a 61-year-old woman who had collapsed. The deceased was an epileptic, and undertakers took her to the mortuary at nearby Hinchingbrooke Hospital, Huntingdon. Four hours after she was pronounced deceased, however, and just minutes before she was to be put in the mortuary freezer, an undertaker – who happened to be a family friend – noticed a twitching in a leg vein. After she was heard to snore, she was rushed to intensive care but after 48 hours was well enough to be transferred to a general ward. It appeared that she might have slowed down her metabolism by mixing epilepsy tablets and sleeping pills, thus making her pulse hard to find. The case received a huge amount of publicity, but by 10 January she had recovered well enough to give a press conference, although the chain of events had naturally distressed her family very much. The unnerving aspect of all this is just how close she came to being interred alive – a nightmare of urban myth and horror film proportions that is perhaps a wider, more ingrained fear among the human race than we care to admit.

CURIOUS NATURAL CURES

In the past, many remarkable rituals were reckoned to effect cures upon the peasantry of Cambridgeshire. We have seen that miraculous 'healing wells' were employed by the wealthy in the past, but what of the ordinary villagers who could not afford to pay for their supernaturally-ascribed curative powers? They had to rely on time-tested remedies that today would make us shudder.

In February 1861 a young woman named Stacey was either desperate, gullible or very devious. To cure herself of her fits, she wandered round the neighbourhood of Middle Moor showing people a barely-legible piece of paper signed by 'the order of Mr Bates' in which it was stated she must collect nine sixpences from nine separate married men. These were to be smelted into a ring for her to wear in order to stop her fits, any of which might signal her final moment. Mr C.P. Bates was an actual person, although he had nothing to do with Stacey; outraged, he had her sent before the magistrates at Ramsey where she was reprimanded. Amazingly, however, this would not seem to have been a begging scam – Huntingdonshire folklorist W.H. Bernard Saunders wrote that she obtained the 'magical number' of sixpences and did indeed have them fashioned into a ring.

In 1863 Cuthbert Bede visited friends in a Huntingdonshire village. He was suffering with a sore throat, and his hosts told him of a sure cure. When he retired to bed, he was to take off his stocking (as was the fashion for men then) and place the sole on his throat before wrapping the rest round his neck. His throat would be well again by morning. Bede was doubtful, and suggested that a hot flannel might effect the same remedy; however, he was assured that it *had* to be a stocking, as this was what his hosts did – and furthermore, they declared, 'We know hundreds that it has cured!' He was further told that a clean stocking would not do, nor the leg-part of a worn stocking: 'It's the sweat of the foot as does it!' he was told. Unfortunately, Bede did not write in his piece to *Notes And Queries* whether this peculiar ritual worked on himself.

Cuthbert Bede also wrote to the same periodical of other charms, designed to ward off smallpox. One way to avoid the pox was to carry a small piece of camphor wood in a bag tied to one's neck, as this would ward off any infection. If the disease was caught, then the option was always there to open all windows at sunset and allow the gnats to swarm around one's person, biting and 'stealing' the infection. They would thus fly off and die, and the sick person would get better. And we have already seen that snakeskin was supposed to cure headaches.

The question this all poses is: to what extent did such humble cures actually work? Presumably some must have worked to one degree or another, to have persisted for so long. At any rate, one wonders who the brave, desperate and indeed stupid people were who first attempted them on what must have been

John Clare's memorial in Helpston — where Will-o'-the-Wisps haunted the fields at night.

it was of a mysterious terrific hue' but admitted that he was terrified as he fled through the rushes. He also observed that it had, curiously, approached him but then – as he perched petrified on the stile – it had suddenly darted away. He also noted that the lady who kept the inn at Helpston had seen from her upper chambers as many as 15 of these 'Whisps' dancing in and out at once in the distance.

It is at once clear from this that with Will-o'-the-Wisps, as with crop circles, we are at a juncture where possible explanations for various phenomena recounted in this book all converge. The villagers at Helpston may have taken similar 'Whisps' for the ghost of the old lady, while the ones observed by Clare appear to demonstrate behavioural patterns that *could* be attributed to UFOs in some cases. They have also been suggested as an explanation for belief in fairies, the blazing eyes of black shuck and trickster sprites like the Shag Foal. The Will-o'-the-Wisp's Latin name is the *ignis fatuus* ('foolish fire'), and although a real, documented natural wonder, its exact nature is still the subject of some debate among environmental historians. Most consider it caused by vapour rising from the foul air of decaying vegetable matter combusting in marshland areas. It is, however, the subject of much folklore in its own right. The ghost expert Peter Underwood, in *This Haunted Isle* (1984), learned that in Wicken Fen the 'Lantern Man', as the *ignis fatuus* was called, also haunted church graveyards, and was reputed to be attracted to the noise of a whistle. One old fisherman would tell how he had actually had to throw himself to the ground to dodge a Lantern Man when it had been attracted by his whistling. Others had it that they were in fact evil spirits in and of themselves, which would lure those lost in the Fenland to a watery grave. This behaviour is entirely reminiscent of the Shag Foal, and it is clear that a lot of supernatural phenomena and folkloric belief may cross paths at this point.

However, it is only a partial explanation. Will-o'-the-Wisps, Lantern Men, or whatever name they go by, are, like fairies, seldom seen these days. This prompted these words from a contributor to *Fenland Notes And Queries* during the last decade of the 19th century: 'These phenomena were witnessed, I understand, at Lolham Mills [a still water-logged region in the vicinity of Helpston], soon after the disappearance of a severe frost in the past winter. I understand that old residents in various parts of the Fens state that Will-o'-the-Wisps were very commonly seen in their younger days, but have gradually ceased to be observed. Is this due to the improved drainage of the fenland?'

Even less easy to explain is the spectacle loosely known as ball lightning. This is still a hotly debated natural wonder whereby an amalgamation of atmospheric electrical conditions combine to form a luminous, spherical lightning-type effect.

Just such an extraordinary combination of factors must have come together to produce ball lightning in September 1816, when it is written that the start of that month suffered a snowfall of such heaviness that the Huntingdon and Cambridge roads became impassable. All the crops around Ely were ruined by the frosty temperatures. Such weather had never been observed at harvest time before, and the weird conditions were compounded two days later by a ferocious hurricane that pelted the county with hail. At Alconbury Weston, north-west of Alconbury itself, the cornfields were virtually annihilated; but amidst the devastation some sheaves of corn in the fields were scorched by a fireball that came from nowhere and managed to burn parts of the field to stubble despite the otherwise dreary conditions.

Some scientists do question the very existence of ball lightning, even despite an incident in August 1982 when some staff members at the world-renowned Cavendish Laboratory in Cambridge declared they had actually seen the building struck by ball lightning.

REMARKABLE PRESERVATION OF LEAVES IN COFFIN

A rather ghoulish anomaly was discovered in the chancel of St Mary Magdalene's Church at Brampton in December 1822. While workmen were excavating there they unearthed the 150-year-old coffin of one Humphrey Sylvester who had died on 25 March 1673. The coffin bore a skeleton, but also contained a quantity of very fresh looking laurel leaves. This was put down to the fact that the coffin was lined with lead, and their remarkable preservation must have been 'owing to the chemical properties and dryness of the earth.' The leaves were still of a dark green colour and some string that had apparently bunched them up was also observed to be in good condition – which, although interesting, did not explain the puzzle of why the corpse and other materials in the coffin had all deteriorated naturally over 150 years but the laurel leaves had not.

STATUES THAT COME TO LIFE

There is a famous story from Stamford that tells us that Roger Bacon, the celebrated Franciscan friar who died in 1292, resided for a time at Brazenose College. The knocker on the College gate was a brazen head with a heavy ring through its mouth, and Friar Bacon ordered his servant to keep watch on it since it was supposed to mumble prophetic utterances. The legend goes that if the servant had snatched the ring from the mouth of the brazen face while it was talking, then by some magical occurrence Stamford would have been instantly ringed with a wall of brass! This unlikely story is largely a fairytale, but there are other legends in Cambridgeshire itself of inanimate objects that seemingly posses the power of movement. The early 18th-century school at Burrough Green displays two niches above its central

One of the sets of lions on the portal of the Fitzwilliam Museum.

187

doorway, in which can be found the quaint stone figures of a little boy and a little girl, both carrying psalm books. Every child who attends this primary school for four to 11-year-olds knows that these two figures are supposed to come alive and dance on the village green on the last day of April, and in the past children have been told that any footprints found in the damp grass are those of the statues. At the 14th-century Longthorpe Tower, off Thorpe Road, Peterborough, I understand that children are told that one of the mediaeval wall paintings – the yellowed image of King David – 'steps down to play his harp at night' in the vault.

With this storytelling in mind, on 21 June 2009 I visited the prestigious Fitzwilliam Museum on Trumpington Street, Cambridge. Here, where among a remarkable repository of treasures are displayed works by such notable artists as Picasso, Monet, Constable and Hogarth, I had in reality come to see the exterior of the building itself. The museum was founded in 1816, and at either side of the impressive main entrance facing out onto Trumpington Street can be found two sets of huge stone lions that guard the steps up to the building.

It appears there is a fascination with these mighty sculptures generally, above and beyond my own; many tourists will sit atop them to be photographed, and others about the grounds clearly considered them striking enough to be put to canvas. It is doubtless their imposing stone presence that has inspired 'generations of children, certainly until the 1950s' to believe that they are somehow possessed of life. According to Enid Porter's *Cambridgeshire Customs And Folklore* (1969), when the bells of the Catholic church chimed midnight these four lions were thought to either open their mouths and roar or to step down off their plinths and roam the museum grounds, or else wander into the museum itself. Some said that they walked out into Trumpington Street to drink the water that in days gone by used to run along the road and originated from the springs known as Nine Wells, south-east of Trumpington.

There is something of a charming, fantastical element to this belief that appears to capture the imagination of children quite sincerely, much in the manner of Father Christmas or the Tooth Fairy. My eight-year-old niece insisted on having her photograph taken while stood next to one of these lions at the southern portal, and upon subsequently viewing the lions from a different vantage point in the grounds she became *convinced* that they had somehow moved, or shifted position, since we had last looked at them. This was entirely unprompted, and upon being told that they were, in actual fact, supposed to roar, she then insisted repeatedly on going back to them and looking at them from different angles to see if they had moved 'once again.'

It would appear that this belief is very well known – someone even told me that at midnight the lions were supposed to drink from the River Cam itself. I suspect that this superstition, which seems particularly suited to children, might have something to do with the fact that at first glance the lions all appear to be in the same pose; closer inspection, however, reveals that there are small differences in their positions. It might also have something to do with the belief that the architect of Fitzwilliam, George Basevi, never saw the completion of his great work – for he fell through scaffolding at Ely Cathedral in 1845 while supervising work on the nave and was killed. Hence, maybe the lions are destined to pad through the building looking for their creator who never returned.

I doubt whether Trumpington Street is ever quiet enough at midnight these days for the lions to move about unhindered: so, as my niece prefers to believe, they will lay there in silent, dignified stillness…for the time being.

SPONTANEOUS COMBUSTION

On 13 January 1993 the *Cambridge Evening News* reported that the emergency services had received a call from a household in Graveley declaring that a pair of socks in the bathroom had somehow burst into flames without any reason. Although fire trucks from St Neots and Papworth screamed to the address following the early morning call, by the time they got there the emergency was over and the mysterious 'socks fire' was out.

There was a similar phenomenon in 2002, when a number of newspapers carried the bizarre story of the origin of a fire that destroyed a conservatory in Peterborough. The house owner had placed a 10in-high Chilean cactus in the conservatory that April, in hopes that it would benefit from the sunlight and temperature in the room. However, it spontaneously exploded, bursting into flames and setting other plants in the conservatory on fire. The roof melted and for a while it was feared the blaze might spread through the house, but a fire crew managed to bring it under control before it did too much damage.

The phenomenon, although not entirely unknown in scorching hot climates, had reportedly never before been observed before in the UK.

A MILLION TO ONE

In March 1825 Samuel Seaton ventured into a pond near Sawtry to collect water in his bucket, but he slipped and, floundering hopelessly, quickly drowned. It was recalled at the time that his two brothers had also died in the same manner, and at the same pond: one in 1810 and the other in 1821.

One wonders what the odds of this are. Nearer our own time, there are curious instances of million-to-one chances that almost defy belief. The *Daily Mail* of 23 December 2005 was just one of a number of newspapers that reported the amazing journey of a missing George Cross medal. The medal had been awarded to Anthony Tollemache at the age of 26 for his heroic efforts in saving the passenger in his Blenheim fighter plane after it had crashed in 1940. But following his death, the heirloom was lost in 1988 – stolen from his heartbroken widow's home in Waterbeach during a burglary.

It seems that fate, however, intended the medal to be returned to its rightful owners. In 2005, someone found the medal on a beach on the other side of the world – lying in the sand at Maroochydore, on Queensland's Sunshine Coast, deposited as though dropped out of some sort of vortex. The beach-walker who found it handed it in to the Australian police, who contacted both the British authorities and the Victoria Cross and George Cross Association.

Gradually it was worked out whom the lost medal belonged to, and before long it was handed over to the Consulate General in December 2005 to be returned to the UK and its rightful owners.

Surely the strangest story of this nature concerns the phenomenon of so-called 'postal black holes'. In May 2006 it was widely reported that a faded letter was collected by porters at Trinity College, Cambridge, that was postmarked London and dated 3 March 1950. It read: 'George, will meet at Monty's next weekend. Is 2pm acceptable? Love Gwen.' The addressee was George Green and it was possible he had been a student, but the letter had the College and the Royal Mail scratching their heads in puzzlement. A Royal Mail spokesman stated, 'As it has a postmark, it is extremely unlikely that it has been in our system all this time. A postmark shows it has already been through so it must have been put back again only recently. It is possible that it may have got caught up in a large envelope and sent to a wrong address. It is certainly a strange one.'

This again is a new form of folklore, the question being where on earth such letters have been for half-a-century. It is almost as if they have been in some kind of vortex, waiting patiently to be delivered in the wrong historical period, but to the correct address.

Wonders will never cease.

A SHORT CONCLUSION

In travelling to the four corners of Cambridgeshire, I have found that the county hides a wealth of curious anecdotes and strange mysteries behind the façade of splendour that Cambridge presents, or beyond the historical treasures immediately apparent in the surrounding towns. Some mysteries take the form of historical riddles: for instance, there is a story that a young woman named Letitia Woodville travelled from St Neots to London in 1654 and fired a pistol at Oliver Cromwell in an attempt to assassinate him. Cromwell, apparently merciful, recognised the girl was 'melancholly' and allowed her back to St Neots under her father's care; his agents later poisoned her. The Georgian traveller Edward Brown heard this was 'pure fiction'.

Then again, some stories are traditional folklore. One of the Fellows at Clare College kindly told me an interesting legend behind a drinking vessel called the 'poison cup' that is kept within the Master's Lodge: 'The "cup" is actually a tankard, with a hinged lid, and the lid is ornamented with a large clear crystal. This is shaped and polished in the manner of a jewel, and is possibly quartz. The legend is that, if there is poison in the cup, the crystal becomes cloudy. I don't think anyone has put this to a scientific test, and there is no known basis on which it might be thought to work.'

Other mysteries, if true, are nightmarishly perplexing. *The Terrific Register* (1825) remarks that an awful, parasitic creature unknown to science was discovered living in the heart of a horse that had recently died in Spaldwick in 1586. Upon being removed and laid out, it was observed that its head was in a kind of membrane, and resembled that of a toad. The body was the colour of a mackerel and three and a half inches round, appearing to taper into 50 or so small tentacles that 'spread from the body like the branches of a tree'. It was made of 'many grains' and from its snout to its furthest extremity it measured 17 inches. Red water leaked from it at four points. It was killed with a dagger as it tried to slither away.

It would perhaps take a highly sceptical person, with no sense of faith, to dismiss *everything* complied in this book as fanciful or utter nonsense. What I have found somewhat reassuring is that many, many people were eager to provide me with information, and even their own experiences. A staff member at Flag Fen made reference to witnessing 'some strange phenomena which, in reverence to our ancestors, are best expressed around a log fire in a roundhouse' at this 3,500-year-old site of religious antiquity near Peterborough. In Cambridge itself, Sarah Keys, the proprietor of the Haunted Bookshop, explained to me that the place was haunted by 'a lady who occupied mainly the middle floor area and who would walk around and at times look out of the window. Also, books would be misplaced and jump around etc. This has happened on one or two occasions and I have seen the lady walking up the stairs and vanishing into nothing…I have to say that the presence such as it is, is thoroughly benign.' There is clearly still a place for the supernatural and the downright inexplicable in modern Cambridgeshire, and hopefully complete scepticism of such oddities will not overtake us too soon.

INDEX OF PLACE NAMES